W9-CZW-846

JOHN BERRYMAN AND ROBERT GIROUX

John Berryman

and

Robert Giroux

A Publishing Friendship

PATRICK SAMWAY, S.J.

University of Notre Dame Press
Notre Dame, Indiana

University of Notre Dame Press
Notre Dame, Indiana 46556
undpress.nd.edu
All Rights Reserved

Copyright © 2020 by the University of Notre Dame

Published in the United States of America

Library of Congress Control Number: 2020940881

ISBN: 978-0-268-10841-0 (Hardback)
ISBN: 978-0-268-10844-1 (WebPDF)
ISBN: 978-0-268-10843-4 (Epub)

In memory of my former mentor and good friend,

JOSEPH L. BLOTNER

(1923–2012)

CONTENTS

In writing this book, I would like to thank especially Robert Giroux, my editor and dear friend, who, before his death, assisted me in annotating a good number of the letters enfolded into this book. I am also grateful to the staff of the Manuscripts and Archives Division of the New York Public Library; the staff of Rare Books and Special Collections, Firestone Library and the Seeley G. Mudd Manuscript Library, Princeton University, Princeton, New Jersey; Alan K. Lathrop, professor and curator of the Manuscripts Division of the University of Minnesota Libraries; Kathleen "Kate" Donahue Berryman; Cara Donaldson; Nadine and Ben Forkner; Annemarie Gervasio; Kathryn Samway Lang; Svilen Madjov; Hugh James and Dorothee McKenna; the extended Robert Miss family; Trish Nugent; Charles Reilly; Dominic Roberti; Brian and Thomas Samway; Eileen Simpson; Sara White; Megan Wynne; the Jesuit community of Saint Joseph's University in Philadelphia; Professors Thomas Brennan, S.J., and Peter Norberg of the English Department of Saint Joseph's University in Philadelphia; les Soeurs de Jésus au Temple in Vernon, France; and especially my thoughtful literary agent, Albert LaFarge.

Some of the letters that John Berryman received from Giroux are in the Elmer L. Andersen Library at the University of Minnesota. The bulk of the letters that Giroux received from Berryman, plus carbon copies of letters he sent to Berryman, are in the Farrar, Straus & Giroux Collection in the New York Public Library; unless identified otherwise, readers can assume that these letters are in this library.

A few months after Giroux's death on September 5, 2008, Hugh James McKenna, the executor of the estate, found a box hidden in the back of Giroux's bedroom closet. In it we found a small cache of early letters that Berryman had written to his friend—letters that Giroux at some point clearly treasured, but whose existence he had seemingly forgotten about over the years, since he had never mentioned their existence to me. In addition, a number of cards and letters that Giroux kept in his personal files before leaving Harcourt, Brace in the spring of 1955 are housed in the Robert Giroux Collection, Special Collections Room, Monroe Library, Loyola University, New Orleans. By incorporating either sections or the entirety of letters between Berryman and Giroux into this book, I have tried to make available the exact, detailed historical record of their relationship—something too often missing in quick-turn-around emails. Some information about Giroux's life and career can be found in my *Flannery O'Connor and Robert Giroux: A Publishing Partnership* and "Tracing a Literary and Epistolary Relationship: Eudora Welty and Her Editor, Robert Giroux," as well as in the introduction to a book I edited, *The Letters of Robert Giroux and Thomas Merton*. Bibliographical information about books that Berryman kept in his library can be found in Richard J. Kelly's *John Berryman's Personal Library: A Catalogue*.

Where dates of letters are incomplete or missing, I have relied mostly on internal evidence in establishing a date. I have tried to preserve the physiognomy of the letters in order to allow the reader to appreciate the stylistic habits and preferences of the writers. Minor typographical infelicities have been silently corrected, but I have made every effort to retain the creative spelling and usage wherever the meaning can be gleaned from the context. Since Berryman sometimes changed the numbering of the Dream Songs, as is clear from his letter to Giroux of March 10, 1968, his numbering of certain poems can seem at variance with those found in the printed texts. I have retained the numbering of Berryman's poems as found in his letters except when it is clear that they refer to the published versions. Handwritten marks are presumed to be made by the sender unless otherwise noted. Editorial interpolations—missing words and corrections of obvious errors affecting sense—are enclosed in [square brackets], as are any contextual annotations other than endnotes. The following reflect some of Berryman's stylistic abbreviations: abt / about; bk, bks / book, books; cd / could; fr / from; Mpls / Minneapolis; ms or mss / manuscript; no / number; yr / your or year; shd / should; wd / would; w / with; wh / which.

During the twenty-plus years that I knew Robert Giroux, he sometimes repeated informally the same stories and anecdotes about his authors, and thus I do not provide a specific date for each of the hundreds of times we met. I taped a two-hour interview with him in 1997, during which he related much of his personal life, and Jonathan Montaldo videotaped Giroux for sixteen hours over a period of several months a few years before this noted editor's death. Both of these interviews are housed in the Robert Giroux Collection, Special Collections Room, Monroe Library, Loyola University, New Orleans. I note, too, that I have profited greatly from the writings of John Haffenden, Paul Mariani, and Eileen Simpson.

Giroux edited and published the following works of Berryman: *Homage to Mistress Bradstreet* (1956); *77 Dream Songs* (1964), which was awarded the Pulitzer Prize in 1965; *Berryman's Sonnets* (1967); *Short Poems* (1967); *His Toy, His Dream, His Rest* (1968), which won the National Book Award and the Bollingen Prize for Poetry; *The Dream Songs* (1969); *Love & Fame* (1970); *Delusions, etc.* (1972); *Recovery* (1973); *The Freedom of the Poet* (1976); *Henry's Fate and Other Poems: 1967–1972* (edited with an introduction by John Haffenden, 1977); *Collected Poems: 1937–1971* (edited with an introduction by Charles Thornbury, 1989); and *Berryman's Shakespeare* (edited with an introduction by John Haffenden, 1999).

I am particularly grateful to the estate of Robert Giroux for permission to publish from Giroux's poetry, short stories, and essays, as well as his letters to Berryman and to other friends and colleagues. Likewise, I wish to thank Mrs. Kate Donahue Berryman and Mrs. Martha Berryman Mayou for permission to quote from Berryman's poetry, interviews, speeches, and essays and to publish his letters, either in part or in whole, to Giroux and other friends and colleagues. Lastly, Professor David Wojahn, a former student of John Berryman, has graciously given me permission to quote from his poem "A Fifteenth Anniversary: John Berryman."

Reprinted by permission of Farrar, Straus & Giroux, LLC: Excerpts from *Collected Poems: 1937–1971* by John Berryman © 1989 by Kate Donahue Berryman. Reprinted with permission by Farrar, Straus & Giroux. Excerpts from *The Dream Songs* by John Berryman © 1959, 1962, 1963, 1964, 1965, 1967, 1968, 1969 by John Berryman. Reprinted with permission by Farrar, Straus & Giroux. Excerpt/s from *Homage to Mistress Bradstreet* by John Berryman © 1948, 1958, 1959, 1967, 1968 by John Berryman. Reprinted with permission by Farrar, Straus & Giroux. Excerpt/s from *The Freedom of the Poet* by John Berryman. Reprinted with permission by Farrar, Straus & Giroux. Excerpt/s from *Henry's Fate and Other Poems: 1967–1972* by John Berryman © 1969 by John Berryman. Copyright © 1975, 1976, 1977 by Kate Berryman. Reprinted with permission by Farrar, Straus & Giroux. Excerpts from *Recovery* by John Berryman © 1973 by the Estate of John Berryman, foreword by Saul Bellow, foreword copyright © 1973 by Saul Bellow. Reprinted with permission by Farrar, Straus & Giroux. Excerpts from *Collected Prose* by Robert Lowell © 1987 by Caroline Lowell, Harriet Lowell, and Sheridan Lowell. Reprinted with permission by Farrar, Straus & Giroux. Excerpts from *Letters of Robert Lowell* edited by Saskia Hamilton © 2005 by Harriet Lowell and Sheridan Lowell. Reprinted with permission by Farrar, Straus & Giroux.

ABBREVIATIONS

AT	Allen Tate
Berg	Henry W. and Albert A. Berg Collection of English and American Literature, New York Public Library, New York, NY
BKQ	Robert Giroux. *The Book Known as Q: A Consideration of Shakespeare's Sonnets*
BS	John Berryman. *Berryman's Shakespeare*. Edited with introduction by John Haffenden
CT	Charles Thornbury
DS	Paul Mariani. *Dream Song: The Life of John Berryman*
ES	Eileen Simpson (married names: Berryman, Simpson, Baine)
FS&G	Farrar, Straus & Giroux
JB	John Berryman
JBCC	John Haffenden. *John Berryman: A Critical Commentary*
JH	John Haffenden
JL	James Laughlin
L&F	John Berryman. *Love & Fame*
LJB	John Haffenden. *The Life of John Berryman*
ML	Seeley G. Mudd Manuscript Library, Princeton University, Princeton, NJ
MVD	Mark Van Doren
NYPL	Farrar, Straus & Giroux Collection, Manuscripts and Archives Division, New York Public Library, New York, NY
PM	Paul Mariani
PS	Patrick Samway, S.J.
PTY	Eileen Simpson. *Poets in Their Youth*
PU	Rare Books and Special Collections, Firestone Library, Princeton University, Princeton, NJ

RG	Robert Giroux
RGPF	Personal files of Robert Giroux, Special Collections Room, Monroe Library, Loyola University, New Orleans, LA
RL	Robert Lowell
SB	Saul Bellow
TSE	T. S. Eliot
UM	Archives and Special Collections, Andersen Library, University of Minnesota, Minneapolis, MN
WDH	John Berryman, *We Dream of Honour: John Berryman's Letters to His Mother*. Edited by Richard J. Kelly
WM	William Meredith

Balloon

It takes just a moment
for the string of the gas balloon
to tug itself loose from the hand.

If its string could only be caught in time
it could still be brought down
become once more a gay toy
safely tethered in the warm nursery world
of games, and tears, and routine.

But once let loose out of doors
being gas-filled the balloon can do nothing but rise
although the children who are left on the ground may cry
seeing it bobbing out of human reach.

On its long cold journey up to the sky
the lost balloon might seem to have the freedom of a bird.
But it can fly only as a slave
obeying the pull to rise which it cannot feel.

Having flown too high to have any more use as a plaything
who will care if it pays back its debt and explodes
returning its useless little pocket of air
to an uncaring air it has never been able to breathe.

—Robert Lowell

CHAPTER ONE

The Early Years and Columbia College

[Berryman was] the most brilliant, intense, articulate man I've ever met, at times even the kindest and most gentle, who for some reason brought to our writing a depth of insight and care we did not know existed. At a time when he was struggling with his own self-doubts and failings, he awakened us to our singular gifts as people and writers. He gave all he had to us and asked no special thanks. He did it for the love of poetry.
—Philip Levine, "Mine Own John Berryman," in
Recovering Berryman, edited by Richard J. Kelly
and Alan K. Lathrop, 40–41

*Like many people who worked with him, I called him "Mister Giroux."
To the literary world, he was Robert Giroux, the greatest living editor.*
—Paul Elie, author of *The Life You Save May Be Your Own*,
at the December 2008 Memorial Service for
Robert Giroux, Columbia University

Of the writers whose lives intersected with Robert Giroux, former editor in chief of Harcourt, Brace and editor in chief and chairman of the board of Farrar, Straus & Giroux, poet John Berryman had the longest impact on him both on a personal and professional level, beginning with their student days at Columbia College in New York. However, this was no ordinary friendship. Giroux had a deep-seated secret desire to surpass the essays written about Shakespeare by Berryman, as well as the book on Shakespeare written by their mutual professor Mark Van Doren.[1] From the time of his graduation in 1936, it would take Giroux forty-six years for his work, entitled *The Book Known as Q: A Consideration of Shakespeare's Sonnets*, to come to fruition and be published.[2] Such unacknowledged competition between a college student, his classmate, and their professor has never been seen before in the annals either of publishing or of Shakespearean scholarship. Giroux's letters to Berryman were often filled with editorial details and pertinent observations emanating from his genuine affection for his friend, whose talent he never doubted. Giroux gave Berryman the greatest gift he could: sustained encouragement to continue writing without trying to manipulate or discourage him in any way, even while harboring for many years a silent grudge against him and enduring a nearly five-year estrangement after the publication in 1956 of Berryman's *Homage to Mistress Bradstreet*.

During the final days of Herbert Hoover's Depression-ridden presidency, as millions of Americans were desperately seeking employment of any sort, Berryman and Giroux, both eighteen years old in 1932, enrolled in Columbia on Morningside Heights.[3] A few blocks north, Harlem was suffering from a devastating 50 percent unemployment rate. In spite of great social and political unrest not only in New York but throughout the entire country, Columbia, protected by the rectilinear boundaries of 114th Street and 120th Street, and Broadway and Morningside Drive, provided its incoming students a place of quiet refuge and heady elitism, inspired by the presence of such distinguished faculty as Jacques Barzun, Irwin Edman, Douglas Moore, Lionel Trilling, Mark Van Doren, and Raymond Weaver. Among all of them, Van Doren, known as a calm and steady mentor, stayed in touch with these two students more than did any other member of the faculty.

Poetry and the works of Shakespeare, beginning with reading and analyzing Shakespeare's plays and poetry in Van Doren's class, as well as publishing in the *Columbia Review*, brought Berryman and Giroux into close contact. David Lehman, who wrote the foreword to a reprint of Van Doren's book on Shakespeare, gives an honest and widely accepted appraisal of Van Doren:

> But the reason Van Doren's students loved him had little to do with his relatively high public profile and even less with his poetry, which

many regarded as orthodox and lyrical at a time when modernity itself seemed to require a rough assault on poetic convention. No, the reason Van Doren exerted such a strong force on students, especially those with big literary and intellectual ambitions, was that he had no agenda, no outsized ego, and he treated them as grown-ups. He wanted to talk to them, not compete with them. He sought not disciples but dialogue; not imitators but independent minds in the Emersonian tradition.[4]

Giroux likewise mentioned in an interview with Lehman that he and Berryman took every one of Van Doren's classes, including the American literature course in their junior year and the two-semester course on Shakespeare, in addition to Professor Weaver's Colloquium on Important Books.[5] Van Doren's Shakespeare course in the fall of 1935 and the spring of 1936 covered thirty-seven plays, studied in chronological order, in addition to the two major narrative poems, the sonnets, and "A Lover's Complaint" and "The Phoenix and the Turtle."[6] This course transformed Giroux's life and opened up to him the comic heights and tragic depths of the human spirit.

Van Doren's *Collected Poems: 1922–38* and *Shakespeare*, both published in 1939, provide evidence of the poetic talent and critical ability of this noted professor. When invited to write an essay on Berryman for the special issue of the *Harvard Advocate* (Spring 1969), Van Doren replied that Berryman was complex to say the least: high-strung and nervous, though devoted to his friends and often relaxed in their presence; sensible, yet morally indignant; always witty, yet seemingly bristling at times. Beginning with *Homage to Mistress Bradstreet* and going through the *Sonnets* and *Dream Songs*, Berryman handled with ease the world that he knew.[7] Heavily influenced by Van Doren, Berryman imagined that after college he, too, could become a poet.[8] He even reviewed Van Doren's *A Winter Diary* in the April 1935 issue of the *Columbia Review*—a bold step for a student to take.

Van Doren, whose reputation was validated on almost every page of the May 1932 issue of Columbia's *Varsity Review*, later wrote about four of his most talented students from the midthirties:

If anyone supposes that the Depression produced only bitterness in students, and savagery, and wrath, such cases as Berryman and

[Thomas] Merton and [Robert] Lax refute the supposition. . . .
There were bitter cases, granted; though again there was Robert
Giroux, whose nature was as noticeably sweet as that of Merton or
Lax, and as modest and as charitable. Giroux . . . thought then that
he would never be interested in anything but movies. He saw all the
films, and made sure that I saw the best of them; scarcely a week
passed without his coming to tell me of one I must not miss.[9]

Van Doren spotted something in Giroux's character that would be developed over the years: a strong, discerning visual imagination nurtured by
attending Saturday matinees in the two enormous movie theaters in his
native Jersey City, New Jersey: Loew's Jersey Theatre and The Stanley,
as well as the Thalia on Manhattan's Upper West Side. Giroux once sent
a film script to Fox Film Corporation on West Fifty-Sixth Street about a
character named Robert who remembers the Armistice of World War I,
goes to college in the East, and becomes a determined pacifist. Unfortunately, everyone he knows turns against him. Later, after not receiving an
answer, Giroux wrote to D. A. Doran at Fox, explaining the significance
of the storyline: "It is a situation in which many a young man, including
myself, has found himself."[10] At Columbia, Giroux also learned to evaluate
fiction and poetry, as well as other forms of creative expression, particularly the operas broadcast live each Saturday afternoon from the stage of
the Metropolitan Opera. Over the years, he grew to appreciate the complexity of operatic performances in recitative form, arias, duets, and en-
sembles as expressed in the extraordinary musicality inherent particularly
in the Italian language. In short, his ears confirmed the validity, truth, and
beauty of what his eyes were seeing and reading.

The fragments we know of Berryman's early life reveal unabsorbed
trauma leading to an endless succession of personal struggles. Born on
October 25, 1914, in McAlester, Oklahoma, John Allyn Smith Jr. (Berry-
man's original name) was the son of Martha Little Smith and John Allyn
Smith (sometimes called Allyn), who had married two years before in All
Saints Catholic Church in McAlester. At the time of her marriage,
Martha converted to Catholicism, the religion of her husband, though
their religious beliefs seemed to make them incompatible with each other.
Martha later maintained that Allyn, seven years her senior, had previously
raped her, but this could have been a fabrication, for she was known for
dissembling certain events in her life.[11] (Giroux told me that, on the oc-

casion of the baptism of Berryman's daughter, Sarah, for whom Giroux served as godfather, Berryman's mother had confirmed to Giroux that Allyn had indeed raped her and that only after she had become pregnant did she agree to marry him.) She even wrote to her son, John, something that no son ever wants to hear from his mother: "I did not love him [Allyn] and have long felt wretchedly guilty because of what came of us to him [*sic*]."[12] As Berryman grew, he tried relentlessly to decipher, without success, the import of these words.

As the Smiths moved around the state, Allyn worked in local banks in Lamar, Wagoner, and Anadarko (where, it seems, he was forced to resign) and then briefly, and not always successfully, as a state game and fish warden and captain in the 160th Field Artillery at Fort Sill. While in Anadarko, the Smiths, including John's younger brother, Robert Jefferson, born on September 1, 1919, attended Holy Family Church, where John made his first communion in 1923 and served as an altar boy. Two years later, Martha and Allyn moved to Tampa, Florida, where Martha's mother had given her daughter and Allyn some property as a wedding present. After half of this property had been sold to purchase a restaurant, Allyn unloaded the rest at a loss against his mother-in-law's wishes. In the interim, John and Robert briefly attended a mission boarding school, Saint Joseph's Academy in Chickasha, run by the Sisters of Saint Francis. These were not the happiest times for either boy as they coped with separation from their parents.

Once in Florida, the four Smiths adjusted to the postwar economy during the presidency of Calvin Coolidge. Government aid to the depressed agricultural sector seemed shortsighted as nearly five thousand rural banks in the Midwest and South shut their doors in bankruptcy. Thousands of farmers lost their lands. Tax cuts contributed to an uneven distribution of wealth. The economic prosperity within Florida created conditions for a real estate bubble, as outside investors from around the country considered Florida a glamorous, tropical paradise. Land prices were based solely upon the expectation of finding a customer, not upon land value, and, in the midtwenties, the inevitable slowdown began in the real estate industry as new customers failed to arrive and old customers sold their land. During this time, the Smiths experienced marital problems and contemplated divorce. John's father took up with a Cuban woman, and John's mother began an affair with John Angus McAlpin Berryman, sixteen years her senior, the owner of the Kipling Arms on

Clearwater Island across the bay from Tampa.[13] After the family moved to an apartment at the Kipling Arms, Allyn, according to his wife, admitted being unfaithful. On June 26, 1926, he shot himself in the chest with a .32 caliber revolver, though, curiously, no traces of the usual powder burns were detected.

Soon transplanted to New York, Martha married John Angus (sometimes called Uncle Jack) on September 8, 1926, in the Church of the Transfiguration in Manhattan—just ten weeks after the death of young John's father. Though Martha reverted to her Episcopalian roots for her second marriage, most likely in an effort to develop stronger spiritual values, she never succeeded in creating a strong family unit. Her relationship with her new husband grew more unsettling as time went by. Perhaps she pretended to love John Angus during the thirteen years of their marriage, or perhaps she just wanted to avoid having her sons grow up fatherless, or perhaps she never knew how to reciprocate the love he had for her and her boys. Most likely the nature of their alliance remained unclear—even to her.[14] However much John Angus tried, he could never fill the deep void left in young John's heart by the death of his biological father.

Many questions went unanswered after Allyn's death. Martha had previously taken her husband to see a psychiatrist, and, after sensing imminent danger, she removed five of the six bullets from his revolver.[15] One could well ask: why did she not remove all of them? Eileen Simpson (Berryman's first wife, who later preferred to use the last name of her second husband) believed that her former mother-in-law periodically reworked the ever-changing myth about Allyn's death, resolutely repeating to her son what seemed to be a constant refrain: "In the name of God, John, it is my deepest conviction that your father did not intentionally kill himself."[16] Years later, Giroux met John Angus, whom Mrs. Berryman introduced as her husband but not as John's father. It took a while for Giroux to figure out that John Berryman's biological father was the late John Allyn Smith. Gradually, Giroux put the pieces together, confirming what he had suspected for years: Mrs. Berryman, whom he referred to in my presence as "crazy paranoid" and as someone who ruined John's life, had *murdered* her husband. John Angus's oldest sister, Cora, known as Aunt Code, believed likewise.[17] According to a brief statement in Berryman's private journal, it crossed his mind, too, that his mother had killed his father, though, as late as July 1967, his mother explicitly denied this.[18] Giroux was more circumspect on this topic years later: "Though Berryman's tragic illness (alcoholism) crippled his later years and ended in suicide, I repeat my conviction, as his close friend, editor, and publisher, that biographers have underrated his lifelong torment over his father's suicide, as well as the sinister role of his possessive mother."[19] Martha also recounted to Giroux how Allyn had once tried to drown John and perhaps also Robert, then a child, though only John seemed to recall such an incident, something that his mother had earlier described to him.[20] Simpson, who undoubtedly knew Giroux's views because they remained close friends throughout the years, reserved judgment in her final comment on the tragedy of Berryman's father: "The circumstances of his death I heard recounted so often, and so variously, that to this day they remain a puzzle."[21]

All his life, Berryman was plagued by the never-fully-explained death of his father, as evident in his 1971 poem "Tampa Stomp," in several letters to his mother (particularly one written from Minneapolis, Minnesota, in November 1970), and in his posthumous, semiautobiographical novel, *Recovery*.[22] In Dream Song 143 he wrote of his father, "I put him down / while all the same on forty years I love him / stashed in Oklahoma / beside his brother Will." Furthermore, Berryman's "Henry's Confession" (Dream Song 76) and especially Dream Song 384 capture the unassuageable raw emotion caused by his father's death:

> The marker slants, flowerless, day's almost done,
> I stand above my father's grave with rage,
> often, often before
> I've made this awful pilgrimage to one
> who cannot visit me, who tore his page
> out: I come back for more.
>
> I spit upon this dreadful banker's grave
> who shot his heart out in a Florida dawn
> O ho alas alas
> When will indifference come, I moan & rave
> I'd like to scrabble till I got right down
> away down under the grass
>
> and ax the casket open ha to see
> just how he's taking it, which he sought so hard
> we'll tear apart

the mouldering grave clothes ha & then Henry
will heft the ax once more, his final card,
and fell it on the start.[23]

Charles Thornbury, editor of Berryman's *Collected Poems: 1937–1971*, who has written with great insight about Berryman's reaction to his father's death, believed that, in addition to imagination, talent, and love for the sound and the feel of words, his father's suicide made a poet out of Berryman.[24] While some of the Dream Songs might be critiqued as assorted tidbits from the past or self-conscious verbal petroglyphs testing the limits of the imagination, those that deal directly with his father reveal sustained, focused, reiterative, filial anger.[25]

Giroux spent the early years of his life in circumstances that made him sympathize with Berryman, who, because of his mother's serial relationships and husbands, grew up without an attentive, ever-available father. Born on April 8, 1914, in Jersey City, Robert was raised in a decidedly blue-collar city that looked longingly to New York on the other side of the Hudson River. Originally settled by the Dutch, Jersey City had by that time developed into a large city with approximately 275,000 residents, many of them Roman Catholics who had migrated from Ireland, Germany, Italy, and other European countries. Robert attended the impressive Saint Aloysius Church, an almost exact duplicate of the church of Santa Maria della Grazie in Rome. Robert entered first grade in 1919 at Saint Aloysius School, run by the Sisters of Charity of Saint Elizabeth of Convent Station, and remained there until he finished eighth grade. When a new Saint Aloysius grammar school opened in September 1923, he was one of seven hundred and fifty students. Nearby, the new convent had enough rooms for thirty-six nuns! While outward displays of piety and academic discipline were considered basic values, students applied themselves to the work at hand in an effort to gain an education that their parents often lacked. The Catholics of Jersey City took great care to see that their burgeoning schools combined basic pedagogy and religious values that were appropriate for that time and place—and Robert felt most comfortable in this environment, as did his two sisters and two brothers. Few of Robert's classmates ever suspected that he suffered from the absent-father syndrome. His father, Arthur, had abruptly stopped working as the foreman of a silk factory in Paterson—some say because of the advent of synthetic fibers—thus causing an interlocking series of financial and emotional strains on the Giroux family. Arthur grew distant from his family—and inaccessible to his five children—spending idle days at home poring over scratch sheets and handicapping horses. Thus, Robert's mother, Katherine, provided for the family's needs by doing fine sewing.

The Berrymans lived briefly in Gloucester, Massachusetts, and then took up residence at 89 Bedford Street in Greenwich Village while Mr. Berryman worked on Wall Street as a bond salesman.[26] The family eventually moved to an upscale apartment in a recently constructed building complex called Spanish Gardens on Eighty-Third Street in Jackson Heights, Queens.[27] Each school day, John walked six blocks to attend P. S. 69, where he was known as a studious child, even winning a prize for writing an essay on cruelty to animals. As Martha Berryman became the family's breadwinner by assuming positions of more and more responsibility in several business and advertising agencies, she wanted John to have the best education possible. After finishing eighth grade, he entered the Second Form at South Kent School in South Kent, Connecticut, in September 1928.[28] In typical British fashion, South Kent, run by an Anglican Benedictine monastic community known as the Order of the Holy Cross, had five "forms" (the equivalent of eighth to twelfth grade). This all-boys boarding school, located on 650 verdant acres 25 miles due north of Danbury on the New York border, had the look of a country club, though some students who came from affluent families might have felt it resembled an academic detention center. John did not relish living in a dormitory that resembled a military barracks. The priests promoted an intense regime of prayer, study, and athletic activities and were known, at times, to paddle students and make them crawl on their hands and knees over gravel while reading assigned books.

It seems, however, that John adapted fairly well to his South Kent environment, though he sometimes appeared withdrawn and demoralized from being harassed and intimidated by the older, stronger boys. One of them once beat him up so severely as he went for a run along the train tracks that he threw himself in front of a train; fortunately, two others dragged him away before his suicidal impulses could be realized. He related the incident in his poem "Drunks."

I wondered every day about suicide.
Once at South Kent—maybe in the Third Form?—

I lay down on the tracks before a train
& had to be hauled off, the Headmaster was furious.[29]

After the Berrymans moved in late 1928 to a suburban home on Burbury Lane in Great Neck, New York, on Long Island, John enjoyed the vacations he spent in his new environment. But that all changed during his second year at South Kent as a result of the Wall Street crash on October 29, 1929. Billions of dollars were lost, wiping out thousands of investors and causing panic throughout the country. As a result of the crash, John's parents grew further apart, and he brooded on the events surrounding the death of his biological father as his stepfather grew more marginalized from their family life.

Because of his excellent record at Saint Aloysius, Giroux entered the Jesuit-run Regis High School on East Eighty-Fourth Street just off Park Avenue in Manhattan. This school provided a totally free education for boys, with special consideration given to those who could not otherwise afford a Catholic education. Since Robert had to commute daily from his home to Regis, he spent a good deal of time in the subways rather than playing after-school soccer in Central Park with his classmates. Unlike South Kent, all students attending Regis lived at home with their parents or guardians. If one of them misbehaved, he was normally sent to "jug," which often meant marching in file around the gym or writing out repeatedly "I will not talk in class" for an hour or so. The Jesuits did not believe in corporal punishment. During his first year at Regis, Giroux had classes in Latin composition, Latin literature, English composition, English literature, history, Christian doctrine, and algebra, achieving an overall average of eighty-six. His second year repeated the same subjects, though he added Greek composition and literature and sight-reading Latin. In his third year, his course load included subjects from the first two years, plus plain geometry and French grammar. As someone in the literature track, he took no courses in science. His final grades at Regis, which included those of the first three months of his senior year, showed an average of eighty-nine, a gratifying achievement given the school's emphasis on academics.

An important mentor for Giroux during his teenage years was Lillian Brown, an editor at the *Jersey Journal* who recognized his incipient talents and took him and his friends to concerts, museums, and sites of historical interest. She encouraged him to apply to Columbia, since none of his four siblings had gone to college. In the year between high school and college, Giroux assisted Brown in collecting and editing informative articles for the newspaper's Club section, which discussed social and literary gatherings on topics ranging from chess to drama, cartooning to editorial writing. In retrospect, Giroux saw his work at the newspaper as the perfect apprenticeship for entering the world of publishing, giving him a chance to value the written word. This formative time also instilled in him a sense of his own worth, something often missing at home, due mainly to his father's indifferent attitude, which embarrassed him so enormously that he rarely invited classmates home or allowed them to see how he lived his private life.

School routine continued without major incidents for Berryman at South Kent and Giroux in New York, something rather remarkable given the uncontrollable turmoil and malaise throughout the country. Like Giroux, Berryman had classes in English, math, ancient history, Latin (one of his favorite subjects), and French, as well as obligatory attendance at certain religious services that used the King James version of the Bible, allowing him to read and especially hear the resonant dignity of time-honored English. During his second year, he wrote his mother that he could not get enough of church services, and though he felt they were almost identical to the Roman Catholic ones, he preferred the Episcopal ones. In June 1929, Chaplain Jasper H. Kemmis gave him William Hole's *The Life of Jesus of Nazareth* as the Sacred Studies Prize. In addition, he received a copy of Rudyard Kipling's *Stalky & Co.* as head of the second form; a copy of Sir Thomas Malory's *Le Morte d'Arthur* as head of the third form; and a copy of Laurence Sterne's *A Sentimental Journey through France and Italy* as head of the fifth form in June 1932. These awards clearly indicate that the priests and teachers at South Kent recognized Berryman as a student with great potential. At the beginning of the fourth form (or his third year at South Kent), he was first in his class.[30] Though Berryman had expressed an interest in a Wall Street career, perhaps due to Uncle Jack's influence, he was genuinely taken by literary studies but unable to see how he could become an author, since he knew "absolutely nothing about human nature."[31] He felt that his sound and excellent knowledge of English literature, which he sensed would undoubtedly develop in the ensuing years, might lead him to become a professional in that field.

Before leaving South Kent, Berryman wrote his mother on April 13, 1932, about a short paper on John Millington Synge's play *Riders to the Sea* that he had written for Albion Patterson's English class: "As you know, I consider English the only subject I'm taking this year that is really of vital importance, and this term I am doing it justice, the first time I have ever done myself justice in any subject."[32] Unlike Giroux, Berryman gave little credit to his early schooling; his time at South Kent devolved in his mind over the years, even though he profited from his younger brother's presence during the 1931–1932 academic year. He later told Simpson that he hated South Kent and did not remember a single book he had read there, something he repeated in a slightly different vein to his mother, though he had seemed to relish reading as a teenager the fiction of Charles Dickens, George Eliot, Ernest Hemingway, D. H. Lawrence, and Sir Walter Scott.[33] Yet, Berryman so excelled in his studies that after four years at South Kent (an undistinguished final average grade of seventy-eight notwithstanding), he skipped the sixth form and went directly to Columbia (not to Princeton, his other choice) after receiving a partial scholarship.

Giroux similarly went to Columbia without a high school diploma. He quit Regis in his senior year after being accepted, feeling sure that Columbia would not revoke its decision. In late June 1932, he received the first Nicholas Murray Butler Scholarship sponsored by the Columbia University Alumni Club of Hudson County, New Jersey, after obtaining the best grade in an exam taken by fifty other students. Though the larger world was quickly opening up in front of him, Giroux knew he would still have to live at home as a college student. In point of fact, he lived almost his entire life in Jersey City (except for two different apartments in Manhattan and a short time in Pittstown, New Jersey), commuting back and forth in the Jersey "tubes" while studying at Regis and Columbia and then during much of his career as an editor in New York. Thus, his life had an extraordinarily predictable routine, each day beginning and ending with subway rides that allowed him to rub shoulders with thousands and thousands of other people, ranging from the prosperous to the poverty stricken. Whether arriving at Columbia or his office in New York, he brought with him a knowledge of his place in the world that allowed him to sort through with common-sense wisdom the myriad variables of the task at hand. Jersey City rooted Giroux in a complex, diverse network of values that would be important to him during his entire professional life.

Berryman's mother and stepfather continued to move often, from Great Neck to East Sixtieth Street in Manhattan, then to East Twenty-Fourth Street, and finally to a less-expensive apartment at 119 East Eighty-Fourth Street. Living on the Upper East Side during his first year on campus gave Berryman a buffer from those eking out an existence in deplorable Depression-era shantytowns, such as nearby Hooverville in Central Park, where many dwellings were pieced together from crates, cardboard, and flimsy scraps of metal. Berryman's closest friend at Columbia, Ernest Milton "Milt" Halliday, wrote about the private, post–Jazz Age aspects of Berryman's life at this time, especially his girlfriends Jean Bennett and Garnette Snedecker, students at Hunter College; Elspeth Davies, a student at Barnard College; and Jane Atherton, a student at Smith College, Northampton, Massachusetts.[34] In addition to an active social life that included heavy drinking, Berryman enjoyed various sports, particularly swimming, track, and wrestling; his participation on the Columbia crew team, however, left him with nagging memories of torn leather straps and bloody thighs. He later put his thoughts about his first months at Columbia into a poem entitled "In & Out."

> After my dismal exile at my school
> I made at Columbia a point of being popular,
> by mid-November already I knew by name
> most of the nearly 500 men in my class,
>
> including commuters, touchingly pleased
> to have a soul recognize them.
> I liked them, a man of the world, I felt like them,
> barring my inordinate desire.[35]

What Berryman failed to mention in this poem was the awkwardly intrusive presence of his mother. Giroux was not the only one astonished and perplexed to see Mrs. Berryman assuming at times the role of an undergraduate at campus activities.[36] She even rented a dilapidated, three-bedroom apartment at 408 West 115th Street in the fall of 1934 in order to be close to campus. At times she made a rather glamorous figure, haunting the quadrangle in front of the impressive Hamilton Hall or attending one of her son's poetry readings, with her modish clothes, dangling earrings, and youthful appearance, even to the point of passing herself off as her son's sister. Halliday paints a similar picture of her: "She was naturally a good-looking woman, I think, but in any event she was always skillfully made up, and she wore what impressed me as elegant if slightly bizarre costumes. She spoke in a bright, cheerful way, perking the conversations with quips and with allusions to what the *New Yorker* called 'goings on about town.'"[37] In his poem "Unwanted," Robert Lowell depicts Berryman's mother from a different perspective, as someone who remained quite inaccessible:

> I read an article on a friend
> As if recognizing my obituary:
> "Though his mother loved her son consumingly,
> She lacked a really affectionate nature;
> So he always loved what he missed."
> That was John Berryman's mother, not mine.[38]

Nor was Mrs. Berryman beyond visiting Professor Van Doren's office to check up on her son's progress. When she gave a big champagne party on October 25, 1935, to celebrate her son's twenty-first birthday, Mark and Dorothy Van Doren, Robert Giroux, Elspeth Davies, Jane Atherton, and Professors Edman and Weaver were among the invited guests. One can easily get the impression that Mrs. Berryman was recasting in and around Columbia the Academy Award–winning film *Grand Hotel*.

In an essay entitled "Three and a Half Years at Columbia," Berryman recounts the highlights of his "lost years" and "the need to sit at the feet of exceptional men."[39] Pulled more to the social life—the thrill of spending a night in a speakeasy or going to Harlem to hear Duke Ellington or Ella Fitzgerald—than the academic one, Berryman flunked Van Doren's English 64, an eighteenth-century literature course, and left college for a while, as partly explained in his poem "Down & Back":

> I wrote a strong exam, but since it was Mark
> a personal friend, I had to add a note
> saying of the 42 books in the bloody course
> I'd only read 17.
>   He liked my candour
> (he wrote) & had enjoyed the exam
> but had no option except to give me F in the course—
>
> costing my scholarship.[40]

Flunking this course was a heavy blow to Berryman, who felt he had let down this thought-filled professor. Dean Herbert Hawkes, known to be crusty but nice, granted Berryman a leave of absence in early October 1934: "I regret to learn that you are obliged to drop out of college for a little while. I enclose a leave of absence as you request and hope that we may see you back in school before long."[41] In preparation to retake the exam, Berryman read all the required texts over a period of several months and kept a notebook that included a thirty-page digest of one of John Locke's essays. When Berryman handed Van Doren this substantial manuscript, hoping that it would repair their friendship, it did even more. Van Doren was so impressed that he showed it to the dean. They agreed to change Berryman's mark, restore his scholarship, and welcome him back to the college. In writing about this in mid-February 1935 to Halliday, Berryman mentioned he had averaged about four hours of sleep a night and was practically a shade. "However, there it is—I gave him [Van Doren] yesterday noon the whole course, and Milt, it was 166 pages, something over 52,000 words! . . . I'm so proud that I can scarcely touch the ground."[42] Dean Hawkes subsequently could not have been more considerate. When Berryman resumed taking courses, wiser in the ways of academia, he drew close to Van Doren, who had recognized his student's incipient literary strengths and willingly changed his grade after a successful three-hour oral exam. "John Berryman was first and last a literary youth," Van Doren wrote in his autobiography, "all of his thought sank into poetry, which he studied and wrote as if there were no other exercise in the human brain."[43]

When Berryman returned to Columbia, supported in part by some money Uncle Jack had made on the stock exchange, he started reading the quarterly *Hound & Horn*, originally titled in 1927 *A Harvard Miscellany*, which Giroux considered the best literary magazine of its day. Beginning in 1928, Richard Palmer Blackmur, an autodidact known for his courtly manner and tweedy jackets (memorialized in Dream Song 173), whom Berryman later considered the "only writer" at Princeton, became one of its editors.[44] Berryman once wrote to his mother, "Blackmur is the supreme example of [a] really magnificent intellect without hieratic base, spending himself on triviality."[45] Impressed by the magazine's content, Berryman eventually referred to it in his poem "Olympus":

I found this new Law-giver all unknown
except in the back numbers of a Cambridge quarterly

Hound & Horn, just defunct.
I haunted on Sixth Avenue until

at 15¢ apiece or 25
I had all 28 numbers
& had fired my followers at Philolexian & Boar's Head
with the merits of this prophet.

Berryman, together with Robert Lax, later an excellent minimalist poet who lived for eighteen years on the island of Patmos, and Thomas Merton, a future Trappist monk and prolific spiritual writer, helped to organize a short-lived poetic antisociety, a counterpart to the Philolexian Society, the oldest undergraduate literary society in the United States. Founded by Alexander Hamilton at Columbia before the Revolutionary War, the Philolexian engaged in a wide range of literary activities, including debates, theatrical productions, and essay contests. After some reflection, however, Berryman realized that he needed to be associated with the Philolexian to have any legitimate standing as a budding poet, and so he joined this society and served as its president in 1936.[46]

In their sophomore and junior years, the individual literary and aesthetic interests of Berryman and Giroux became apparent, especially in writing for the *Columbia Review*, which had briefly enfolded *Morningside*, an independent review that ceased publication in 1931.[47] Before Christmas 1933, the *Columbia Review and Morningside*, for which Giroux is listed as one of three associate editors, printed a short vignette by Giroux entitled "Prelude," depicting a boy of thirteen walking home from the library. When a stranger confronts him and wants to look at his books, the boy suddenly realizes that the stranger is the Devil. Eventually reaching home, he wonders whether he should mention this event in the confessional at church but finally decides not to, "since he had only resisted temptation and committed no sin."[48] Though pious juvenilia would have had little appeal to college students of his day, Giroux's foray into the publishing world clearly indicates that he felt it important to communicate to his classmates a subject rooted in his own spiritual environment. A similar theme, repeated in Giroux's second vignette, entitled "End of the World," placed first in the prose group category for a contest sponsored by the Philolexian. Here, Giroux depicts a scene in which another boy, Tommy, serves Benediction in a Catholic church after Midnight Mass on New Year's Eve. In this story, the local paper predicts that the end of the world would occur that very evening. When this does not happen, Tommy returns home with his parents, who give him a pan to beat on so he can join in the local New Year's festivities. Isolated from other revelers, Tommy decides to go into his house. If anything, this vignette depicts a lonely boy, whose pious family lives by monotonous, all-too-predictable routines. Tommy finally joins his parents, knowing, no doubt, that his world has not ended, as he bides his time until he might find some communal joy and happiness. Both vignettes show boy protagonists returning home and avoiding real or potential dangers, though life at home, hidden behind closed doors, apparently has little to offer.

Similarly, Berryman's "The Ball Poem," written in blank verse and first printed privately about December 1942, reveals an unnamed boy's backward glance at his short life, his willingness to accept loss, and the painful knowledge of an irretrievable childhood possession of a lost ball and its suffused attendant lesson. This poem provides a crucial insight into Berryman's poetic development (emphasis mine).[49]

What is the boy now, who has lost his ball.
What, what is he to do? I saw it go
Merrily bouncing, down the street, and then
Merrily over—there it is in the water!
No use to say 'O there are other balls':
An *ultimate shaking grief* fixes the boy
As he stands rigid, trembling, staring down
All his young days into the harbour where
His ball went. . . . I am everywhere,
I suffer and move, my mind and my heart move
With all that move me, under the water
Or whistling, I am not a little boy.[50]

The boy in the poem suffers a tremendous defeat all alone. One could well ask: is Berryman really talking about himself—as the boy in Florida who lost his father, who throughout the rest of his life experiences "ultimate shaking grief"?

In any discussion Berryman had with Giroux about his family, Berryman's mother, not his father or stepfather, stood out in Giroux's mind. As a sign of their growing friendship, Berryman gave Giroux in July 1934 copies of four sonnets he had written to honor his mother on her birthday on July 8 ("I sing a mother's love," "Full-blown, gentle and wise, today she stands," "And she's grown beautiful on the rocky road," and "Paradox, that she should claim her wit").[51] The figure of this meddlesome mother, as Giroux often observed, haunted every moment of her son's existence.[52] Giroux rarely spoke about his own mother except to indicate that in a quiet and unobtrusive way she kept their family together, especially during and following the Great Depression. Regardless of certain similarities in their younger years, Berryman and Giroux, as adults, radically diverged in the ways they sought companionship and intimacy, the first by constantly seeking the companionship of women, whether inside or outside of marriage, and failing to deal adequately with chronic alcoholism and resulting bouts of depression, and the second by living soberly with his close companion, Charles Reilly, whom he had known as a teenager, in spite of a short-lived marriage with a woman who had worked at the United Nations.

At the end of his sophomore year, a special issue of the *Columbia Review and Morningside* printed Giroux's "Score One," an eight-line poem about death and time. It concludes with an observation, "We can do no more, Marcel Proust," a line that Berryman remembered and twice quoted back to Giroux:[53]

> Inconsequential, gentle these deaths . . .
> Later we look, lamenting. Know you knew
> And tried to snap the camera, congeal
> The fleeting flow and feel it full. How few
> The scores, with strong-armed Time giving the push,
> Rushing us on in one swift breathless boost.
> Cry "Zut! Zut!," waving an umbrella;
> We can do no more, Marcel Proust.[54]

The name of the French author and the repetition of the French word *zut* refers to a draft version of Proust's *À la Recherche du temps perdu*, entitled "Combray," in which the narrator recalls the adolescent sexual fantasies that set up barriers between himself and his mother. He is sent to bed without receiving a kiss from her, though his father encourages the mother to spend a night in the narrator's bedroom. This draft resembles the final version, in which the narrator stops to gaze at a pond with a chicken nearby fluffing its feathers. He points his umbrella, exclaiming, "Zut, zut, zut, zut."[55] By itself, Giroux's poem is almost indecipherable until one thinks about the words "Know you knew" in the poem—that is, Giroux knew that Berryman knew what had happened to his father. This most tragic event in Berryman's life flowed by too quickly, causing infinite regress, and remained deeply imbedded in his memory. If this is the case, the allusion to Proust, when linked to the death of Berryman's father, reveals that Giroux intuited early on in their friendship Berryman's complex and unresolved (and unresolvable) relationship with his mother and her first husband. Most likely, Giroux remembered this reference to Proust from a class discussion in which Berryman also participated. Subsequently, it became a private code between the two of them. Giroux avoids interpreting the Rorschach inkblot of the father directly in his poem but, like Proust, just points to it.

At the end of 1934, a regular issue of the *Columbia Review and Morningside* featured Giroux's short essay on art and propaganda, in which he prodded communist sympathizers on campus to show their true colors— his way of ferreting out those who were naïvely smitten by revolutions:

> For what will become of the poetic imagination when the revolutionary will has achieved its goal? It will continue the same as it did before the revolution, as it does now, as it always has. It will continue to see a way of looking at things, at people, at human nature. People will always be Yahoos and Houyhnhnms in any society, despite all the educating in the world, hating each other and loving each other. And Gulliver, the artist, will be there to translate it into terms of art. Art is a weapon, art is an escape, art is a way of looking at things. Certainly it is all three right now. Will the first two always be necessary? That is a question which only time can decide.[56]

Most likely, Giroux was reacting to a gathering of some five thousand members of the Communist Party who had rallied at Madison Square Garden in mid-February to protest the massacre of Austrian socialists by the fascistic regime of Engelbert Dollfuss. Rather than getting caught up in the Sturm und Drang of this riot between communists and socialists, or any demonstrations by the communists for that matter, Giroux, an unabashed Jersey City Democrat, questioned the underlying political strategies of the communists and the implications such policies might have for art in American society. His focus, as it would be throughout his life, was on the perennial role of the creative imagination.

As Berryman and Giroux began their junior year, the November issue of the *Columbia Review*, as it was now called, published Giroux's reviews of a number of films, including *Our Daily Bread*, directed by King Vidor.[57] He would return years later to a closer study of King Vidor in his *A Deed of Death*. By venturing into the world of fiction, poetry, and essay writing, albeit in a very limited way, Giroux realized inchoately that he need not remain an outlier to creativity in the printed form. (Berryman's uncollected poem "Homage to Film" suggests that some filmmakers might be considered artists equal to John Donne or Henry James.)[58] These college publications helped Giroux to realize that he would be better suited to develop his skills as an editor, not as a creative writer, as demonstrated in the March 1935 issue containing his six-page article "On Being a Film Crank," in which he discusses various contemporary films, such as *David Copperfield*, *The Lives of a Bengal Lancer*, *Chapayev*, *Sequoia*, *The Scarlet Pimpernel*, *Man of Aran*, and *Musical Moods*. Giroux reveals here his theory of film criticism, noting that a film critic needs to be a crank. But if one were to replace *film* and *cinema* in his words below with *literary* and *literature*, then it would be possible to sense his incipient theory of the role of an editor as a pioneer in a new field of endeavor, one who insists that works of art have a character of greatness about them that can best be evaluated by his own particular standards.

> Crank, of course, is another word for critic. A film critic demands a masterpiece every time he goes to the movies, for he insists on not only a good picture but a great one. He knows that in all likelihood [that] he won't be accommodated, and he knows the reasons why. But he insists, and all the films he sees are measured by this insistence. He has a great respect and love for the cinema, if not for most of the people in it. He is a pioneer and must devise his own critical standards, for the art is new—the newest—and the confusion and cant which surround it is endless. He is a crank indeed, but only because he believes the cinema capable of great things, and expects them.[59]

Giroux concludes by mentioning the talks given at the twentieth annual conference of the National Board of Review of Motion Pictures held that March in New York, a foreshadowing of his fifty-four years of service to this review board.

As Giroux and Berryman talked in the offices of the *Columbia Review*, each tried to locate within himself what direction he might like to pursue. They began to learn more about themselves as they saw their essays and poems in print. In the same March issue, the editors published a controlled and highly self-conscious poem by "John A. McA. Berryman" entitled "Essential," which attempts to penetrate the darker recesses of the mind, a theme that would remain with Berryman throughout his life (emphasis mine).

> The unresolved angular
> Of deep mind-lying stone
> Contains the only singular
> In mass that mind can own.
>
> When waters of expression
> Have rounded the boulder,
> Transmitted the impression
> Is falsely thin and older
>
> In platitude than its unique [*sic*]
> Which cannot wash away—
> As one would judge by his tunic
> A man, who cannot fray.
>
> And sanguine fingers searching deep
> Into the dark of mind
> Will not away from ever-sleep
> This stone: and will not find
>
> A fracture-edge that it can hold
> Or weakness it can bend
> To service—hand however bold
> Will fail *to comprehend.*

The solid stone, with fractured edges that make it ungraspable, represents something deep within the poet's mind, something that cannot be given its own proper name but is nevertheless objectively solid and real. But try as the poet might, he will fail "to comprehend"—from the Latin "to hold" and "to understand"—the stone, an everyday object that, according to the inscape theory favored by Gerard Manley Hopkins, S.J., has a distinctive being (*haecceitas*) all of its own.

Giroux gradually fell under the spell of Professor Weaver, not only because his colloquium expanded Giroux's awareness of the Greek and Latin classics (he had been introduced to them at Regis), but also because Weaver was someone who had made—in Giroux's eyes—a genuine contribution to the history of American letters. Weaver had found the manuscript of Melville's unfinished novella *Billy Budd* in a trunk while visiting Melville's granddaughter's house in Manhattan in 1919. Weaver produced a text that would later be published in 1924 as the first edition of this work. A colleague once wrote of Weaver, "To see him cross the Van Am quadrangle was to have the sense that one was witnessing some striking detail of a moment in history, or the representation of that moment on a stage."[60] When Weaver told Giroux that *Moby-Dick* had not been recognized as a masterpiece when it was first published in 1851, Giroux had a great insight: he would search out new works of literature that, even if not immediate best-sellers, would later become dominant texts in expanding the American literary imagination. Weaver inspired Giroux to become a book editor and publisher. For Berryman, on the other hand, Weaver, an amateur boxer, was a bit of a tyrant whose distinctive voice and pedagogy were not at all helpful to a budding poet: "One day he [Weaver] walked into our classroom on the third floor of Hamilton and boomed, 'Write me out the first canto of the *Inferno* in the style of Homer, and bring it down to my office.' I spent half an hour at this and went down to his office. 'Put it there,' he said, 'there' being his wastepaper basket. His marking must have been the Dean's despair: only if he actively disliked you did he give you an A minus."[61] If anything, Weaver's scholarship and mannerisms affected Giroux and Berryman in opposite, highly telling ways, the one articulating a desire to find and edit genuinely important literary texts and the second reacting negatively to the summary rejection of his poetic efforts—traits that lasted all their professional lives.

It took a while for Giroux to realize that the tenets and values Berryman had brought with him to campus were not what they seemed to be. During their first two years on campus, Giroux felt that Berryman looked on him as a "grind from New Jersey whose classical studies under the Jesuits had resulted in a scholarship" and saw Berryman's self-centered charisma turning him into an "insufferable snob."[62] Moreover, Giroux was turned off by Berryman's initial interest in campus politics (as a freshman,

Berryman lost the election for class vice president by a few votes), sports (he was a member of the freshman wrestling team), and social activities (stemming, to some extent, from being a member of the Phi Kappa Psi fraternity).[63] In those Depression years, Berryman flaunted his advantages at a prom as the only undergraduate to wear tails and a white tie, a tux that his mother had purchased for him while he was at South Kent, while Giroux had neither the financial resources for nor an interest in ostentation in dress. Giroux likewise avoided verbal grandstanding; in any situation it seemed he went through a process of discernment, articulating his thought process in clear, crisp, and controlled English that reflected an abiding love of the language. Nor did his Jersey City background ever leave him as he coped with the poverty he experienced at home. To earn some pocket money, he wrote publicity for the Cinéma de Paris, a downtown movie house that showed French films exclusively, while also distributing samples of Philip Morris cigarettes, then a new product, for which he was paid ten dollars a week plus two cartons of cigarettes (though he was always a confirmed nonsmoker).

As a serious student of poetry, Berryman became enthralled by poets other than Shakespeare, including Gerard Manley Hopkins (celebrated in Dream Song 377), whose posthumous collection of poetry, in its second printing in 1930, had been receiving considerable attention in the States. (Merton, who entered Columbia as a sophomore in January 1935, once considered writing a doctoral dissertation on Hopkins.)[64] The "terrible sonnets," a group of untitled poems probably written between 1885 and 1886 and found after Hopkins's death, reflect the deep despair and spiritual anguish the poet experienced, analogous to the later, prolonged depressive periods endured by Berryman. One must quickly add, however, that soon after writing these sonnets, Hopkins wrote the magnificently uplifting "That Nature Is a Heraclitean Fire," not unlike the "Eleven Addresses to the Lord" that Berryman composed toward the end of his life. In doing so, both poets contributed to the achievement of new vernacular idioms by carving out autonomous literary spaces, both dark and luminous, where they remained the sovereign rulers. Berryman was also influenced over the years by the poetry of T. S. Eliot, A. E. Housman, Robert Lowell, Ezra Pound, Dylan Thomas, W. B. Yeats, and Walt Whitman. He was particularly taken with the poetry of W. H. Auden (whom he met in November 1936 while studying at the University of Cambridge), as reflected in his poem "Shirley & Auden":

I recognized Auden at once as a new master,
I was by then a bit completely with it.
My love for that odd man has never altered
thro' some of his facile bodiless later books.[65]

At one point, Berryman maintained that Hopkins, Lowell, and Pound were equally important to him; he would not choose the best among them, and yet his ongoing rivalry with Lowell provided both of them "a continuing stimulus to originality."[66] Any jealousy either might have felt about the other ultimately melted into genuine friendship, as seen in Lowell's touching, elegiac poem "For John Berryman (After reading his last *Dream Song*)."[67]

The April 1935 issue of the *Columbia Review*, for which Giroux continued as coeditor, reveals his inchoate role as Berryman's editor: he published two poems by Berryman that came in second for the Boar's Head prize, "Ars Poetica" and "Blake." The same issue also featured two other poems by Berryman, "Apostrophe" and "Lead Out the Weary Dancers," followed in the May issue by "Ivory." The November issue contained two poems by John McAlpin Berryman, "Thanksgiving" and "Elegy: Hart Crane." (On April 27, 1932, Crane, in his early thirties, jumped over the rail of the steamship *Orizaba* ten miles east of the Florida coast. His body was not recovered.) Yet, Berryman wanted a larger readership beyond the confines of Columbia, as he mentioned to his friend Halliday on October 23, 1935: "I've somewhat begun on a career, though—I got the proofs of my review [of three novels] of [James Branch] Cabell, [Harry] Sackler and [Carl Christian] Jensen (called Types of Pedantry) from *The Nation* this morning, and am still joyous about it."[68] As might be surmised, Van Doren had made the contact with Joseph Wood Krutch at *The Nation* for the publication of this review, and it was written with Giroux's assistance. Though Berryman had received considerable recognition on campus as a poet and reviewer, he also had his fair share of rejections, notably the five poems he sent the *Atlantic Monthly* and the six to the *New Yorker*. At one point in the spring of 1935, he put together a manuscript of his poems that he hoped the Yale Younger Poets series would publish, though this turned out not to be the case. In the summer after his junior year, he sent poems to one of the best literary magazines of its day, *Poetry*, edited at the time by Harriet Monroe, who did not accept them but took the time to explain why.

In another letter to Halliday in October 1935, Berryman mentioned the difficulty of fitting his Shakespeare course into a heavy academic schedule: "My course is the acne of Hell College. Three seminars—Senior Colloquium, Edman's Metaphysics, the last year of the Lit sequence—and three others: VD's [Van Doren] wonderful Shakespeare, Weaver's Renaissance and [George C. D.] Odell's Modern Drama."[69] It was said that Professor Odell, whom Berryman considered "a peach of an old fellow," had seen every play of importance on Broadway since the 1880s; by the time he died, he had compiled fifteen volumes of his *Annals of the New York Stage*.[70] Edman's philosophy class—a course that Berryman considered one of the most important ones he took at Columbia—met once a week in the professor's apartment and was normally introduced by Brahms's chamber music before students engaged Plato's writings in chronological order. Berryman was pleased that Edman gave him a copy of John Donne's *Complete Poetry and Selected Prose* in October 1935. Yet he never forgave Edman for interpreting some of his self-termed "lousy" poems as "philosophical poetry" before a large, but unspecified, audience in the McMillan Theater.[71]

This apparent posturing to Halliday, however, does not reveal Berryman's capacity to touch clearly and without pretension the bass strings of his personal life. The opening of another Berryman poem, "Words to a Young Man," in the December issue of the *Columbia Review*, with Giroux as coeditor and Berryman now as one of four associate editors, reflects a dilemma that prefigures much of the personal anguish in his life. In it, he seems to refer to his relationship with his biological father as he poetically beckons his father to come into the sunlight as the two of them walk away from his father's creditors (emphasis mine):

Your roads are trampled by desires
Mixing mud with conflict. Clear,
Swift would be the passage for the State
Officials and the messengers of purpose.

Passionless and prey to any letter
From province or a friend, you seem
The many man when none. Walk with me
Out of this elaborate, simply into the sun.

And let the *light like guns* solve
Creditors, the framework of desire:
Cancel history, be altar for
The iron elate religion of the soul.

The sunlight unfortunately resembles the gun used by his father to kill himself.

If, in a cryptic way, Berryman was using autobiography in his poetry, he likewise saw the value of creating a poetic alter ego. In his review of books in the same issue, entitled "Notes on Poetry: E. A. Robinson, and Others" (featuring authors as diverse as Robinson, Archibald Fleming, Robinson Jeffers, Edgar Lee Masters, Muriel Rukeyser, A. E., and Audrey Wurdemann), Berryman shows a firm grasp and appreciation of contemporary poetry. One Berryman poem in particular, "Note on E. A. Robinson" (who died on April 6, 1935), which appeared in *The Nation* (July 10, 1935; later reprinted in *Columbia Poetry 1935* and the *Literary Digest* [February 1936]), was the recipient of the Mariana Griswold Van Rensselaer Prize. In analyzing Robinson's narrative poem "King Jasper," Berryman highlights the relationship between the subject of the poem and the poem's author; that is, the author comments directly on events in his own life: "The plan of the poem is very simple and comparatively little symbolism is employed: what is thus lost in range is more than compensation for by the great and devious complexity of the few elements used. This is the bare statement toward which he has been working. . . . And the depth of his vision has finally overcome his personal refusal of experience, the influence of which on his work Robinson must have known—a sinister parallel between Jasper and his creator can be pointed out."[72] It is as if Berryman is intimating his later poetic persona, Henry, as himself.[73] Such a reference provides an apperceptive background to Berryman's literary mindscape and landscape, making sure that the reader understands that the creator of the poem portrays at times impenetrable references that have autobiographical bases, something that Berryman would develop with sustained intensity and impressionistic linguistic bravado in his Dream Songs as he espoused poetry as personal memoir.

On March 28, 1936, on personal stationery from West 115th Street, Berryman, as chairman of the Boar's Head Poetry Society, wrote to Blackmur in Boston, giving him some background on the society and inviting him to be a guest of honor, for which he would receive an honorarium of twenty-five dollars. Berryman mentioned that he was familiar with *The Double Agent: Essays in Craft and Elucidation* and inquired if Blackmur would be willing to submit an essay to the *Columbia Review*.[74] In reply, Blackmur agreed to write a critique of Allen Tate's *Reactionary Essays*. At the twenty-sixth annual poetry reading sponsored by the Boar's Head Society on the last day of April 1936, Van Doren said that what keeps the society together "is the desire of students to write poetry and test it on each other's judgment."[75] Berryman read his poems "Notation," "The Witness," and "The Ancestor" before the assembled group and received the first prize for his poem entitled "Trophy."

> On a winter night
> The cold is apt to awaken
> Ambiguous memory: a man who is gone
>
> Who has not moved
> Heart nor made a gesture this
> Nine years of peace constructing calm
>
> Throws up a hand
> Where a bird sings in
> An ash in spring, a shadow in the sun.

This poem shows great lyric control as Berryman's imagination transforms past experience—and the nine years intervening since the death of his father—to reveal its significance in the present without revealing how this memory might play out in some indefinite future. Those present could well have reflected on Van Doren's words of praise for Blackmur, cited as one of the most distinguished critics of poetry, as relevant to Berryman's poetic sensibility. In addition to Berryman's four poems, the final issue of the *Columbia Review* (April 1936), coedited by Giroux, also contained a favorable book review by Van Doren, entitled "A Critic's Job of Work," on Blackmur's *The Double Agent*. Van Doren asked a series of questions that reveal his admiration for Blackmur. What does a poet mean in any given poem, and what does a poet say? How much of any poem is clear and thus knowable by the reader, that is, by fairly ordinary terms? What is the relationship between one poem and other poems by the same poet? "And if all these things are one, what is its character, what are its limitations, what is its final value?"[76] Van Doren emphasized that Blackmur arrives at no conclusion without an exhaustive and critical study of the poet's diction, imagery, and patterns. At the finale of his college career, Berryman could not have asked for more incisive observations about the relationship between poetry and readers of poetry.

Van Doren's critique of Blackmur's essays gives a glimpse of the thinking of two eminent academics who were for years part and parcel of Berryman's life. Blackmur's method, Van Doren notes, is implacably keen, delightful, and tempered, always full of valuable perceptions that would prove useful to future poets. In particular, one sentence reveals much of Van Doren's own philosophy of poetry: "It has not been understood that poetry at any time is at once simple beyond analysis and complex beyond paraphrase; that a full account of what any poem says must include as many articulate statements as can be made concerning the art with which the saying has been achieved, and concerning the total effect in which the artist was interested."[77] Van Doren did not subscribe to the theory that a poem should be easy, though he defended the notion that a poem should say something. If Pound's 1935 injunction to *Make It New*, the title of a collection of his essays, was the touchstone of the Modernist movement that dismissed, to some degree, the obsolete culture of the realistic past, then Van Doren believed that poets and other artists who experimented with innovations, reflecting perhaps an ahistorical sensibility and nontraditional forms, should be judged, both positively and negatively, on their accomplishments. This was a difficult task, to say the least, especially for poets eager to put aside accepted, reliable precedents to find new modes of expression. In short, Van Doren acknowledged the value of radically experimental prosody as long as it made sense from a human and epistemological point of view.

In her own way, Mrs. Berryman perceived something of what was happening when she gave her son his 1935 Christmas present: a copy of Blackmur's book. Would Berryman grasp the views of these learned mentors as he struggled over the years to find his own mode of creative expression? Would he break new ground while integrating the views of these scholar-poet-critics who never disappeared from his thought processes? Could he balance the energy of instinct with the necessity of form? It should be noted, however, that once Berryman had commenced his graduate studies, he began to see that Blackmur was preoccupied with relatively minor aspects of certain poets who were not always outstanding in their craft.[78]

The May–June 1936 issue of the *Columbia Review* contained both Giroux's bibliography of film criticism, "Books on Film Theory," and Berryman's review of six dance plays by Yeats entitled "The Ritual of W. B. Yeats." Giroux told me that Berryman while in college "sopped up" everything of Yeats he could find.[79] Berryman even once considered editing a collection of essays on Yeats. Unfortunately, his projected book of elegies, essays, and interpretations, as he mentions in a letter to Tate written on March 5, 1939, shortly after Yeats's death, was turned down after an interview with James Putnam at Macmillan.[80] Berryman's Dream Song 312, a monologue addressed to Yeats, reflects his forceful desire to confront this great poet, who remained for many years his hidden mentor.

As a leading journal of opinion that then rarely published poetry, *The Nation* featured reviews at this time by Van Doren, Carl Van Doren (Mark's older brother), and Dorothy Van Doren (Mark's wife), the latter serving primarily as the journal's associate editor. Just before Mark Van Doren became the journal's film critic, replacing William Troy, Van Doren asked Giroux to write two essays on film in October 1935: "Taxidermy on the Screen," a review of *Anna Karenina*, and "Novel into Movie," about *Maria Chapdelaine*, *William Tell*, and *Red Salute*. Once he assumed his new role, Van Doren continued writing book reviews and articles on various literary topics; he asked Giroux to substitute for him three more times (June 24, 1936; July 25, 1936; August 8, 1936). Thus, Giroux's name appeared more often in *The Nation* than did Berryman's during the years they were in college. At the 182nd graduation exercises in June 1936, John Angus Berryman gave his adopted son a copy of Whitman's *Leaves of Grass*, a volume the younger Berryman highly praised. In a prescient manner, Giroux gave Berryman a similar gift: H. L. Mencken's *The American Language: An Inquiry into the Development of English in the United States*. Not unexpectedly, both Berryman and Giroux were elected to Phi Beta Kappa. Berryman succinctly summarized his senior year: "I remember the general excitement of running things in my senior year: Philolexian, Boar's Head, and, with Bob Giroux, the *Columbia Review*, which made me practically professional."[81] In all, the collaboration of Berryman, as a published poet, and Giroux, as his editor (as well as a published film critic), presages one of the most extraordinary personal and professional relationships in the history of American poetry.

Before the beginning of the second semester of Giroux's senior year, Van Doren informed him that he was being considered for the Euretta J. Kellett Fellowship at Clare College, Cambridge University. Giroux incorrectly had the impression that recipients of the fellowship were subsequently required to teach, as did his friend and previous recipient, Andrew Chiappe, who returned to Columbia in 1938 and later replaced Van Doren as the university's Shakespeare scholar. Since Giroux wanted to become an editor and book publisher, he turned down the offer. Van Doren had failed to tell him, however, that a two-thousand-dollar stipend was available to cover living expenses. Had Giroux known this, he might have decided differently. By the time he found out about the stipend from Jacques Barzun, Van Doren had approached Berryman, who had done exceptionally well in eleven of the twelve courses he took in his senior year.

The twelfth, Professor Emery Neff's yearlong course on Romantics and Victorians, was the sticking point. There was a side of Neff's personality that curiously attracted Berryman, particularly the ways he articulated the elegant music of Wordsworth's poetry and taught "the vile Carlyle" with such unabashed enthusiasm. However, Berryman had made Neff's life most uncomfortable during the course, and he was not prepared for the C he received. It meant, in effect, that he could not graduate, because for every six credits of an A one received an extra credit, provided that one received no grade below B. After turning in his grades, Neff promptly set sail for Europe, having left instructions with his assistant to post the marks at the last possible moment, something that was not normally done.

Berryman, not unexpectedly, thought of Neff as a "villain," "a great ass," and the "worst teacher" he had ever known.[82] He subsequently complained to the dean, who offered his support, as did members of the English and Philosophy Departments, and a second exam was arranged. Berryman never knew that he received a grade of B- (just barely enough to pass); his large notebook had proved that he had been following the course with attention. After thus overcoming the C, Berryman was awarded the Kellett Fellowship, as he explained in his poem "Crisis."

Finally, a command decision:
They'd give me a second exam, invented by themselves,
& judge it, & if my paper justified,
They'd elevate the highly irrational mark.

I took it—it was fair, hard—& I killed it.
I never knew what I got, but the course-grade
Cranked upward to a B. I graduated.[83]

Exhausted by the experience, Berryman spent the summer in Canada before going to England. His savior had been Van Doren. Berryman considered him, as he mentions in his essay "Three and a Half Years at Columbia," the "presiding genius of all my work," mainly because his courses were "strongly structured, lit with wit, leaving ample play for grace and charm." Berryman admired Van Doren's common sense and disciplined approach, especially applauding the professor's decision to walk out of the classroom when only two or three students out of a class of thirty had read the play they were to discuss. "If during my stay at Columbia I had met only Mark Van Doren and his work," he claimed, "it would have been worth the trouble."

Giroux often said that Van Doren treated his students as equals, and they, in turn, tended to respond positively to the material he presented in class. Yet, all through his life, Giroux harbored a low-key resentment against this former professor for not being upfront about the Kellett Fellowship and for preferring Berryman over him. Giroux realized, too late, that going to Cambridge would have indeed advanced his career prospects as an editor, but to the credit of his evenhanded spirit, he never let his suppressed feelings enter into his relationship with Berryman. "It doesn't matter now," he once told me, "but it mattered a good deal then."

When Halliday, a transfer student at the University of Michigan since September 1934, wrote to Berryman after having received the latest copy of the *Columbia Review*, he remarked, "It was, indeed, a demonstration of how thoroughly [Berryman] and Bob Giroux, with Mark Van Doren as mentor, dominated literary events on the Columbia campus in the spring of 1936. . . . I was properly dazed."[84] What Halliday never suspected was that Giroux, in an unconscious way, felt that he was in competition with Berryman and needed to prove that to himself; he wanted to become as competent a Shakespearean scholar as was Van Doren and as Berryman would later become.

Van Doren wrote to Berryman that he liked Berryman's long postgraduate poem, again concerning the death of his father, entitled "Ritual at Arlington," written as a 360-line tribute to Tate in July 1936 for a poetry contest sponsored by the *Southern Review* (Tate and Van Doren were the judges). Tate, however, was not impressed by the theme (it was "mechanical, not dramatic"), which Berryman interpreted as condemning the poem "for length & formlessness."[85] Robert Penn Warren, editor of the *Sewanee Review*, echoed Tate's opinion of Berryman's poem, though he encouraged Berryman to consider sending his poetry to his review in the future.[86] Curiously, Berryman's poem has similarities to Tate's "Ode to the Confederate Dead," which exhibits an inquiring intellectual posture steeped in Southern history, no doubt the result of doing research for his biographies of Stonewall Jackson and Jefferson Davis. Tate depicts a former Confederate soldier ruminating on issues of honor, heroism, and mortality—in short, his place in the world as he looks over a Confederate graveyard.[87] In a weeklong summer session taught by Tate, which Berryman audited the summer after graduation, he was greatly impressed by the poetry of the Southern Fugitives, a literary group that included Tate, Warren, and John Crowe Ransom. This group promoted formal techniques in poetry and defended the traditional values of the agrarian South against the effects of urban industrialization. As Berryman and Giroux went their separate ways after graduation, Van Doren wrote to Berryman that Columbia was going to be "barren bricks" that winter without him.[88]

After the graduation ceremonies had finished, the world beyond the boundaries of Columbia started to become increasingly bleak as Nazi Germany used the 1936 Olympic Games for propaganda purposes. There had already been a riot at Columbia when the German ambassador denounced critics of the Hitler regime.[89] Reich Chancellor Adolf Hitler saw the Olympics as an opportunity to promote racial supremacy and antisemitism, feeling humiliated each time Jesse Owens received one of his four gold medals. The spectacle and hospitality offered in Berlin, however, awed many visiting athletes and spectators and sent them home with warm impressions of the host country. Apparently unfazed by the political drama taking place in Germany, Berryman began his new adventure. His poem "Recovery" depicts him leaving Pier 42 in the East River and embarking for England.

> . . . I kissed Jean [Bennett]
> & Mother & shook hands with old Halliday
> and I mounted the *Britannic's* topmost deck
> O a young American poet, not yet good,
> off to the strange Old World to pick their brains
> & visit by hook or crook with W. B. Yeats.[90]

Undeterred by the remilitarization of the Rhineland and the ominous bond of friendship between Hitler and Mussolini, Berryman sailed into uncharted waters that might just offer him an unparalleled education. In hindsight, however, he was beginning a literary voyage whose consequences he could never have anticipated.

CHAPTER TWO

The Post-Columbia Years

Once Berryman disembarked from the *Britannic* in late September 1936, he stayed briefly in London before moving into two comfortable, well-furnished rooms with a kitchenette in Memorial Court at Clare College, Cambridge, fortunately located near the new university library.[1] The day before lectures began, he wrote a rather disjointed letter to "Dear Blackmur" in Harrington, Maine, giving him an update on his health and activities, especially his reading of the poetry of Yeats, Robert Frost, and Emily Dickinson. Tucked into the middle of the letter is the hope that Blackmur and Tate would travel to Cambridge and stay there for a few months.[2] On October 11, he wrote a letter to Tate, perhaps trying to get into his good graces by noting he was writing a paper "refuting Johnson and his moral vigilance contra Donne."[3] He also talks about profiting from the tutorship of George Rylands, a Shakespeare expert and author of *Words and Poetry*, whom he saw once a week at King's College. He quotes a few lines from an article he had been reading by Ramón Hernández (*The Dial*, March 27, 1936) that could well serve as a preliminary *ars poetic* for him: "Art & literature are operative in the world of quality. The more things are qualified, diverse, irreducible one to another, the more the artist feels at ease and breathes freely." During Berryman's two years in Cambridge, as revealed in his voluminous, often highly personal correspondence with his mother, he focused intently on his studies, particularly drama and poetry. In his second year, he was supervised by Herbert Lionel Elvin of Trinity College, author of *An Introduction to the*

Study of Literature (Poetry), who became better known as a theoretician of education and society. In addition, discussions with E. M. W. Tillyard, a renowned authority on the works of John Milton (whom Berryman admired very much), as well as with other Cambridge dons opened up for Berryman a textual literary world, from Aristotle to Chaucer, from Donne to William Blake, and even to Robinson Jeffers and Archibald MacLeish—giving him solace and comfort as the dreary English winter grayness descended. He read omnivorously and acquired an incredible collection of books, which later he shipped to the States to be integrated into his ever-expanding personal library.[4]

After receiving his college diploma from President Nicholas Murray Butler on June 2, Giroux desperately wanted to become an editor and thus visited a number of publishing houses, but he received no job offers. Through contacts made by Van Doren, he felt pleased to start as an apprentice at CBS in August, earning twenty-five dollars a week. The daily commute between Jersey City and New York meant that Giroux, in effect, could not develop an active social life beyond occasional discussions with two lifelong friends from Jersey City, Arthur Sturke and Charles Reilly, neither of whom had gone to Columbia. Giroux's earliest letter to Berryman, written from 33 Romaine Avenue in Jersey City and dated October 10, is one of the oddest he ever wrote in his life; it reflects not only the snazzy college lingo of its day but an overwhelming desire, bordering on a plea, to continue his friendship with his former classmate.

> First of all you have to go to the Hall and buy Lengley a drink.[5] These are explicit instructions from Peter Monro Jack.[6] Lengley, it seems, was his gyp (a shady aura surrounds the office, if you ask me) when Mr. Jack studied at Trinity Hall [College]. So for old times' sake you must treat Lengley—the new generation passing the cup for the old or something.
>
> I wish I had had the sense to have you meet Jack before you sailed. He not only would have been a charming person to know but would have been infinitely useful as a former Cambridge man. But in my dense way I even neglected to keep in touch with him myself, until recently when I wrote him about Blackmur's review of Tate (I remembered his own on Tate in the [New York] Times) and he asked me to drop in some evening. I did so and had a wonderful talk: he not only suggested to the Times that I review Mortimer Adler's

forthcoming "Art and Prudence"—a movie book, of course; the one Van Doren let me read; in MS—but also referred me to some members of the musical department here at the Columbia Broadcasting System! [J.] Donald Adams is away from the city and C[harles] G. Poore wrote me that the book would not be assigned until his return but that he, frankly, believed that Edward Alden Jewell, the ancient Times art critic, would get the job.[7] This is manifestly unfair, now isn't it? I bet the geezer never even saw Mickey Mouse. But there's still hope, and even if nothing comes of it I shall feel that it was very nice of Jack to have recommended me. . . .

My work at CBS is very steady and unexciting. But I am really grateful to have the job. There's a marvelous policy of laissez-faire here which leaves one's privacy unmolested, and if I get a few spare literary chores to do outside from time to time then I shall be happy for the present. I am more fortunately situated than [Gilbert] Godfrey and [Robert Paul] Smith here, I think.[8] They do "creative" work in the script department—crap of purest ray serene, of course, and it is very harrowing (lists of adjectives and nouns for instance, from which they must choose in writing musical continuity: "exotic," "vignette," "lilting air," "measured cadence"—well, you've listened to the radio); while I work with statistics and other dispassionate paraphernalia and remain oh so detached.

All is forgiven of Giroux by Van Doren. Prodigal son may come home, having squandered his birthright—chance of being Nation's film critic.[9] Van Doren stated he "didn't know exactly what the trouble was" and decided "let's forget it," when he should have been mortally offended and harbored a lasting resentment against the wretch. He addressed wretch for first time in letter as "Dear Bob" which gave wretch courage, after great struggle, to reply to "Dear Mark" instead of "Dear Mr. Van Doren" (these trivial precedents by which history is changed!) and hope to see you soon.

I hope to see him, as a matter of fact, Monday which is Columbus day and a holiday for us woikers but not for them perefssers and collidge stewdents [sic]. I haven't been around since June to the scene of our scholastic crimes (remember that Great Hoax, Jake, by which we swindled a university out of two sheepskins?).[10] I hope Monday to avoid [Columbia] Review office, but probably won't. Also Professor Weaver, whom I couldn't look straight in the eye, with

one unwritten Machiavelli paper imprinted in scarlet on my con-
science. [Robert] Gibney tells, by the way, the story of [Professors
James] Gutmann and Weaver having such a violent discussion of
Plato that it actually ended by the one giving the other a slight push.

And Lax tells the story (true-life) of Edman visiting his apartment and Bob Burke coming in roaring drunk and recounting a hor-
rible story of pickets and bastards and the class struggle, with choice
and very unmentionable references to capitalists until the air was so
livid that Edman left.[11] And Sy [Seymour] Freegood tells the sequel
of Edman walking home in ominous silence to his home and playing
Beethoven for two straight hours on the gramophone without a
word, so as to get back into the realm of spirit.

Burke is having lots of torch-parades and demonstrations on the
campus, by the way, but I doubt if there's a chance in the world. I
doubt too if a certain fellow named Thomson is active in the t.p.'s
and the d.'s [torch-parades and demonstrations].

I saw "Horse Eats Hat," the new WPA play which is very rau-
cous, obscene and unfunny. Dialogue built on gigantic double en-
tendres like the hero being mistaken for an organist by a decadent
French countess and she, coaxing him to play, saying "I understand
we must pamper your organ." [The John Gielgud] Hamlet, not yet,
but I hope to [see it] soon. The reviews were mixed, unexpectedly
enough. The movie of "Dodsworth" surprisingly good. Character
acting never been better done than by Walter Huston and Ruth
Chatterton as Dodsworth and Fran.

Let me know how you're settled and what it's like. I haven't
heard nor has anyone from [Leonard] Robinson.[12]

Berryman was so put off by Giroux's chummy letter, as Giroux told me,
that he simply did not reply. In addition, Berryman was most reluctant to
answer letters he received from friends and former faculty (his mother
and Halliday were the exceptions), since it meant that he would need to
type more or less the same letter to multiple recipients. It simply would
take too much of his time.

Once situated at Cambridge, Berryman adapted quickly to his new
environment, as he expressed glowingly on his twenty-second birthday in
a letter to Halliday: "Yesterday and today have been beautiful beyond any
days I have ever seen: full Autumn, but green, green lawns and parks, un-

diminished glory of gardens, and the complex splendor of the leaves falling and fallen. I've been on the river both days, yesterday in a punt and today in a canoe—it's like a dream, drifting along the quiet Cam, under ancient bridges and the shadows of stone and wood, into the clear sunlight bordered with green, and the light that struck the shore along the water!"[13] For a budding poet, Cambridge provided an ideal physical and academic environment. Berryman had a chance to hear T. S. Eliot lecture at the English Club on November 13 on "The Idiom of Modern Verse." Two days later, W. H. Auden addressed the Spenser Society, followed by a gathering in Rylands's rooms, where students briefly conversed about a number of topics: John Crowe Ransom, Ireland, *The Ascent of F6: A Tragedy in Two Acts*, and the nature of the English dons to remain insular, with barely a glance from them at American literature. For a time, however, Berryman stopped attending lectures, focusing more on his private study; this led to long days of little contact with others and the consumption of more alcohol than normal, resulting in mood shifts and insomnia. Like many expat students, he went through protracted periods of homesickness, accentuated by a daily monotonous routine. He once wrote to his mother that he "*frightfully*" wanted to see her, the family, and Jean Bennett.[14] But all was not self-imposed isolation. On February 11, 1937, for example, he gave a two-hour talk to the Dilettante Society, at the invitation of Andrew Chiappe, on the complex topic of Yeats's symbolism. He also met Dylan Thomas twice, first in March on the occasion of a reading by the Welsh poet at the Nashe Society in Saint John's College, and again just before he was to meet up with Yeats in April in London.[15] His encounter with Yeats proved to be unfocused as Yeats bounced from one topic to another. Yet, personal encounters with some of the greatest poets of his day allowed Berryman to listen to their distinctive cadences and thus reevaluate his own work and the nature of poetry itself.

Ambitious to become better known as a published poet, Berryman sent Warren at the *Southern Review* twenty-five poems in early 1937, an attempt that would have positive results after his return to the States.[16] His inner drive was rewarded when he received the prestigious Charles Oldham Shakespeare Scholarship in November 1937, worth 83 English pounds (then approximately $425), for excellence in writing four three-hour essays. This scholarship plus funds remaining from the Kellett Fellowship assured his second year in England. One could well wonder whether his seventy-seven-page essay, "The Character and Role of the

Heroine in Shakespearian Comedy," for the Harness Prize was inspired, at least in part, by his involvement with Beryl Eeman, a twenty-one-year-old amateur actress and student at Cambridge's Newnham College, who soon became his fiancée.[17] In his essay, Berryman demonstrated that he could articulate a sustained thesis involving interlocking relationships on a topic that could be approached from multiple perspectives. The Harness was not awarded to him, however, and that rejection may have prompted him to reflect negatively on the value of his education: "I have made an almost total hash of my years at Columbia and at school, and I have done little better over here [in England]; my character is a disagreeable compound of arrogance, selfishness and impatience, scarcely relieved by some dashes of courtesy and honesty and a certain amount of industry; I have been, I believe, thoroughly disliked by most of the people whom I have not known intimately."[18] In spite of such negativity, Berryman tried hard to be recognized as a well-read, up-and-coming poet, even summoning up the courage to send some poems to Eliot's *Criterion*; these were rejected in April 1938, though Eliot provided a few comments on them. After receiving an Upper Second rather than a First Class university degree, he had little desire to continue living and traveling in Europe, particularly as World War II loomed large on the horizon. Who would have ever suspected that Hitler, Mussolini, French premier Édouard Daladier, and British prime minister Neville Chamberlain would soon sign the Munich Pact, virtually handing Czechoslovakia over to Germany?

When Berryman returned to New York on the *Île de France* on June 21, 1938, with regrets about not paying all of his bills at Cambridge, his mother and Milt Halliday met him at the dock. Both were somewhat astonished by his umbrella prop, temporary English beard, and slight British accent. He took up residence for a while at his mother's apartment on West 115th Street, hoping that he might teach at Columbia. When that fell through, Van Doren contacted Scott Buchanan, founder of the Great Books program and dean of Saint John's College, Annapolis, Maryland, inquiring about a possible position for Berryman.[19] Buchanan's reply gave Berryman hope, though no offer was forthcoming.

With no income at his disposal and no genuine prospects of employment, Berryman faced increasing bouts of depression due, most likely, to a lack of friendships or intimacy in his life. Seeking to escape his mother's domineering mannerisms, he sought refuge for part of the summer with the Van Dorens in Falls Village, Connecticut, enjoying the company of

Tate, his wife, Caroline Gordon, and their teenage daughter Nancy in their rented house nearby. Not long afterward, Tate, who had recently published his *Selected Poems* and his only novel, *The Fathers* (Berryman thought it "an excellent very strange and carefully done novel"), invited Berryman to visit him in August in West Cornwall, Connecticut.[20] There he had another chance see the Van Dorens and to meet up again with James "Jay" Laughlin, a Harvard graduate whom he had encountered in Cambridge in June 1938. Laughlin's family had amassed a huge fortune in the steel business, allowing him in 1936 to start New Directions, a firm that became increasingly important by publishing works by Elizabeth Bishop, Marianne Moore, Ezra Pound, Wallace Stevens, Dylan Thomas, and William Carlos Williams, among others. Before long, New Directions earned a reputation as a preeminent publisher of Modernist literature. Four of Berryman's poems appeared in *New Directions: 1938* and seven in *New Directions: 1939*, both volumes edited by Laughlin.

Berryman's contacts with Van Doren and the Tates kept up his hopes of entering the academic literary world. Though he had a first-rate European education, his prospects for employment in the United States were slim, and he felt crestfallen after being turned down for teaching posts at Queens College and Princeton. His only recourse was to continue writing and try to break into the publishing market on his own. While the *New Yorker* rejected five of his poems, Warren accepted four for the summer 1938 issue of the *Southern Review* and five for the spring 1940 issue.[21]

The war news intensified as England prepared for an attack by the powerful Wehrmacht. The horrors of Kristallnacht in early November 1938, when German civilians and members of Hitler's Sturmabteilung destroyed thousands of businesses and burned hundreds of synagogues, served as an advance warning of further brutality. Since the United States had not entered the war, Berryman and Giroux, along with millions of others, could only keep an eye on what was happening on the other side of the Atlantic. They had both survived the Depression almost completely unscathed, but would the same be true for them if Hitler's dictatorial quest for more territory were to have a direct impact on the United States? It was not surprising that Eeman, seeking refuge, decided to join Berryman after a five-month separation. After arriving in New York in late October just in time to celebrate Berryman's twenty-fourth birthday, she took up residence in Mrs. Berryman's new apartment at 41 Park

Avenue. Five months later, Eeman set sail for home, distraught over John's emotional outbursts and anxious to be closer to home, should England declare war on Germany. Uncle Jack, under great pressure of a different sort and estranged from his wife, decided to live with his sister, Ethel Bird, in Reisterstown, northwest of Baltimore.[22]

That Thanksgiving, Berryman caught up with Giroux, spending time, as Giroux related to me, in discussing his incomplete, semiautobiographical play, *The Architect*, which Berryman had started thinking about two years before in Paris. Set in a bar in New York, the play featured a character modeled on Jean Bennett and another named Hugh Severance. (Berryman would later name the protagonist of his novel *Recovery* Alan Severance, M.D., Litt.D.)[23] Though unpublished, this play shows Berryman tapping into a part of his private life that would later find expansive, dynamic expression in his Dream Songs. In the spring of 1939, he accepted a temporary teaching assistantship at Columbia for the upcoming academic year with a stipend of $1,000, which would last through late June, but he sought release from this contract when he learned that he would be spending most of his time correcting student papers.[24]

Fortunately, Berryman was about to make a breakthrough that would change the course of his life. Delmore Schwartz, poetry editor at the *Partisan Review*, stopped by the Park Avenue apartment in late April 1939, and during the course of an engaging discussion, Berryman reiterated his pleasure that two of his poems would appear in the summer issue.[25] Perhaps this visit impelled Berryman to accept a part-time position at the end of May, after consulting with Van Doren, as the poetry editor of *The Nation*.[26] Producing rather than appearing in its pages must have tugged at his envious heart, especially when he read the poetry of such notables as W. H. Auden, Elizabeth Bishop, Wallace Stevens, and rising star Robert Bhain Campbell, Halliday's leftist-leaning friend and roommate, whom Berryman first met in July 1938 and once called his "closest friend."[27] With Campbell's help, Berryman landed a position at Wayne University in Detroit, with an initial salary of $1,700 a year, teaching three classes of English composition and one evening course. It is not surprising that he accepted Campbell's "Of Gramatan's Transaction" for publication in *The Nation* (September 30, 1939).

In October, Berryman moved into a roomy apartment near the university with Bhain and Florence Campbell. After two years of regulating his own schedule at Cambridge, he was not prepared for the arduous task of teaching more than one hundred students in the first semester. The demands of lecturing, leading discussions, correcting endless student essays, and wasting his literary talents, in addition to the tight living conditions—and some tension between John and Florence—caused Berryman to become "so bizarre, withdrawn, suspicious, irritable, explosive and depressed, that Bhain called in a psychiatrist," though this condition, which lasted well into February, could have been attributed in part to petit mal seizures.[28] From this time through the rest of his life, Berryman was plagued by incandescent outbursts and perilous bouts of depression, which subsequent psychological therapy never fully corrected nor allayed.

Sadly, whatever he attempted at this point in his life failed to come to fruition. During the Christmas season of 1939, he reached such a low point while visiting his mother in her new apartment on East Thirtieth Street in New York that Tate came from Princeton to take him back to New Jersey to recuperate.[29] Most likely, Tate was not aware of Berryman's simmering animosity toward him at the time over an unanswered inquiry. Berryman had written Tate that April to inform him that James Putnam at Macmillan had turned down his volume of forty poems and inquire whether the University of North Carolina Press would be interested in publishing it.[30] Although Tate agreed to read Berryman's manuscript, he decided not to accept it for publication, perhaps concerning an issue over royalties. Berryman wrote to his mother that August, "And if Tate thinks he can get my book by sitting tight on some grievance, he is wrong; I'll burn or give it to *Harper's* first."[31] But this did not prevent Berryman from pursuing his dream. On January 10, 1940, he wrote to Van Doren to ask whether he should accept Laughlin's offer to include his work in a new anthology, *Five Young American Poets*, for poets under thirty who had not published a book of verse.[32] If all went well, this volume would also include poetry by Randall Jarrell, W. R. Moses, George Marion O'Donnell, and Mary Barnard—thus giving Berryman the visibility he so desired.

After Berryman returned to Detroit, the Campbells decided to move out of the city in late February, due mostly to Berryman's continued nightmarish and frightening behavior, accentuated by his gaunt appearance and violent headaches. As Bhain's health declined due to testicular cancer, Berryman proved ever solicitous. By early April, Berryman had moved into an apartment of his own at 4827 Second Avenue on the southern edge of the campus, with "six windows at one end [of the room] and incessant activity at the other."[33] He continued writing and sent his poetry to the *Kenyon Review*, the *Southern Review*, and the *New Republic*, encouraged by Schwartz, whose fame at an early age had escalated due to the success of an eclectic volume of stories, poems, and a play entitled *In Dreams Begin Responsibilities*, published by New Directions. Berryman's determination never seemed to falter. That spring, after taking two graduate courses at the Horace Rackham School in Detroit, he registered at the University of Michigan in Ann Arbor, where he submitted a play and a booklet entitled *Twenty-Five Poems* for the Hopwood Awards in drama and poetry (which Milt Halliday had received in June 1937).[34] Though upset that he did not win the award, he took consolation in a new ray of light: Schwartz, who was teaching then at Harvard, wrote in May to say that Harvard might be interested in offering Berryman a teaching fellowship.

In the aftermath of Hitler's massive attack on Warsaw in September 1939, no American could remain indifferent to what was happening in Europe, though life in the States, nevertheless, retained a degree of normality. Giroux gradually became more involved with the war effort, which oddly enough proved to be his entrée into the professional world of publishing. He worked at CBS for three years under the supervision of Victor Ratner, director of sales promotion, mainly assisting in the production of a monthly program guide. Two of the guides resulted in the booklets *Vienna March, 1938: A Footnote for Historians from the Columbia Broadcasting System Crisis* and *Crisis, 1938: A Report from the Columbia Broadcasting System*. Though neither booklet listed him as the principal compiler, he was especially proud of the latter, which recounted Chamberlain's "peace journey" and the ill-fated Munich Agreement. While at CBS, Giroux met Stanley Preston Young, a senior editor at Harcourt, Brace, who introduced him to his colleague Frank V. Morley, a former Rhodes scholar who had worked at Faber & Faber in London until early 1939, when Donald Brace asked him to return to the States to become head of the trade department of Harcourt, Brace.

Having impressed Morley, Giroux started working at Harcourt, Brace as a junior editor in early January 1940 in a newly arranged editorial bullpen. He soon felt part of an important editorial team, though he knew that the U.S. book publishing industry might radically change due to the anxiety brought about by the declarations of war on Germany by France and England. That summer, Berryman sent a group of fifty poems to Harcourt, Brace—as Giroux told me—nine from 1937, twelve from 1938, twenty-three from 1939, and six from 1940.[35] Though Giroux wanted to see this manuscript accepted for publication, he had some reservations because of Berryman's insistence that the book be published in the very near future, an impossibility since even junior editors knew that only established poets stood even the slightest chance of having books published while war raged in Europe. As John Haffenden, a biographer of Berryman, states, "For his part, Giroux was wary of Berryman's sense of haste and emergency about gaining acceptance for the volume, but he was not the less enthusiastic."[36] No doubt conflicted and unwilling to discourage his former classmate, Giroux wrote to Berryman—perhaps without the nuance such a letter deserved—that he was "ready to battle for the volume to the bitter end. I'm delighted to; it will be the first occasion since I've been here that I really want to see a book published."[37] Further consultation with other editors prompted Giroux not to act precipitously. After Berryman revised his book, Schwartz took it upon himself to submit it to Harcourt, Brace, where Morley, *not* Giroux, decided against publishing it, as Giroux explained it to me.[38]

Even without a book of poetry of his own, Berryman's luck was about to change as he began to think more about his academic future. He had sent Blackmur a carefully typed letter in April 1940, trying to reestablish contact with him by asking, perhaps as a ploy, about the quality of the revisions of the Henry James works in the New York Edition: "I ask it only because I suppose you [are] familiar with the changes and I don't quite know whom else to ask."[39] Were their correspondence to continue, Berryman might venture to ask him more directly about help in finding a teaching position. There were two outside possibilities, Kenyon College and Harvard; Columbia was not a real possibility because Berryman's mental problems had become known there. In a letter, dated June 3, 1940, Berryman informed Van Doren he did not want to go to Columbia and attached no importance to the "action," that is, the *negative reaction* to this appointment by Harrison Steeves, chairman of the English Department.[40] Thus, thanks to a recommendation from Schwartz—and references from Van Doren, Tate, and Dean Hawkes at Columbia— Theodore Morrison, chairman of the Harvard English Department, offered a position to Berryman on June 11. Berryman was on a seemingly failsafe course to success—from Cambridge University to Cambridge, Massachusetts.

Willing to join the war effort, as reflected in a poem written that June, "The Moon and the Night and the Men," Berryman wrote to Van Doren from his mother's apartment in New York, "I am trying to get from Harcourt & Brace & The Nation money for an English summer."[41] Berryman asked Giroux whether Harcourt, Brace would be interested in publishing a series of letters he might write from England, as a short-term war correspondent, to record "the death of our kind of life."[42] Giroux was a bit perplexed when another poetry manuscript, rather than a collection of wartime letters, arrived at his office. Berryman had decided not to go to England. For his part, Giroux knew instinctively that Berryman needed more time to adjust to his new surroundings at Harvard and establish a reputation there before Harcourt, Brace would agree to accept such a manuscript. Berryman, having registered for the draft as required by law and been rejected for military service (classified as 4-F by the U.S. Army), wrote another letter to Van Doren from Detroit on August 7, indicating that he would choose the plausibility of the lower choice by rotting away his time teaching at Harvard.[43] After France capitulated to the German invaders in June, followed by the Battle of Britain and the savage Luftwaffe raids over England's air bases and military posts, Harvard provided Berryman, counter to his expectations, with a safe refuge. He wrote to Van Doren on September 29, from his rented apartment in a house at 10½ Appian Way in Cambridge, saying that his classes had begun and he was adjusting to a new academic environment. "Schwartz for a miracle," he added, "is enjoying his [classes] also."[44] Berryman's close quarters were made even tighter when his brother, Bob, who had transferred from Columbia College to Boston University, and eventually Bob's wife, Barbara, joined him. His brother's presence saved him from the paralyzing loneliness that he felt in such new environments.[45] Yet Berryman remained isolated from the social life of Cambridge, since the married faculty tended to form tight friendships among themselves. After beginning to teach three sections, he was grateful that Howard Baker, author of the autobiographical novel *Orange Valley*, would eventually take over one of them in January, even if it meant a decrease in his $2,000 salary.[46]

As Campbell's health declined further, Berryman took a train to Detroit to see him in August and then again during the Thanksgiving break. He was so distraught over the death of his twenty-nine-year-old friend on December 3 that he could not bring himself to attend the funeral. Campbell's death, and that of Berryman's father—both thematically linked in the poet's subconscious to Milton's pastoral elegy "Lycidas" (in honor of Edward King, who drowned in the Irish Sea in 1637)—found expression in his poem "Relations": "Bhain Campbell was extracted from me / in dolour, yellow as a second sheet / & I have not since tried to be the same."[47] Berryman found no real consolation when his "Twenty Poems" and a problematic introductory note were published in *Five Young American Poets* in November. Nor did he make his poetic breakthrough after five of his poems appeared in *New Poems, 1940: An Anthology of British and American Verse*, since he knew that New York's Yardstick Press had no funds to publicize this book. Still and all, he cooperated with the editor, Oscar Williams, who would include Berryman's poetry in the 1943 and 1944 volumes as well.

While at Harvard, Berryman ventured to New York on occasion, even reaching out to Giroux to include him in his rather restrained private life. At this time, he introduced Giroux to Eileen Patricia Mulligan, whom he had been courting, though he was still engaged to Eeman. Berryman initially met Mulligan, then rooming in a brownstone on West Twelfth Street and Sixth Avenue, at a New Year's Day party in New York in 1941.[48] (To avoid confusion, I will continue to refer to her as Eileen Simpson, the name under which she wrote her seminal *Poets in Their Youth*.) She was attracted to him the first time she first saw him: he entered the crowded room, tall, wearing a black-and-yellow muffler, sporting a jaunty bow tie, having the slim body of a runner, and later, after they had come to know each other better, she was swept up by his apparent self-contained maturity and comportment.[49] That summer, Berryman spent some time in New York, living in a rented, damp basement room at Lexington and Thirty-Sixth Street to be closer to Simpson. They particularly enjoyed the rooftop bandstand of the Hotel Astor, swaying to the tunes of Tommy Dorsey and enjoying the captivating voice of Frank Sinatra. Her memories of those times with John remained vivid in her mind: "At five o'clock, when I left the office where I was working on lower Broadway, we met in the Jumble Shop on Eighth Street for a drink. Or went to rundown, airless, steaming movie houses on the Lower East Side to see films like *Potemkin* and *Alexander Nevsky*. Or to the Apollo on Forty-Second Street for any picture with Louis Jouvet or Jean-Louis Barrault."[50]

One day Berryman radically changed Simpson's life. She had often been humiliated in school for her inability to write correctly, from fourth grade through graduation from Hunter College, and she often felt ashamed in the company of her peers until he pointed out something about a note she had sent him:

Deare

Time for olny a hurried note. M. [Marie Mabry, her sister] and children well. Swimiming every day despite gary skies. Tomorrow we calabrent M.'s birthday. See you Thursday.

In haste,
Love
E.[51]

Berryman told her forthrightly that she was not functionally illiterate but rather suffered, as did one of his former students, from dyslexia, a disorder that had always seemed to her like a pesky mechanical flaw. Though she knew that her condition would not change, she could, over time, learn ways to compensate and she felt incredibly liberated.

When Berryman's mother went on vacation, the couple stayed together for a month in her agreeable studio apartment on East Thirtieth Street, where they entertained at times Giroux, Van Doren, Jean Bennett (a former Berryman fiancée who was Simpson's closest friend while they were students at Hunter), and Mabry (who had married James Mabry while at Hunter and lived in New York with her husband and children).[52] (Simpson once told me, when Giroux and I visited her in her New York apartment, that in the early years of her friendship with Berryman, Van Doren kept Berryman from swinging too high or too low.)[53] Simpson traveled periodically to Boston to see Berryman while working for the Canadian Aviation Bureau in New York's Waldorf Astoria Hotel. In mid-September, he vacated the Appian Way apartment after Bob, Barbara, and their baby daughter, Shelby, had moved out; he rented a fairly comfortable apartment in a four-story converted townhouse at 49 Grove Street, in the Beacon Hill area, a fair distance from the university. If he continued to see Simpson, as he hoped, they would need more congenial surroundings.

Meanwhile, the long wait was over, and the U.S. Congress declared war on Japan on December 8 in response to the attack on Pearl Harbor. The subsequent days brought Berryman and Simpson even closer as they tried to envision what a future life together might mean. By February 1942, he had introduced her to Schwartz, who had, she was delighted to learn, graduated from the same New York high school as Simpson. She came "to love Delmore for his thoughtfulness and generosity."[54] The gregarious, often argumentative Schwartz would become increasingly important in Berryman's life, as living proof of a young, successful, published writer who had begun receiving praise from Eliot, Pound, Tate, and William Carlos Williams, all signaling high expectations of his incredible talent. "Delmore," Berryman once said, "was extremely beautiful and miraculously brilliant, one of the best talkers I ever heard in my life; but he became well-known too soon and came to count on fame. He began to plan his career, but a literary life is not to be planned that way."[55]

These were unsettling times for Berryman on a number of levels. He had made few friends among the Harvard faculty, and teaching seemed less attractive now that the war had started. His mother had lost her job, and his brother left for Pearl Harbor in a fruitless search for work. (In 1944, Berryman's eighteenth-month-old nephew Charles Peter accidentally drowned in his parents' bathtub, and Bob left Barbara for another woman.) Even while falling more in love with Simpson, Berryman's letters to his mother over these months reveal an unsettling congeries of preoccupations: fear that he might not be invited to continue at Harvard, tension between Bob and Barbara, unease about his lack of financial resources, and stress in consoling Schwartz over the devastating loss of his manuscript *Genesis*, which had disappeared after he sent it by way of Railway Express in early January 1942 to Jay Laughlin, then skiing in Utah.

In a letter written from the Grove Street apartment, with a curious salutation to "Beloved Robert," Berryman thanked Giroux for his visit the previous day and for allowing him to read and quickly comment on the works of various young British poets.[56] He enclosed an unpublished poem about his wasted life, entitled "A Point of Age," which he had written in February 1940. This poem—along with "The Disciple," both highly praised by Schwartz for their "richness and complexity"—reveals something deep within Berryman's psyche, especially in its sixth and eleventh stanzas. The desire to be "prepared to start" could well have been his way of signaling to Giroux that, though flawed as an individual, he wanted to begin writing poems that would be taken seriously—and, of course, be published by an acknowledged first-rate firm, such as Harcourt, Brace (emphasis mine):

> Slow spent stars wheel and dwindle where I fell.
> Physicians are a constellation where
> The blown brain is a fascist to the heart.
> Late, it is late, and *it is time to start.*
> Sanction the civic woe, deal with your dear,
> Convince the stranger: none of us is well.
> We must travel in the direction of our fear. . . .
> In storm and gloom, before it is too late
> I make my testament. I bequeath my heart
> To the disappointed few who have wished me well;
> My vision I leave to one who has the will
> To master it, and the consuming art;
> What else—the sorrow, the disease, the hate—
> I scatter; and *I am prepared to start.*[57]

But rather than be too explicit with Giroux, Berryman merely asked him to contact the poetry editor of the *New Republic* and see if this poem could be published there. Knowing that he stood a better chance of having a collection published by Laughlin, Berryman anticipated finishing by mid-June a manuscript (his "actual first book"), which he had been working on the previous spring (first entitled *Poems 1936–42* and then *Poems 1939–1940*).[58] This volume, containing eleven poems, including "A Point of Age," would be published by New Directions in midsummer 1942 simply as *Poems*, a title that annoyed Berryman because he hoped that it would be used later for a more substantial volume of his poetry.[59]

In June Berryman anticipated another visit to his Grove Street apartment from Giroux, Reilly, and Bennett (now married to Edwin Webster).[60] This tight-knit group would also have tea together in Mrs. Berryman's New York apartment, where Berryman and Simpson lived on and off for a while. As Simpson told me, "We all saw one another frequently and informally before John and I married." What she unfortunately tended to overlook was that Berryman had remained in contact with Eeman, despite being physically separated from her for the past three years.

After editing important works of at least seven major authors at Harcourt, Brace, including Hannah Arendt (*The Origins of Totalitarianism*), W. E. B. Du Bois (*Dusk at Dawn*), Randall Jarrell (*Blood for a Stranger*), William Saroyan (*Three Plays*), Jean Stafford (*Boston Adventure*, initially entitled *The Outskirts*), Edmund Wilson (*To the Finland Station*), and Virginia Woolf (*Between the Acts* and *The Death of the Moth, and Other Essays*), Giroux felt it was his civic duty to serve his country militarily, once General Dwight Eisenhower had taken command of U.S. forces in Europe. He applied for enlistment in the navy in late March 1942 and received a commission as a lieutenant (junior grade) on April 18. After three months of training at the naval base at Quonset Point, Rhode Island, he was assigned to the USS *Essex* at Norfolk, Virginia, then about to engage in a series of shakedown cruises. For almost two years, he served as an aide to Lieutenant Commander Charles D. Griffin, in charge of the Air Group Nine aboard the *Essex*, which had a crew of 3,400 and carried just over one hundred aircraft. The *Essex* left on May 10, 1943, for the Panama Canal on its way to Hawaii. Though Giroux sometimes shared with me his naval experiences in the Pacific, he preferred not to put the spotlight on himself, for he realized that he was but one of hundreds of thousands fighting for their country.

On July 6, 1942, Berryman wrote to Van Doren from Grove Street, indicating that he would be in Cambridge all summer, teaching summer school, but not sure whether Morrison would continue to keep him on for the fall semester.[61] While living with this uncertainty, he proposed to Simpson in early August, just after Eeman broke off her engagement to him. Berryman agreed to be married in a Catholic ceremony, though he leaned toward agnosticism. The wedding ceremony, presided over by the Reverend Michael Deacy, took place on Saturday, October 24, in the Lady Chapel, directly behind the main altar of Saint Patrick's Cathedral in New York.[62] The ceremony cost thirty-five dollars, which the married couple considered almost prohibitive, especially as Simpson, after working temporarily at the advertising company founded by Charles W. Hoyt, was having problems in securing permanent employment. Before heading to the Pacific, Giroux, having obtained a travel pass and looking gallant in his naval uniform, met up with Berryman and Simpson at a prenuptial party given by a Russian émigré couple, Vladimir Sokolnikoff and his wife. Simpson had known the dashing Vladimir since her teenage years, when he would accompany her to the ballet and opera.[63] Giroux later wired Berryman from Virginia that he could not make it to the wedding, nor could Berryman's brother, who might lose his job if he came.[64] During the wedding liturgy, Van Doren substituted for Giroux as best man. The few invited guests included Mrs. Berryman, Charles Reilly, Jean Bennett Webster, Florence Campbell, and Marie and Jim Mabry.

As husband and wife, the Berrymans lived in the Grove Street apartment and seemed to be an ideal couple with a promising future. Simpson thoroughly enjoyed walking with her husband through Harvard Yard, going to his office in the two-and-a-half-story Greek Revival Beck-Warren House, and browsing together in the Coop. They occasionally went to cocktail parties hosted by the Mark Shorers and spent delightful evenings with Schwartz and his wife, Gertrude, in their apartment on Ellery Street. Berryman's mother, now working for Associated Manufacturers, Inc., in Washington, DC, remarried, this time to Army Lieutenant Colonel Jack Lemon. Simpson had a new job in the legal department of Liberty Mutual Insurance Company in Boston for twenty-two dollars a week. She had been losing weight and feeling lonely, and John thought a projected trip to Brattleboro, Vermont, to visit Bob and Barbara would do her good, perhaps even serving as a sort of second honeymoon for them. Upon learning of the death of Simpson's granduncle Charles Tully in February 1943, however, they called off this trip. The strains on their marriage continued to increase.

With Giroux out of the picture for the next few years, Berryman had to rely on his wit and ingenuity if he wanted to be recognized as a talented and published poet. That February he finally put together "a whole book" of his poems at Schwartz's urging, though he thought it was a waste of time to do so.[65] Schwartz, with his star rising even higher, asked Berryman and Simpson to read the proofs of his recently recovered epic poem *Genesis* before it was published in the spring of 1943.[66] For four months, the manuscript of the poem had lain hidden under the floorboards of Laughlin's station wagon. The contrast between the two poets could not have been greater. By March, Berryman had received signals that he would not be rehired by Harvard, causing him enormous distress, though his students considered him a mesmerizing lecturer. Since his salary would cease at the end of June, he desperately needed to find another job, preferably an academic appointment. He wrote to Van Doren on April 13, indicating that Morrison ("a Master bore") was letting him go; Harvard would not keep anyone longer than three years without giving that person a five-year faculty instructorship.[67] The only one available was the one Schwartz had, as the Briggs-Copeland instructor in English composition.

Though Giroux was thousands of miles away, somewhere in the Pacific, Berryman had been thinking again about his friend. Giroux's sole wartime communication with Berryman, an official navy postcard postmarked May 16, 1943, indicates how lonely he had been at sea. He reached out to Berryman, whom he thought was living a fairly normal life, far from the unimaginable horror that he was, at times, enduring. The postcard contained generic, preprinted phrases that Giroux would have nuanced and expanded, if he could have done so: "Well and safe, regards, all my love," "Greetings, give my best regards to all my friends," "Writing at first opportunity," and "Have not heard from you, lately, for a long time."[68] He crossed off three other phrases that he thought did not apply—about birthday greetings, receiving letters and parcels, and being sick or wounded. Because of censorship regulations and the difficulty of sending letters to the States, Giroux rarely communicated with anyone during his naval career, even his family.

Before leaving Harvard in June, Berryman submitted his poetry manuscript to Harcourt, Brace, and Morley again rejected it.[69] Noted critic Arthur Mizener had little positive to say about Berryman's published accomplishments up to this point of time:

Mr. Berryman is a writer of considerable natural talent who has modelled himself, in most of these poems, with painstaking—indeed humorless—literalness on Yeats. It is unfortunately the case, however, that Mr. Berryman is quite unlike Yeats in both personality and conviction. This is most obvious where his liberal sympathy for strikers takes the incongruous form of "Words for Music Perhaps" ("River Rouge, 1932"), or where, by extension, the lurid, full-scale tragedy of "Edward, Edward" is reduced to a commentary on the Nazi-Soviet Pact ("Communist"). The effect of this is to make Mr. Berryman's respectable and commonplace feelings look silly. Something of this same kind, though to a less distressing extent, goes on in the long poems too. It was one thing for Yeats, with his dignity, his humor, his profoundness of mind, to dramatize himself as "a sixty-year-old smiling public man." But Mr. Berryman mediating solemnly over a game of Chinese checkers is too small for Yeats's boots. Where Yeats could catch his whole poem up in a bold burst of romantic imagery, Mr. Berryman seems only to be playing tricks.[70]

Whatever cards Berryman tried to play at this point in his life, he realized, unfortunately, that he held a worthless hand. Willing to help his friend, Schwartz contacted Tate, now the curator of American poetry at the Library of Congress and on his way to becoming the editor of the *Sewanee Review*. When the chance to replace Tate came through in March 1944, however, Berryman turned down the post.[71] He moved instead to New York at the end of the 1943 academic year and stayed first with Simpson in her aunt Agnes's apartment in the Bronx and then with the Mabrys on East Eighty-Second Street until the end of October. Desperate, he applied to fifty schools and colleges, but with no success. He resigned himself to selling the *Encyclopedia Britannica* door-to-door in Harlem, which left him with feelings of self-hatred and nausea. One night at the opera with Simpson, he sat in front of Reilly, Chiappe, and Robert Paul Smith. Had Giroux been there and not in the Pacific, he might have discreetly offered some illuminating advice about Berryman's chance of publishing a book of poems. After securing a brief stint teaching English and Latin at Iona Preparatory High School in New Rochelle, New York, Berryman felt the need to realign his priorities. He could not wait to be out of the "Hell-in-New-Rochelle."[72]

CHAPTER THREE

Berryman's Princeton Years

In search of more suitable employment, Berryman visited Van Doren to seek his counsel, especially in light of a book of verse he had put together at the urging of Schwartz. At Van Doren's suggestion, he again wrote to Blackmur at Princeton, giving his credentials and asking if Blackmur would inquire about a teaching position for him.[1] Berryman's letter to Professor Gordon Gerould, chairman of the English Department at Princeton, likewise asked about a possible appointment, adding "I prefer even a part-time or small-paying position there to anywhere elsewhere."[2] Blackmur was able to arrange a four-month instructorship for Berryman beginning in the fall of 1943 at a salary of $225 per month.[3] Once on the Princeton campus and happier, at least at the beginning, than he had ever been, though still quite poor, Berryman and his wife initially found a one-room apartment, barely big enough for their red leather chair and maple table, at 36 Vandeventer Avenue, similar to Berryman's former living arrangements at Appian Way. Seeking something more suitable, the couple moved temporarily to a cramped studio apartment at 120 Prospect Avenue around Thanksgiving and then into a larger one in the same apartment building in June the following year. They lived there for the remainder of their time together in Princeton.[4] Berryman was pleased that his brother wrote, at least temporarily, a column called "Milestones" for *Time* magazine and that Simpson found employment in Fuld Hall in the economics section of the League of Nations at Princeton's Institute for Advanced Study. After Berryman started teaching, he wrote to Halliday on December 2 with a short appraisal of his situation:

We like Princeton, too, which is a place altogether, morally & humanly superior to Harvard. Through the accident of friendship with Blackmur, who has been here for two years and has carefully gone through the University looking for interesting people, being the most obsessive conversationalist of our time, we have got to know automatically an extraordinary group of men, mathematicians, historians, philosophers, refugee novelists, musicians—I suppose it sounds entertaining; and it is; but I am not in repair for it. I never felt the need of solitude so sharply as now when it is absolutely inaccessible.[5]

Blackmur, unlike most of his peers at the university, possessed no doctoral degree, yet he served as an exemplar of someone whose native talent and intellectual commitment brought him continued success—as the Alfred Hodder Memorial fellow at Princeton during the 1943–1944 academic year, fellow in the School of Economics and Politics at the Institute for Advanced Studies, resident fellow in the creative writing program from 1944 to 1946, associate professor, then full professor of English beginning in 1951. If Blackmur proved too formidable and meticulous to some, Berryman held him in high esteem: Blackmur's "intelligence and moderation and wisdom, displayed endlessly in charming and spacious conversation," he confided to Van Doren, "have astonished me every day since I came here."[6] As Berryman assisted Blackmur with his seminar on Joyce's *Ulysses*, he had the opportunity to read Blackmur's manuscript on Henry Adams. Left incomplete at Blackmur's death in 1965, it would be edited by Giroux and finally published in 1980.[7] With a professorial corps of distinguished literary figures and historians at Princeton, including Carlos Baker, Francis Fergusson, Christian Gauss, Erich Kahler, and Willard Thorp (not to mention Albert Einstein, whom Simpson would see each morning at precisely 10:30, striding sockless in his moccasins down to his office two doors away from hers), Berryman felt intense pressure not only to teach well but also to prove himself by becoming a poet who could compete with the very best. Being in close association with Blackmur, it is understandable that he went through periods when he considered his mentor more admired than himself. He hoped, however, that his academic post would be renewed, thus providing him with financial relief to pay off some of his debts, including those from his Clare College days. However, he felt discouraged when a Guggenheim Fellowship fell through, perhaps foreclosing the possibility of remaining at Princeton.

Even though Princeton decided not to renew his appointment in March 1944, Berryman would remain associated with the university and the township, either formally or informally, until he took up a post at the University of Minnesota for the 1954–1955 winter quarter. He would cope, as best he could, with its stuffy, scholarly, orderly Presbyterianism, since it provided an unparalleled environment to grow intellectually. Fortunately, historian Douglas Southall Freeman had read Berryman's review of W. W. Greg's *The Editorial Problem in Shakespeare: A Survey of the Foundations of the Text* in *The Nation* (August 1943), and he brought Berryman to the attention of the Rockefeller Foundation, as had Blackmur, as a candidate for a fellowship.[8] That May, awarded this one-year research fellowship with a stipend of $2,500, Berryman looked forward to working on a new, updated, critical edition of *King Lear*, a project that had been on his mind since leaving Columbia.[9] His initial investigation of the *Lear* quarto of 1608 revealed that he had indeed found a worthy and challenging subject for the months to come, since the quarto was garbled and riddled with errors. He theorized that Shakespeare, in a fit of amnesia, "reported" his own play, thus destroying all distinctions between prose and verse before selling it to a printer.[10] Berryman envisioned cleaning those parts of the text affected by the negligence of those who reprinted Shakespeare's plays, much as an art conservator removes the debris from a masterpiece. Naturally, this honor boosted Berryman's self-worth, since teaching positions at other colleges and universities— including Bennington, Smith, and Oglethorpe—had not materialized.

Robert Lowell, called "Cal" by his friends, gives a close-up, picture-perfect snapshot of Berryman at this time:

> We met at Princeton through Caroline Gordon, in 1944, the wane of the war. The moment was troubled; my wife, Jean Stafford, and I were introduced to the Berrymans for youth and diversion. I remember [that I] expected, probably false, images, the hospital-white tablecloth, the clear martinis, the green antiquing of an Ivy League college faculty club. What college? Not Princeton, but the less spruce Cambridge, England, John carried with him in his speech rhythms and dress. He had a casual intensity, the almost intimate mumble of a don. For life, he was to be a student, scholar, and teacher. I think he was almost *the* student-friend I've had, the one who was the student in essence. An indignant spirit was born in him; his life was a cruel fight to set it free. Is the word for him courage or generosity or

loyalty? He had these. And he was always a performer, a prima donna; at first to those he scorned, later to everyone, except perhaps students, his family, and Saul Bellow. . . . John had fire then, but not the fire of Byron or Yevtushenko. He clung so keenly to Hopkins, Yeats, and Auden that their shadows paled him.[11]

As depicted here, Berryman had become the consummate scholar, externally fusing the roles of teacher-student, though desperately seeking inner contentment and satisfaction, while living with feelings of inferiority and relentless anxiety—in short, seeking a personal freedom beyond the distant horizon that he could not, and would not, ever reach.

By the time the *Essex* pulled into San Francisco in early March 1944 for refitting and some R & R for the sailors aboard, it had taken a number of kamikaze hits and participated in raids on strategic islands in the Pacific: Marcus, Wake, Tarawa, the Gilberts, and Kwajalein—in short in nearly every major carrier action in the theater up to that time. During the raid over Truk in February 1944, for example, Air Group Nine destroyed thirty-six enemy planes in the air and many more on the ground, in addition to sinking four ships and damaging twenty-four others with bombs, torpedoes, and strafing.[12] Giroux headed back to the Pacific again, now even tougher as he faced the possibility of death, and finally returned stateside in early fall 1944, when Commander Griffin was detached to plan operations in the Pacific theater as a member of the Joint War Plans Committee of the Joint Chiefs of Staff. Giroux finished his naval career at the Naval Air Station Jacksonville in Florida, where he was assigned to work for Commander John "Jack" Raby, a highly decorated combat pilot. Giroux was eventually decommissioned with the rank of lieutenant commander, well versed in dialoguing with superiors and subordinates about crucial daily business.

The battles of World War II, particularly the D-Day landing of Allied troops on the beaches of Normandy, France, in June 1944, had added to the strain on the lives of all Americans—and the Berrymans were no exception, especially as John's deepening psychological problems took a toll on them both. He isolated himself as he worked on his *Lear* project in a basement room of the old Princeton library. Given the vagaries and pressures of his academic milieu, he always seemed to be considering options, sometimes in a tortured way, and without much discipline, especially not in clearly articulating his alternatives. One case in point, expressed in a letter to Van Doren, reveals Berryman's inability to state clearly possible reasons for contacting William Sloane, who along with three colleagues from Henry Holt & Company, was in the process of establishing the publishing house of William Sloane Associates.

> If it is for the future, perhaps I should see Sloane, although the conditions of publishing, at best, appear to me unpleasant and degrading—being unable, I mean, to publish books that should be published (there is no great number of these, but each would be a sword) while one prints beautifully and trumpets books which are not worth even their authors' time of composition; treading, bargaining, competing; the intolerable reading painful rejections, uncomfortable interviews—into all this I would not wish to go if it could be helped. I don't know that it can.[13]

Van Doren was anticipating publishing a study of Nathaniel Hawthorne for the William Sloane Associates' American Men of Letters series, and he recommended that Berryman write the Stephen Crane volume for them, even going so far as to send Berryman in the fall of 1945 his twelve-volume set of Crane's works.

Berryman's Rockefeller Fellowship had been renewed for the academic year 1945–1946, so he turned down an offer to teach at Bard College in Westchester, New York. Subsequently he began working on his biography of Crane, a nineteenth-century American realist writer best known for his novels *The Red Badge of Courage* and *Maggie: A Girl of the Streets*. The publication of this work, perhaps, might advance Berryman's pursuit of permanent employment. Since he could not hold out any longer for Giroux to return officially to Harcourt, Brace, he signed a contract with William Sloane Associates on June 12, 1945, with an advance of $1,000, though the Crane book would not be officially published until December 1950.[14] When Berryman later inscribed an advance copy of his book to the Van Dorens, he indicated a sense of having failed to write a biography that adequately showed his filial gratitude for all Van Doren had done for him: "Mark & Dorothy with love / Crane's relation w. [Hamlin] Garland tells me something about mine with you. Rebellion & guilt suffocating the gratitude. Will you forgive me ever & can we meet? This is better by the way than when you saw it but still lousy. Don't read it. I hope to do something pleasant yet. / John / 14 Nov 50."

While awaiting his formal discharge papers in the fall of 1945, Giroux visited his family and gradually adjusted to civilian life. He caught up with Berryman and his mother, who was newly married to her fourth husband, Nils Gustafsson, a man nine years her junior (they separated not long afterward). She had been working in New York as the editor of the magazine *Sportswear Stylist*, which unexpectedly folded. Berryman, meanwhile, maintained his Columbia connections. He delighted in writing to his mother about a festive surprise celebration at the Algonquin Hotel on May 22, 1945, where about seventy guests honored Van Doren for completing twenty-five years of teaching with great success.[15] Berryman, who gave a warm tribute to his former professor, recalled meeting many friends and some new acquaintances, including Jacques Barzun, Clifton Fadiman, Joseph Wood Krutch, Delmore Schwartz, Harrison Steeves (*not* a friend), William Sloane, James Thurber, Raymond Weaver, Andrew Chiappe, Robert Giroux, and Charles Reilly. A letter to Van Doren mentioned how he and his wife had talked for days of nothing else except of this gathering.[16] In the waning days of the war, Simpson also entertained her mother, her sister, John's mother, the Van Dorens, Giroux, Reilly, Schwartz, and Berryman's former students from Harvard, as well as many of their Princeton friends.[17] In August, images of the bombs dropped on Hiroshima and Nagasaki were shown for weeks on the Pathé News in local movie theaters, proclaiming the end of the war. But Berryman still had no tenured academic appointment.

As the Berrymans celebrated their third wedding anniversary in October, John became terribly upset over news that George Ian Duthie was working on a similar *Lear* project (eventually published in 1949). He doggedly moved forward with his research and writing, but before the end of the year, the Rockefeller Institute wrote to say that they were aware of Duthie's research. It was hard for Berryman to admit that Duthie had beaten him to his cherished project, which over the ensuing months and years would change the trajectory of his career. Abandoning his Shakespeare project now would mean that his future reputation would depend on writing outstanding poetry. Columbia, Cambridge, Harvard, and Princeton had given him environments in which to evaluate the scholarly and literary achievements of others, but the perennial question remained: could he match or even surpass the successes of his friends and colleagues?

In early 1946, after resuming his editorial post at Harcourt, Brace, first as executive editor and then in 1948 as editor in chief, Giroux rented a walk-up apartment on East Ninety-Second Street between Madison and Fifth Avenue rather than returning to his parents' Jersey City home, a delayed *rite de passage*. Over the years, he became a consummate editor with a host of distinguished writers—including Djuna Barnes, Colette, T. S. Eliot, E. M. Forster, William Gaddis, Herman Hesse, Paul Horgan, R. W. B. Lewis, Walker Percy, Carl Sandburg, William Saroyan, Mary Lee Settle, Isaac Bashevis Singer, Susan Sontag, Derek Walcott, Robert Penn Warren, and Eudora Welty, to name but a few—all of whom he granted his full attention. He thought in terms of the *formation*, rather than the education, of an editor, as exemplified in the editorial careers of Edward Garnett, who launched Joseph Conrad, D. H. Lawrence, and John Galsworthy in England, or Maxwell Perkins, who published F. Scott Fitzgerald, Ernest Hemingway, and Thomas Wolfe at Scribner's. Giroux commented archly on the great difference between an acquiring editor, who tended to take on the role of a talent scout searching to add names to his roster of authors, and a line editor:

> The truth is that editing lines is not necessarily the same as editing a book. A book is a much more complicated entity, the relation and portions of its parts, and its total impact could escape even a conscientious editor exclusively intent on vetting the book line by line. Perhaps that is why so many books today seem not to have been edited at all. The traditional function of the editor as the author's close collaborator from manuscript to printed book, and through all the aftermath, has too often been neglected, with deplorable consequences, in the current atmosphere of heightened commercial pressures and a largely acquisitive publishing posture. Editors used to be known by their authors; now some of them are known by their restaurants.[18]

In all, for Giroux, a discerning editor is an author's close collaborator; he or she has judgment, taste, and most of all empathy and the capacity "not only to perceive what the author's aims are, but to help in achieving their realization to the fullest extent." He would ultimately be proud to have been the editor of four of the most renowned American poets, John Berryman, Elizabeth Bishop, Randall Jarrell, and Robert Lowell, who, surprisingly, never met at the same time under one roof.

By March 1946, Berryman had grown more anxious as he tried to figure out what he would do once his fellowship expired. He fretted about his *Lear* project and how it could be salvaged. While he had received recognition in literary journals, he nevertheless felt deep anguish at not having a published book of poetry. Before the termination of his Rockefeller Fellowship, his interest in the *Lear* project reached its peak, as he mentioned in a letter written in mid-May 1946 to his mother: "I scarcely even try to remember anything unconnected with my work, for fear of losing some of the labyrinth I have got to thread. I posted fifty pages of tough close argument to [W. W.] Greg the other day and am now rushing though the text proper; this week so far I've written twelve of text, five of apparatus, eighteen of commentary, and I mean to be done in a month of 15-hour days unless I break up."[19] Apparently, in great denial, he refused to admit that Duthie had bested him, and he seemed incapable of making contingency plans that would result in the publication of some type of book on Shakespeare.

Since the summer after graduation, the lives of both Allen Tate, who had mentored Berryman at Columbia, and Caroline Gordon had become more intertwined with his—and Giroux's. Tate had already established himself as one of America's leading men of letters.[20] Along with fellow Fugitives Robert Penn Warren and John Crowe Ransom, among others, Tate had affiliated himself with the conservative political group known as the Southern Agrarians. Ransom's influence in Southern literature was enormous, especially during his twenty years of tenure at the *Kenyon Review*, in addition to teaching at various times Warren, Tate, Andrew Lytle, Cleanth Brooks, Randall Jarrell, and Peter Taylor. As Tate was leaving the *Sewanee Review* to go to Henry Holt as editor of their belles lettres books in the spring of 1946, he offered his former post to Berryman. Berryman did not accept, most likely because he would be constantly critiquing the works of others and not spending time working on his own.[21] The Tates, not unlike the Berrymans, struggled both privately and publicly to keep their marriage together. They divorced on January 8, 1946, and then remarried three months later in the home of Willard Thorp in Princeton. Giroux often visited the Tates in Princeton, and they visited him at a newly purchased house in Pittstown, New Jersey.[22] Thus, he was fully aware of their marital difficulties, as were the Berrymans and Schwartz and his now-former wife, Gertrude Buckman, all of whom spent part of the summer of 1946 with the Lowells in Damariscotta Mills, Maine, as memorialized in Stafford's 1978 story "An Influx of Poets."[23]

Lowell had talked to Berryman at a party in May 1946 at *The Nation* in honor of Randall Jarrell, who had taken over the position of interim poetry editor. Berryman had not found anyone so pleasant as Robert Lowell and Jean Stafford since he first met Schwartz. For his part, Lowell noted that Berryman was slowly becoming more eccentric, as evidenced in part by his foot-long tresses.

> Too many guests had accepted. We were inept and uncouth at getting the most out of the country; we didn't own or drive a car. This gloomed and needled the guests. John was ease and light. We gossiped on the rocks of the millpond, baked things in shells on the sand, and drank, as was the appetite of our age, much less than now. John could quote with vibrance to all lengths, even prose, even late Shakespeare, to show me what could be done with disrupted and mended syntax. This was the start of his real style. At first he wrote with great brio bristles of clauses, all breaks and with little to break off from. Someone said this style was like Emily Dickinson's mad dash punctuation without the words.[24]

Not long after the Berrymans left Damariscotta Mills (they were there for twelve days), the Lowells' marriage started unraveling.[25] Lowell began exhibiting troubling psychological behavior, even to the point that Stafford considered him "crazy."[26] A bitter divorce followed. Stafford's mental health likewise deteriorated quickly, and she was admitted to New York's Payne Whitney Psychiatric Clinic in November, staying until the following June. Giroux and Simpson were two of her few visitors. Unfortunately, neither Stafford, Lowell, nor Berryman at this point was able to achieve any permanent psychological stability, and thus Berryman now faced a quandary; the more he was recognized for his writing ability, the more he retreated from his role as husband to a compassionate wife. As Simpson notes, their marriage had become a nightmare due to Berryman's "drinking, emotional turmoil, stalling about work, irresponsibility about earning a living."[27] Stafford and Lowell would not be the last of Berryman's literary friends to experience bouts of mistrust, excessively defensive attitudes, irrational self-delusion, prolonged deceptive behavior, and severe alcoholism.

Not welcomed as a professor in the English Department at Princeton, Berryman accepted an offer in the summer of 1946, thanks to Dean

Christian Gauss, to be Blackmur's associate in the creative writing program on the third floor of Pyne Hall, at a salary of $3,750. Donald Stauffer, chairman of the English Department, wrote about Berryman in an in-house memorandum: "He has the particular ability of engaging the respect and rousing the best talents of the specially chosen students who are allowed to elect creative writing."[28] This yearlong appointment afforded him time for his *Lear* edition (never to be completed), for which he wrote a textual introduction, as well as endless revisions of his Crane biography.[29] Fairly isolated from the academic community in general, Berryman fortunately could count on the friendship of William Meredith, a 1940 graduate of Princeton, who, after a military career as a pilot in the Pacific theater, had several teaching appointments at his alma mater from 1946 to 1950, first as instructor in English, then as the Woodrow Wilson fellow in writing, and finally as a resident fellow in creative writing. His first collection, *Love Letter from an Impossible Land*, was chosen by Archibald MacLeish for publication in the prestigious Yale Series of Younger Poets. Meredith praised Berryman simply and directly: "He was formidable in his learning and in his pride of learning."[30] This friendship gave Berryman contact with someone whose acuity and judgment he could always trust.

As he planned for the future, Berryman wrote to Giroux for advice that summer, most likely after meeting up with him in Princeton. After four manuscript rejections by Harcourt, Brace, Berryman knew that he had to be tactful in any correspondence with Giroux if they were ever to have a publishing relationship:

> Give me yr advice. [Henry] Holt have made what seems a reasonable offer for my poems except that Tate writes "we shall publish them in 1947 if possible, but it may be as late as January or February, 1948. I hope you don't object to this possible delay?" Well, I am in no hurry, as my patience hitherto sufficiently attests, but I can't be strongly inclined to sign a contract for so distant an object. What I'd like to know is whether you know other examples of 18 mo [months] predicted delay (=2 yrs? etc) or whether this is exceptional as I think it is; & whether paper tightness can justify it. We are in a sorry way for writers if so. I conjecture Tate [will be] done from Holt by 1948, anyway, & the firm is not otherwise specially attracted to me. Send me a note in care of Blackmur (Harrington), & let both offer and query be tenable in your silence still, as I'll keep yr reply in mine.

I get worse each day of working less, instead of better, & you see Hell's own summer when I stop altogether. "The fifth element: mud" said Napoleon. So the old dichotomy must follow the four elements: man is (1) Body (2) Soul (3) Fatigue. And maligned Death less separates (1) & (2) than cures (3). The only kindness.[31]

After his poems were, in fact, rejected by Tate in November 1946, Berryman immediately contacted Eliot at Faber & Faber and sent him, no doubt as a form of self-validation, ten poems written between 1939 and 1944.[32] It is not clear whether Tate simply did not like the poems Berryman submitted or whether Berryman had overestimated what the publishing houses would accept in the aftermath of the war when money was scarce and rationing continued, though somewhat diminished. Berryman soon wrote another informal, rambling letter to Giroux, with references looping back to their college days together. It should be noted that he did not ask Giroux directly about the possible publication of his book of poetry.

> Many thanks for letting me see the Gibbon [perhaps a 1946 Heritage Press edition of *The History of the Decline and Fall of the Roman Empire*]. His own notes are not much abbreviated, but it won't matter to me because all exact references are omitted, and I have been reading him partly as a cicerone. I was wrong, however, in remembering [John Bagnell] Bury's notes as extensive; they are not. [Illustrator Gian Battista] Piranesi is interesting. But the production I don't greatly like—all that margin, often blank, with the verso showing through and the page dislocated.—My books came! [from England] & amaze me with dozens of volumes I'd forgotten in eight years! The Hound & Horn you want, hélas, not there. Do you collect Southern Reviews? My set is complete again, with these extra: I, 1, 2; II, 2; III, 1, 2, 4—which you can have if you like.
>
> Cal's book [*Lord Weary's Castle*] wonderful, and equally a letter sometime past from Jean [Stafford] saying tacitly that everything is all right. I pray it is, and I hope they can find a place to live.
>
> The Auden-[George] Rylands's Duchess of Malfi is far from good, but the night we saw it enacted the triumph of a great poet over producer, adapter, actors & audience—not even all these could destroy the effect of the mad scene though they made the rest of it hardly more moving than the Harvard [football] game.[33] [Actress

Elisabeth] Bergner's a cold old whore. Why was Hampden not been caught up to be butchered during the meat shortage?[34] Ugh.

Very busy, man, with writing than with students.[35]

His final comment hid the fact that he was privileged to teach at Princeton some very talented students, including future prizewinning authors Bruce Berlind, W. S. Merwin, and William Arrowsmith. Most likely, Giroux read Berryman's review of Lowell's latest book and the *Selected Writings of Dylan Thomas*, along with six other books of poetry, in the Marxist-oriented *Partisan Review* (January–February 1947). Berryman tried to establish in his review that he well knew an American poet who, like Eliot, had an unsurpassed international reputation: "Robert Lowell," he wrote (not without some reservations about Lowell's "heavy rime, and thud-metre"), "seems to me not only the most powerful poet who has appeared in England or the United States for some years, master of freedom in the Catholic subject without peer since Hopkins, but also in terms of this distinction, a thematic poet. His work displays, in high degrees, passion, vista, burden."[36] Furthermore, he had high praise for Dylan Thomas, the subject of one of his poems. Since Lowell believed that Thomas was one of the three best poets writing in England, Berryman suggested that anyone with an interest in these matters should read both Thomas's and Lowell's books. In creating this poetic constellation, Berryman subconsciously left open a vacant spot that he hoped to fill.

As Berryman sought some center in his life, his marital bond became progressively more precarious. At this time, Simpson commenced taking courses, first at Douglass College, the women's division of Rutgers University (two bus rides and an hour's journey from Princeton), and later, after obtaining a proper undergraduate degree to make up for her poor marks at Hunter, at New York University's graduate program in psychology. In addition, she worked part-time at NYU doing research for a statistical survey, all of which increasingly annoyed her husband. She would eventually receive her master's degree in 1950, with a thesis entitled "Poets' Responses to the Rorschach Test," for which Blackmur, Jarrell, Lowell, Meredith, Merwin, Schwartz, Tate, Van Doren, and William Carlos Williams—then recuperating from a recent heart attack; he had graciously allowed the Berrymans to visit with him in Rutherford, New Jersey—served as her subjects. She also had a two-year assistantship at the Rutgers Psychological Clinic as an assistant clinical psychologist working with dyslexics. After three years at Rutgers, Simpson went into private practice with a psychotherapist in Princeton. As her practice grew, she commuted to New York for weekly sessions with a training analyst who supervised her counseling activities.

With his wife absent much of the time, Berryman, not surprisingly, began an intense, short-lived, not-so-secret love affair in May 1947 with "Lise," his pseudonym for Chris, the twenty-seven-year-old wife of a Princeton graduate. His guilt over the affair and reoccurring images of his father's death prompted him to continue seeing his psychiatrist and enter into group therapy.[37] Still, he wrote approximately 115 Petrarchan sonnets to Lise (the intensity of this liaison can be seen in Sonnet 67), and his lengthy unpublished diary reveals the passionate folly of this affair.[38] Further, his drinking increased notably, so much so that Simpson, aware of his extramarital affair (how could she not be when she, Berryman, and Chris and her husband, along with William and Jean Arrowsmith, had spent a day together at the seaside?), wondered whether their marriage could continue.[39]

On the sonnets to Lise, Hayden Carruth wrote,

> Hence the first thing to be said about them is that they are far, very far, from the kind of customary asides that poets dash off to assist the seduction of non-literary females. Dashed off they may have been, some of them; written in an obvious white heat; but they have the power, finish, tension, and verbal originality of the most purposive artistic endeavor. Leaving out matters of concrete style, they are poems of an order that any poet would be glad to have achieved at any time; and this says more, it seems to me, for the quality of Berryman's poetic intention than almost anything else I could imagine.[40]

These sonnets might well have been inspired by women in three other sonnet sequences: Shakespeare's Dark Lady, Petrarch's Laura, and Sidney's Stella.

After Simpson received a letter from Chris in September 1947, however, Berryman realized the full import of what had been happening. His response was predicable: to drink excessively and explode interiorly, not unlike his reaction when learning that John Dos Passos had rammed his car into a parked truck, killing his wife. Before long, however, as the Berrymans celebrated their fifth wedding anniversary, he fell briefly back into Chris's arms—and into other waiting arms that he could not resist—creating more lacerating self-delusion about the consequences of this affair.

As Berryman's Sonnet 5 mentioned, Giroux had invited Berryman to meet Eliot in his Harcourt, Brace office in mid-May 1947. In doing so, Giroux rather blatantly showed that he was a friend not only of Lowell, but also of the best contemporary English poet, who was then staying in his apartment on East Sixty-Ninth Street. The three of them talked about a number of topics: *The Four Quartets*, Eliot's upcoming two lectures at Princeton, and Lowell's *Lord Weary's Castle*.[41] Afterward, Berryman met with Lowell and told him about this important encounter. Personal contact with Giroux now renewed, he needed to proceed with utmost care, if that were possible at this point, since so much was at stake for him. The gaps in his life were turning into ever-widening crevices, as evidenced by two important events. That fall, with the encouragement of Blackmur, he again applied, unsuccessfully, for a Guggenheim. And, in an unwise decision that would put his own publishing future in jeopardy, he turned down an offer from Giroux to publish a volume of his poetry.

William Sloane Associates had agreed the year before to publish Berryman's first collection of poetry, provisionally called *Traditional Poems*.[42] After Thanksgiving 1947, Berryman was advised that the book most likely would be published in six months, with the advance increased to $250. Aware of the situation, and after consulting with colleague Eugene Reynal, Giroux telegrammed Berryman on December 10, care of his mother's address at 338 East Nineteenth Street in New York, offering a contract for this same book of poetry, with standard royalty terms and an advance, provided that Berryman withdraw from William Sloane.[43] Berryman declined. As is clear from Berryman's first two letters to Giroux earlier in 1946, Berryman had not organized his thoughts sufficiently about teaching, writing, and publishing, for he swirled from one topic to another. Had Berryman been more up front about what he had done and what he wanted to do, then Giroux, as he told me, would have been most willing to forthrightly discuss his friend's publishing future.

The problem was at once legal and moral: Giroux could not accept a manuscript that was promised elsewhere. Thus, Berryman's short volume of fifty poems in five parts, entitled *The Dispossessed* (1948), and his *Stephen Crane* (1950) were published by William Sloane Associates.[44] To Berryman's great annoyance, both Schwartz and Lowell were most reluctant to express their views of *The Dispossessed* in nationally known literary journals.[45] Jarrell did review them but vacillated in his appreciation of these poems: "Doing things in a style all its own sometimes seems the primary object of the poem, and its subject gets a rather spasmodic and fragmentary treatment. The style—conscious, dissonant, darting, allusive, always over- or under-satisfying the expectations which it is intelligently exploiting—seems to fit Mr. Berryman's knowledge and sensibility surprisingly well, and ought in the end to produce poetry better than the best of the poems he has so far written in it, which have raw overdone lines side by side with imaginative and satisfying ones."[46] Lowell wrote Berryman a letter, saying in part that he agreed with Jarrell that there are "so many breaks, anacolutha etc. that the whole poem usually escapes me."[47] Rarely did Berryman fully appreciate the written critiques of his work, as expressed in Dream Song 120:

> Foes I sniff, when I have less to shout
> or murmur. Pals alone enormous sounds
> downward & up bring real.
> Loss, deaths, terror. Over & out,
> beloved: thanks for cabbage on my wounds.[48]

For the most part, Berryman tended to see such critiques as written by either enemies or uninformed fools as a way of persecuting him, though neither Lowell nor Jarrell fits into these categories.

In February 1948, after Berryman recorded four of his poems at the Library of Congress at the invitation of Lowell, who was a consultant in poetry there, he and Lowell visited Ezra Pound at Saint Elizabeths Hospital in Washington, DC. Lowell had been attracted to Pound's poetry ever since he first wrote to him in May 1936 as a nineteen-year-old freshman at Harvard.[49] Now, Berryman sat on the floor hugging his knees, asking, at one point, for Pound to sing an aria from his opera *Villon*.[50] Berryman had corresponded with Pound in the late 1940s, as Philip Coleman notes, with the result that Laughlin at New Directions— at the request of Pound himself—had commissioned Berryman to edit a selection of Pound's work.[51] In a letter dated June 27, 1947, Laughlin informed Berryman that "Ezra would like to have you be the editor for the volume of his selected poems to go in the New Classics Series."[52] Although New Directions eventually dropped Berryman as editor for this proposed volume, Pound still considered Berryman an important young writer, as he mentioned in another undated letter, probably written early in 1947.[53] Critic Amanda Golden notes, "Berryman argues, Pound has no matter *of his own*. Pound—who is even in the most surprising quarters conceded to be a 'great' translator—is best as a translator. For Berryman, Pound and poets like him reshape materials like a refinery does. The difference, however, is that a poem's layers are visible. Berryman resolves that 'poetry is a palimpsest,' acknowledging Pound's aesthetic while arguing that all texts allude to those preceding them."[54] Yet Pound flat-out refused to allow Berryman's impenetrable essay to be used as the introduction to his *Selected Poems*.[55] Berryman's second visit to Pound, on November 3, 1948, served as the basis of both his essay "The Poetry of Ezra Pound" in the *Partisan Review* (April 1949), which he had submitted to editor Delmore Schwartz, and also for his poem in *Poetry* (January 1950) entitled "The Cage": "O years go bare, a madman lingered through / The hall-end where we talked and felt my book / Till he was waved away; Pound tapped his shoe / And pointed and digressed with an impatient look." Unfortunately, Berryman's selection of Pound's poems has not been located, nor did Laughlin allow the volume to have any introduction at all, thus putting an end to Laughlin's collaboration with Berryman.

Pound had become a magnet not only for Berryman and Lowell, but for Giroux too. After first encountering Eliot in the spring of 1946 and being impressed by the dedication of his poem *The Waste Land* ("To Ezra Pound, *il miglior fabbro*"), Giroux wanted to meet the controversial poet, which he and Lowell did in September 1948.[56] Since Pound had been influential in the publication in *Poetry* magazine of Eliot's "The Love Song of J. Alfred Prufrock," Eliot on occasion would visit his old friend in Washington. In talking to Giroux, Pound mocked Giroux's Harcourt, Brace colleagues, Morley and Reynal, for he had little tolerance for established editors. Because Giroux had spent stressful months of his life at sea during World War II, he left the short visit vehemently opposed to those who sentimentalized Pound by making excuses for his pro-Axis broadcasts and anti-Semitic tirades.[57]

Without a tenured teaching post, Berryman felt increased pressure as he contemplated whether to continue or conclude his research on Shakespeare. He needed the academic support a university could supply. With backing from his peers, as well as Blackmur, he was appointed in May

1948 the resident fellow in creative writing at Princeton for the academic year 1948–1949 for a salary of $3,750—with no real possibility of a salary increase, as he had previously requested.[58] In light of this, he turned down the offer of a teaching post at the Writers' Workshop, directed by Paul Engle at the State University of Iowa.[59] Furthermore, he won two prizes: the 1948 Guarantor's Prize of *Poetry* magazine for $100 and the 1948 Shelley Memorial Award of the Poetry Society of America for $650. The latter was the most significant recognition he had gained for his poetry since his senior year at Columbia. Two years later, he received an award of $1,000 from the National Institute of Arts and Letters.

In November 1948, Giroux visited Eliot, then sixty years old, at Princeton, where he continued as a fellow at the Institute for Advanced Studies working on his play *The Cocktail Party*. Eliot's workroom was one of the classrooms at the Institute, where Giroux once found him diagramming the frequency of the appearances of the characters in his play in each of its three acts, using letters from each character's names. His writing resembled a mathematical equation, as Giroux told me. "Have you noticed the sign, *Do Not Erase*?" Eliot asked Giroux. "That's because Albert Einstein occasionally uses this blackboard for excursions into the fourth dimension. I wonder what he'll think of my equations."[60] Being in the company of Eliot put Berryman in a most enviable position as well. After taking Eliot to the apartment of Nancy and Dwight Macdonald, Berryman subsequently invited the noted poet, the Macdonalds, and novelist and short story writer Paul Goodman for a drink with himself and Simpson.[61] Macdonald had edited the *Partisan Review* magazine from 1937 to 1943 before he started *politics*, a magazine with a definite leftist editorial perspective. Later, after *The Cocktail Party*'s premiere at the Edinburgh Festival in August 1949, it opened officially on January 21, 1950, at Henry Miller's Theatre in New York. At a party thrown for Eliot by Eugene Reynal and his wife to celebrate this occasion, the guests included Stafford, Lowell, the Tates, Irene Worth, Katherine Anne Porter, and Djuna Barnes, who tried unsuccessfully to take Eliot home with her. What secretly delighted Giroux was the name of the uninvited guest and psychiatrist in the play: Sir Henry Harcourt-Reilly—Eliot's way of tipping his hat to Giroux (at Harcourt, Brace) and Reilly (as in Charles Reilly).

Giroux could not legally sign a contract with Berryman, given that Berryman had already contracted with William Sloane Associates for the publication of two books, so he waited a little over seven years (December 1947 to April 1955) before he felt he could approach Berryman again in a professional role. He knew that he simply had to bide his time until Berryman had a book that he really wanted Giroux, not Laughlin, to edit and publish. He also knew his friend well enough to know that Berryman needed to clarify on his own how and when he was ready to prove himself as a serious poet with a significant manuscript that merited consideration by a major publishing firm. Nothing that Giroux could do would convince Berryman to arrive at this point in his life.

In the meantime, Berryman worked on his Crane biography, for which he had already received an advance of $2,000; he realized, no doubt, that imitating Van Doren in such an enterprise might in the end prove a detour from what he really had wanted to do since his college days. The Crane project had some merit, but not enough for him to see a career as a professional biographer. Thus, he started planning for his first major poetic achievement, "Homage to Mistress Bradstreet," which he began writing toward the end of March 1948. While working on the Crane manuscript, he relied on a regime of Dexedrine, Nembutal, martinis, and sherry—and vitamins.[62] Exhausted and depressed, he sent the final version to Helen Stewart at William Sloane Associates on July 29, 1949. He kept such a stressful schedule during these years that he continued consulting his New York psychiatrist James Shea, M.D., causing him to go further into debt; these sessions covered not only his own and his mother's flamboyant sexuality but the distinct probability that he might be the father of a child born to a woman not his wife.[63] Like many academics, Berryman came to see eventually that teaching, research, and writing could go together, provided that he was not sidetracked by the inevitable and often unforeseen events that came his way. Yet, through writing line after line of the Bradstreet poem, he located and discovered the structure, argument, and language he had been looking for all along.

Berryman continued for years without a tenured academic position, though he anticipated doing further research on Shakespeare, including a biography of the Bard. He was appointed the Alfred Hodder fellow at Princeton for the academic year 1950–1951, in addition to a ten-week visiting post at the University of Washington (Spring 1950, where he replaced Theodore Roethke and again met Dylan Thomas after a hiatus of thirteen years). After his return to Princeton, he gave a highly successful series of four Hodder lectures on Shakespeare, followed by a two-week summer school course in 1951 at the University of Vermont (where he taught with Malcolm Cowley, Irving Howe, David Daiches, and Blackmur). In the spring of 1952, he held the Elliston Chair of Poetry at the University of Cincinnati, where he gave seventeen lectures on Shakespeare and modern poetry, with the final one on the poetry of Eliot. Simpson accompanied him to Cincinnati, having resigned her position at Rutgers, and seemingly enjoyed the acclaim her husband was receiving while feeling terribly hurt by his continual womanizing. When they met up with Tate, who was visiting his brother in Cincinnati, they had a chance to renew their friendship. Tate was particularly delighted to see how well Berryman had adapted to Cincinnati. In fact, Berryman wrote a hundred pages of his Shakespeare biography while working on the Bradstreet poem, though he reported to his mother in April 1952 that the poem was "not going well."[64] Most important, Berryman's inaugural lecture in Cincinnati, "Shakespeare at Thirty," which he had previously given at Princeton, now earned him recognition and credence as an academic professional, so much so that his fifth application for a Guggenheim Fellowship of $3,000 for academic year 1952–1953 proved successful.

Living in Princeton gave Berryman a chance to talk to Robert Fitzgerald, who lectured at Princeton as assistant to Blackmur (1949–1951) and to Schwartz (now descending deeper into depression), who had replaced Fitzgerald in the creative writing program. Saul Bellow, who served as an assistant in this program and whom Berryman first encountered in the fall of 1948, gives a glimpse of Berryman at this time: "The Princeton John was tallish, slender, nervous, and gave many signs that he was inhibiting erratic impulses. He wore a blue blazer, a button-down shirt, flannel trousers, cordovan shoes. He spoke in a Princeton mutter, often incomprehensible to me. His longish face with its high color and blue eyes I took to be of Irish origin. I have known blue-eyed poets apparently fresh from heaven who gazed at you like Little Lord Fauntleroy while thinking how you would look in your coffin."[65] Berryman appeared to others as nervously intense, often exhibiting acerbic dimensions of his personality.

After the publication of *Stephen Crane* in mid-December 1950, Berryman severed his relationship with William Sloane Associates, who had published his two books in two years. He subsequently contracted with Viking to publish his proposed biography of Shakespeare, but whether he would ever finish this manuscript was still up in the air.[66] His erudite, though somewhat rambling, essay in the *Hudson Review* (Spring 1953), based on his inaugural lecture at the University of Cincinnati with a focus on Shakespeare as player, poet, and playwright, indicates that he was doing publishable research on Shakespeare that could well become part of a longer work. His Cincinnati Shakespeare lectures had been so successful that Princeton wanted to publish them as a series of essays.

Berryman maintained, according to Haffenden, that it took him five years to write the Bradstreet poem, which he finished on March 22, 1953, followed by a week in bed from exhaustion.[67] Yet, his letter to his mother in early April 1948 might suggest that the poem had a longer period of gestation: "After eighteen months thought, I came this morning suddenly on the *subject* for the long poem I've been drafting, and am elated; though it will be Fall at least before I can hope to get at it steadily."[68] "Prior to Bradstreet," as critic John North Radway observed, "Berryman's work had been by no means poor—he had achieved relative success and recognition, and was probably well on his way to becoming at least an historically noteworthy 'poets' poet—but a certain coldness of tone prevents many of his early poems from being as moving or memorable as his later achievements."[69] By late July 1952, Berryman had written 75 or 80 pages of notes and more than 125 draft lines, some of them based on the writings found in Helen Campbell's *Anne Bradstreet and Her Time*, Governor John Winthrop's *Journal*, Leo Tolstoy's *Anna Karenina*, and Perry Miller's *New England Mind*.[70] While working on its final stage, Berryman shared this poem with both Tate and Fitzgerald, both of whom "expressed high opinions of it."[71] Anne Bradstreet was an important Puritan known for her volume of poetry, *The Tenth Muse Lately Sprung Up in America* (1650). "For Berryman's purposes," Haffenden notes, "that physicality [of Bradstreet] (which he captures so passionately) serves as the image, the objective correlative of the spiritual pain that he himself suffered in the late 1940s and early 1950s." He adds, "Anne Bradstreet is the type of Berryman's desubstantiated self. His breath is mixed with her agony and consolation. Alienated from her husband, her father, and her religion, unable to quench her longing in the bliss of childbirth, Anne Bradstreet seeks to realize her needs in adultery with the 'poet.'"[72]

In January 1953, Simpson underwent a myomectomy to correct a fibroid condition that might have prevented her from becoming pregnant. She later interpreted Berryman's poem through the optic of his uncontrollable womanizing: "The unbearable impotence and frustration he felt over his work drove him to seek compensatory gratification in women. It made him loathsome to himself but was beyond his control."[73]

In his essay "'Nightmares of Eden': John Berryman's *Homage to Mistress Bradstreet*," Philip Coleman, however, sees that more nuance might be warranted in interpreting the origin of this poem: "Simpson left Berryman, however, only after the couple's return to the United States following a trip to Europe in August 1953, by which time Berryman had completed the manuscript for the poem and deposited it in a vault at the First National Bank in Princeton. Berryman's feverish immersion in the writing of the poem, in the later stages especially, may well have contributed to the failure of his marriage to Simpson, but the poem itself involves much more, of much greater cultural resonance, than the dissolution of Berryman's first marriage."[74] While acknowledging that his wife wanted a child very much, causing strong emotions in himself, Berryman provided his own explanation of the origin of the poem: "The idea was not to take Anne Bradstreet as a poetess—I was not interested in that. I was interested in her as a pioneer heroine, a sort of mother to the artists and intellectuals who would follow her and play a large role in the development of the nation."[75] Furthermore, he told another interviewer that the point of the Bradstreet poem was to take an unbelievably conventional woman and give her every possible trial and possibility of error, including a crazy love affair, and then allow her to forget it. He emphasized that the affair—homage to *Mistress* Bradstreet—is a pun; she is the poet's mistress, ending the affair in the twentieth century.[76]

When Lowell, who had been in Europe for over two years, visited Berryman in January 1953, they talked for twelve hours like old friends who needed companionship. As Lowell had when having a manic breakdown in March 1949, Berryman then reached out to Fitzgerald for help in late February 1953. Fitzgerald was by then teaching at Sarah Lawrence College, an hour's drive from the Fitzgerald home in Ridgefield, Connecticut. The Fitzgeralds graciously accommodated Berryman's request for a two-week visit. Simpson, aware that Sally Fitzgerald was pregnant with their fifth child, later reflected that it was "like asking Sally and Robert if they would be willing to put a lighted stick of dynamite in their room over the garage."[77] As Berryman was killing off Mistress Bradstreet in fifty-seven stanzas, Simpson could well have sensed that John was doing something analogous to their marriage, as articulated in stanza 35:

—I cannot feel myself God waits. He flies
nearer a kindly world; or he is flown.
One Saturday's rescue
won't show. Man is entirely alone
may be. I am a man of griefs & fits
trying to be my friend. And the brown smock splits,
down the pale flesh a gash
broadens and Time holds up your heart against my eyes.

Once back in Princeton, Berryman read "Homage to Mistress Bradstreet" as part of his Gauss seminar in late March 1953, a reading that
thoroughly impressed Edmund Wilson. In a rather predictable way,
Berryman spent part of Holy Week alone in Atlantic City, unwinding by
drinking excessively as he went through his own private passion, though
he was glad that Tate read a carbon copy of his poem and wrote a positive
response to it.[78]

The Bradstreet poem first appeared in the *Partisan Review*
(September–October 1953), where Schwartz was an associate editor and
where Catharine Carver, mentioned in Dream Song 318, worked as an
editorial assistant.[79] Though Carver never claimed the editorial spotlight,
she had a high reputation among her peers, having begun her career at
the *Partisan Review* as a business manager in the spring of 1945 and advancing to editorial assistant in the fall of 1950, managing editor in
January 1954, and finally associate editor in the spring of 1957. Giroux,
aware of Carver's background, hired her to work for him at Harcourt,
Brace as well sometime around 1950, fully aware of the workload involved. Thus, Giroux, most likely through reading the *Partisan Review*
and perhaps through conversations with Carver, knew of the poem. The
moment Giroux had been waiting for had arrived.

CHAPTER FOUR

The New Beginning at
Farrar, Straus & Cudahy

With "Homage to Mistress Bradstreet" completed in mid-March 1953, the Berrymans—with some financial assistance from the Fitzgeralds—sailed to France on April 28, arriving in Paris in early May. They drove south to the Côte d'Azur and then to Florence and Rome, though by mid-July they were in London, where Simpson received treatment for acute pain in her back. Berryman visited Beryl Eeman, still single and living in London, who gave him a book entitled *A Year of Grace: Passages Chosen & Arranged to Express a Mood about God and Man*—perhaps a reminder for him to think more about his spiritual life. Upon learning of Simpson's hospitalization, Eeman went to visit her, as did Tate, who was then lecturing under the auspices of the Fulbright program at Oxford, where he had previously been a Rhodes scholar (1910–1913). He not only paid her hospital bill and the Berrymans' hotel expenses in London, but also solicited the Academy of American Poets in Manhattan to send Berryman a check from the funds they held for needy poets.

Once back in the States in August, Simpson finally summoned up the courage to separate from her husband after ten years of marriage. She stayed in Princeton while Berryman moved into his mother's most recent apartment on West Twenty-Third Street near Ninth Avenue. He had reached such a serious impasse in his life, as Simpson contemplated divorce, that he seriously contemplated jumping off the George Washington Bridge.[1]

Still unemployed, Berryman wrote a rather backhanded letter to the chairperson of the English Department at Queens College suggesting that they hire him. In a more personal letter to Lowell about his experience as the Elliston professor in Cincinnati, he suggested that Lowell might apply for this position. In fact, when Lowell moved to Cincinnati, after a prolonged sojourn in Europe, to take up this post in February 1954, he and his second wife, Elizabeth Hardwick, moved into the same apartment that the Berrymans had occupied two years before.

By November, Berryman had moved into the nearby Chelsea Hotel and took time to visit Dylan Thomas, a resident of the same hotel though barely alive because of severe alcoholism. Thomas collapsed in the White Horse Tavern in Greenwich Village on November 4 and was taken by ambulance to Saint Vincent's Hospital. After returning from Princeton the next day, Berryman was informed of what had happened. Though Berryman desperately wanted to remain by Thomas's side, as others were doing, he withdrew because of a previous commitment. After a speaking engagement at Bard College in Westchester County, Berryman, Ralph Ellison, and Pearl Kazin, a literary editor at *Harper's Bazaar*, drove back to Manhattan to see Thomas. Berryman was in the hospital corridor when the great poet died on November 9 at only thirty-nine years of age. Shaken by this death, Berryman found himself incapable of going to the funeral, though he did attend a memorial service and console Caitlin Thomas. His poetic tribute, "In Memoriam (1914–1953)," reveals the same heartache he felt over the deaths of several others in his life.

Berryman rarely managed his money well, but he struggled especially when alone and in a time of trial. Thus, Giroux, after lending him $120 at this time, invited Lowell and Berryman to attend a performance of *La Traviata* just before Christmas at the Old Metropolitan Opera.[2] After Christmas, Berryman wrote Tate, no doubt as a result of talking to Giroux, that "Harcourt wants to bring out the Bradstreet poem in the Spring, but my Viking contracts have a restrictive clause, and they & I & my agent are all cutting our throats to no result yet. Poem made another convert: [Conrad] Aiken wrote me out of the blue he thinks it one of the best poems ever writ by [an] American. Cal likes it too."[3]

Alone, without Simpson, Berryman predictably sought out the company of at least two other women, all the time distraught at not disciplining himself sufficiently to sit down and write. Beginning in February 1954, he taught a one-semester course on poetry and creative writing at the Iowa Writers' Workshop, where his health seriously declined, again bringing on thoughts of suicide. Simpson summoned up the strength to go to Iowa City and visit him in the hospital.[4] The university medical school gave her permission to participate in staff conferences, enhancing her professional confidence as she evaluated one emotional conflict after another while making rounds. She returned to Princeton, ready to write and publish in her field.

In spite of continued bouts of anxiety, Berryman rallied at times while in Iowa. For future poet Philip Levine, whose classmates there included Donald Justice, William D. Snodgrass, and Robert Dana, the "semester Berryman conducted [was] the most extraordinary seminar I've ever been a part of."[5] In June, Berryman returned to New York, and after helping Simpson vacate the apartment in Princeton, he stayed again at the Chelsea. He next taught a seven-week summer fiction course at Harvard to undergraduates, in addition to a graduate course analyzing twenty-two plays of Shakespeare. After Paul Engle offered him a chance to continue teaching at the workshop, Berryman returned to Iowa City in September and team-taught a course with Marguerite Young, a woman he grew to dislike intensely. (Young's later novel, *Miss MacIntosh, My Darling*, explored the world of hallucinations and the paradise of opium addicts.) As before, Berryman drank heavily, which resulted in a round of fisticuffs with his landlord and a night spent in jail. The university had no alternative but to dismiss him from teaching.[6]

Berryman, at wit's end, contacted Tate, who had replaced Robert Penn Warren at the University of Minnesota in Minneapolis; he considered Tate not only a mentor since his final days at Columbia but "more or less" as a "father."[7] Tate, a tenured member of the faculty since 1953, was then married to Caroline Gordon (their first marriage lasted twenty-one years, 1925–1946, and their second thirteen years, 1946–1959). He would later marry the poet Isabella Gardner, a cousin of Robert Lowell. A philosopher and friend of Tate, Ralph Ross, arranged for Berryman to start lecturing in the Department of General Studies for the winter quarter of 1954–1955.[8] Berryman found an apartment at 2509 Humboldt Avenue South in South Minneapolis, a fair distance from the university but close to the Tates' residence and Lake of the Isles; he enjoyed taking solitary walks around the lake or going to the nearby Minneapolis Art Institute. On his fortieth birthday, he typed a letter to Van Doren, mentioning that he had been helping Tate in selecting material for an anthology and had finished a poetry manuscript that would prove to be his publishing break-through: "Can the next 16 yrs be as painful & useless as the last? <u>no</u>. But I finished last year the old thing I've written so far that's any good, a long poem on Anne Bradstreet, which if you ever see [it again] I hope you like it."[9] The understated conclusion to this letter showed that he wanted the recognition of his former professor—someone who, above all, he wanted anxiously to impress.

Before long, Berryman started seeing Elizabeth Ann Levine, a graduate student who was studying for a master's degree in English at the University of Minnesota. He eventually moved to another apartment at 1929 South Third Street to be closer both to the university and to Ann. If one can judge by the letters he wrote to his mother at the end of the year and the beginning of 1955, he was happier than he had been in a very long time, even while enduring the freezing cold weather (with stretches of 15 to 20 degrees below zero). He enjoyed teaching, spending time with the Tates, and applying himself seriously to studying the Gospels of Saints Mark and Matthew in relation to his work on Shakespeare, which included reworking material on Shakespeare's possible collaboration with William Haughton.[10] Furthermore, he looked forward to teaching the Reformation in the spring quarter, especially the events surrounding Luther's life.

Though caught up by his daily editorial activities, Giroux was never-theless experiencing the most trying time of his editorial career. As a result, he left his position as editor in chief of Harcourt, Brace at the end of March 1955 to join Farrar, Straus & Cudahy. In his new position and ever alert to compete with the very best, he could now sign contracts and bring aboard new authors in order to build up the reputation of this growing publishing house. Giroux's departure from Harcourt, Brace, however, was not without great personal and professional trauma, as he mentioned in a letter to his friend, historian and novelist Paul Horgan. Because Giroux was Catholic, he was not considered "eligible material for the [Harcourt, Brace] board of directors. . . . The firm was quite content to publish Catholic authors, yes; Catholic money was acceptable, yes, but a Catholic director? No."[11] Giroux's unexpected, detailed, "private and personal" letter to Berryman, written toward the end of April, reveals how deeply he felt committed to his friend:

> As you may have heard, I have left Harcourt, Brace after fifteen years to join this firm. I had thought my troubles were over when [Eugene]

Reynal [vice president and director in charge of the trade department] resigned last December, but this was a miscalculation; his leaving only confirmed the ascendency of the textbook people. William Jovanovich (or Don Giovanovich as I like to think of him) and John McCallum are The New Men. Denver Lindley, an old one whom I have always liked, will last as long as they can use him.

In any event, here I am loaded with honors (vice president, member of the board of directors, stockholder) and as excited as Alfred Harcourt and Donald Brace must have been when they left [Henry] Holt in 1919. I've known Roger Straus since we were in the Navy together; John Farrar and Sheila Cudahy are old friends. We're a young firm, and at the same time the oldest survivor (perhaps the only, now that [William] Sloane [Associates] has fragmentized) of the postwar publishers. We publish [François] Mauriac, Edmund Wilson, [Alberto] Moravia, Colette, [Marguerite] Yourcenar, Alec Waugh, and [Giovanni] Guareschi among others.

I want to build up the American list in general (I think our European list has great distinction), and the poetry list in particular. I would like to start with HOMAGE TO MISTRESS BRAD-STREET. I can now sign contracts myself, and there will be none of the Harcourt, Brace ambivalence—editor proposing and management disposing. May I publish your poem? . . . We are going to do Eliot's new play [perhaps a reference to Eliot's *The Elder Statesman*, published in 1959] (he staggered me by cabling "I will come along with you"), and Cal Lowell has agreed to publish the prose book he is working on (a memoir) with us; his poetry, alas, is tied up (I tied it up, of course).

So come on, and join your friends. Will you wire me collect and tell me we can submit a contract for the Anne Bradstreet; I'll offer you good terms.

I plan to come out your way in early May for a brief visit; I have to get back by May 11th when Uncle Tom [Eliot] arrives from London to stay at my apartment. It will be good to see you, and to talk over lots of things, but meanwhile let me know about the poem, by telegram preferably.[12]

Giroux became vice president at Farrar, Straus & Cudahy and then, shortly afterward, editor in chief. Roger Straus, who founded Farrar, Straus in 1945, came from a privileged background and could count on family financial resources (his mother was a Guggenheim and his father's family owned Macy's department store). He said that Giroux's arrival in 1955 was "the single most important thing to happen to this company."[13]

Feeling a sense of liberation and wanting to be more independent than before, Giroux rented a two-bedroom apartment at 219 East Sixty-Sixth Street in Manhattan. Word of his departure spread slowly, through letters to personal friends and by word of mouth. Seeking some companionship, Giroux took a train to Boston and checked into the Hotel Vendome. While there, he visited Lowell to talk about a contract for his autobiography, the first contract Giroux signed on his own with his new firm. He joined Lowell and Hardwick for a drive to Concord, and he also enjoyed cocktails and dinner with Lillian Hellman.[14] When Giroux returned to New York, he spent a good deal of time communicating with the seventeen authors who went with him to his new firm, including Eliot, Stafford, Lowell, Bernard Malamud, Thomas Merton, Jack Kerouac, Peter Taylor, Randall Jarrell, and eventually Flannery O'Connor.

When Berryman replied to Giroux on April 30, 1955, he apologized for not writing sooner; he had been ill and thus had canceled his Monday lecture on the Reformation, a topic, he now admitted, he barely knew. "It seems to have been a combination, far from ordinary, of ingratitude and bigotry," he consoled Giroux.[15] "They are bound to go straight downhill; which, if you feel vindictive, will be agreeable. It is specially pleasing that Eliot went with you. I really think you ought to be proud about this." Berryman wanted very much to sign a contract with Farrar, Straus & Cudahy for the Bradstreet poem, but he was not sure how to do this, as he had not been able to repay Viking for the $1,000 advance for both the projected Shakespeare biography and his *Black Book*, a cycle of poems about the persecution of the Jews in World War II, in the form of a Mass for the Dead, which he once abandoned and then reworked. (Four sections of it were published in *Poetry* magazine in January 1950, and three sections would later be included in *His Thought Made Pockets & the Plane Buckt*.)[16] In addition, he felt bound not to sign with another commercial publisher for any book. "Everything is just the same as it was eighteen months ago," he continued, "except that I heard from them lately for the first time in two years: an amiable letter from [Marshall] Best wanting to know about the biography, just as if nothing were wrong.[17] I have not answered it as yet." Berryman felt discouraged that the most important work he had done to date, the Bradstreet poem in *Partisan Review*, was both unreviewed and unavailable, though parts of it were appearing in anthologies in the United States and England. "Viking didn't refuse it," he added. "They said they wanted to wait & see (two years ago). But I don't want them to publish it and am not prepared to ask them to. I have no resentment against them any more, but after what's passed I just can't see an amicable relation over the several books involved." As a result, Berryman felt no compulsion to write the book on Shakespeare because he was uncertain what would become of it. "I can't get on with anything else with any happiness, because I am not allowed to arrange to publish it. All this is peculiarly exasperating, as owing to my very demanding work here this winter, I am finally recovering my energy and peace of mind, from the chaos of the last few years, and am wild to be writing." He felt the best solution was to repay the advance to Viking, but he lacked the financial resources to do so and did not envision having that much money at his disposal for a year, if then. He said he had been paying off his debts and enclosed a check, thanking Giroux for his kind loan.[18] He would send the remainder as soon as he could.

When Giroux replied on May 2, he took Berryman's words as a renewed token of friendship that moved him deeply. Giroux pursued his desire to publish the Bradstreet poem by offering explicit contractual considerations that would clear the way for Berryman to continue writing and having his works published by a longtime friend who was trying very hard to understand his pressures and problems. Berryman needed, above all, the expertise that Giroux was offering:

> First of all, we will advance you one thousand dollars to obtain the release from your contract. We will advance an additional two hundred and fifty dollars so that there will be some further cash on hand. In return we should like to draw a contract for the Anne Bradstreet poem and the Shakespeare biography, and (if you wish) a third book which can be called your "next work," (this last because I am not now sure what THE BLACK BOOK is). We would want to put the entire advance on general royalty, that is to say, it would be repaid by earnings from any book under the contract. I cannot recall the royalty rate that Viking offered you, but we will offer no less than they, and more if production estimates allow. In this connection, it would help to see the Viking contract once again. I can have it

photostatted overnight and return the original to you within twenty-four hours of receipt; if you can lay your hands on it, would you mail it to me here?[19]

Giroux hoped his proposal would be in general agreeable. If it were, it would seem that the first step would be for Berryman to write Viking for a release. "Is it clear, beyond doubt," he added, "that they want the $1,000 advance?" Giroux counseled his friend to have their answer in writing. Once he had Viking's letter and Berryman's word to the foregoing agreement, then Giroux would send him a check. Giroux felt that it probably would be best that his own name not appear in the negotiations for the time being. "They will doubtless ask who your publisher is to be, and they may also ask to negotiate with that publisher directly; but it is really none of their business and, as far as I am concerned, you do not have to say that another publisher is in the picture." Giroux was glad that Berryman had recovered his energy and peace of mind, aware, too, that Berryman had "lots of writing plans in mind." He continued, "I hope this proposal offers a way out. It's deplorable that the prohibitive clause in the Viking contract has been such a frustrating matter." He concluded his letter by thanking Berryman for his check in partial repayment of the loan, adding that he was in no hurry for the balance and hoping that the new contract would be signed well in advance of the next time they met.

A reenergized Berryman revved up, ready to pick up his career as a poet, and explained his writing philosophy to his mother on May 1: "*Courage* is what writing chiefly takes, when one has not the habit. Just jump in. Draft, without thought of detail or order; then fix. . . . The two great things are to be *clear* and *short*; but rhythms matter too, and unexpectedness. You lead the reader briskly in one direction, then you spin him around, or you sing him a lullaby and then hit him on the head."[20] By mid-June 1955, as Berryman learned that he would continue teaching at Minnesota for a salary of $5,300, his mother wrote to Giroux on stationery from the Chelsea Hotel that she had just learned that Giroux would be her son's editor.[21] In her own not-so-indirect way, she was letting Giroux know that she did not want to be left out of future publishing plans for her son.

During this time, Berryman experienced inner peace and consolation, as evidenced in his reply to Giroux of May 5: "I am about evenly astonished and delighted. I can hardly believe it. I feel like a new man."[22] He informed Giroux of the particulars of the Viking contract:

> Part II, 1A, of the [Shakespeare] biography contract seems explicit upon the advance-back. I have just written to [Marshall] Best claiming, upon this condition, the release he offered verbally two years ago, but I am sending the letter by ordinary mail, so that the contracts can get back in case I should need them. It didn't seem necessary to mention that another publisher was involved at all. I didn't send a copy of the letter because I only took one carbon and anyway there's nothing in it. It's very polite. Damn them though. Only, like all misadventures, this leads to good.

He concluded, "I like the whole arrangement and will give you the best work I can—I hope everything is opening beautifully for you." Berryman would communicate to Giroux the particulars of the unspecified third book he intended to write once he had finished with his Reformation and Counter-Reformation lectures. During the summer break, Berryman, profiting from the research he had done for his classes, spent considerable time reading background material for his Shakespeare biography.

Having accepted Giroux's proposal, Berryman shared with Giroux in a reply of May 24 the letter he had received from Best, indicating that Viking would have been pleased to publish Berryman's books had they arrived on schedule. Because so much time had elapsed since they originally signed the contract, Best was willing to release Berryman from his contractual obligation once the advance had been returned. Berryman went into high gear now that he understood that Giroux would give him the sure guidance he desperately needed:

> So hurrah. I have got intoxicated with the Shakespeare again, since seeing daylight, and have an entirely new view of it; I plan a much more free operation than I did, a book in fact bearing hardly any relation to those stupid old lectures and that boring piece in the Hudson [Review].[23] I am going to document it to the hilt, at the back, but I mean in the writing, and in the intellectual & emotional design. I think now I am going to spend the whole summer producing an entirely new draft of it. I can do this in about three months I believe. That I can then work on next year. I am now very much

against the prolonged strain on the reader's attention that I've always hitherto gone in for in prose. Hit a point, & then move; hitting them in an order that of itself moves the reader's mind (while it satisfies mine as of truth) in a way that can't otherwise be got at. But it wd take hundreds of w[or]ds to describe what I mean, and you'll see; I hope you'll criticize this draft for me. I have located the audience too. I am going to write the book for you & a woman I know [perhaps Sally Appleton] & Edmund Wilson.

I shd think the Shaks[espeare's] Friend ought to follow this, not precede it, supposing it works out; I am anxious to get a draft of it out too; I have no doubt that I am right abt the Taming of the Shrew part, but I can judge much better the plausibility of the other parts after a fresh survey of the whole life & work, especially now that King John seems solidly fixed very early. Here too I want to create a book, not a piece of drab pleading.[24]

In a telegram of June 3, Giroux said that he would both repay the Viking advance and draw up a contract for the Bradstreet poem and the book on Shakespeare.[25] Four days later, Giroux revised his proposal: an advance of $1,500 for both the Bradstreet book and the Shakespeare book, of which $1,000 would go to Viking. Farrar, Straus & Cudahy would offer the same royalty rate, though theirs would be based on the retail price of the books rather than, as Viking had proposed, the whole-sale rate.[26] Yet, in a cryptic private journal written in mid-June 1955, Berryman jotted down notes that perhaps signaled a future strain in his relationship with Giroux:

Giroux cares so little that he
—apologizes by wire, &
—without answering my letter
—takes $500 off the advance.[27]

To his credit, Giroux expressed his willingness to add additional clauses to the contract so that Berryman might feel more comfortable about their arrangement.

In recent months, the communication between Giroux and Berryman had been clear, honest, and straightforward. As the future editor of Berry-man's works, Giroux would remain a loyal friend, never backing away from his commitments to Berryman; his strength of character helped him to accept Berryman's overwhelming personal difficulties. He encouraged Berryman to write poetry during both good periods and difficult ones—even when Berryman went through periods of hospitalization, which became more and more frequent, creating for him a disturbing series of mentally uninhabitable spaces. In addition, he remained a friend to the family, gaining the confidence and friendship especially of Berryman's first and third wives. Giroux paid close attention to the unusually heavy revisions Berryman wanted in the late stages of the editorial process, realizing all the time that he was dealing with an exceptional poet. However, the tone and tenor of Berryman's communication with Giroux was about to change.

Berryman acknowledged Giroux's generosity in his letter of June 18, though, unfortunately, he failed to explain his thoughts about Giroux's contractual offer. His apparent inability to propose systematically what he expected of Farrar, Straus & Cudahy about his financial arrangements revealed a mindset that later proved to be counterproductive. For his part, Giroux sensed this and from that point on indicated how he thought Berryman should proceed, meticulously outlining any proposal he made to Berryman. What was crucial at this point, however, was that Berryman had found both new energy and a seemingly determined focus:

Okay. This wanted a little thinking about, as 500 down from the whole Viking advance, but as that was only coming when the book was delivered I care less; also I was in a lethargy of fatigue for a bit, and have been madly busy since, blasting my way through the problems of King John—I am half-way through the entirely new first chapter and I think it is going beautifully. About details: I don't remember anything much but the indexing and the illustrations. Viking I think was having me respons[ible] for the index, whereas [William] Sloane had the Crane's done, but in this case I think I'll have to do it myself anyway, as remarkably tricky. Then I was worried about Viking's making me respons[ible] financially for the illustrations; I am extremely interested in these—I have some beauties, and also two admirable maps for end-papers if we can—but clearly there is a limit, with publishers' advances in any case paying only a small fraction of the cost of the book manuscript's preparation to go to press, to the responsibility of cost for illustr's [illustrations] I can assume. I am going to sit here straight through the first three chapters, I think; then I'll see. There was a fine third-of-a-rainbow last night, sky elsewhere all pearl & rose, and yellow-white. <u>John</u>, as 1590, makes an unimaginably good point of departure.[28]

Though expressed in a jumbled way, Berryman made one thing clear to Giroux: his renewed enthusiasm for the work at hand.

Giroux, likewise, felt pleased with the trajectory of his life. To keep up his own psychological balance, he often fused his personal life with his professional commitments. He visited the Lowells in early June with Charles Reilly, staying overnight at their new house in Duxbury, Massachusetts, and then later in the month assisted Eliot during his visit to the States, even dining with him in Boston.[29] As usual, Eliot's presence and companionship did Giroux a world of good.[30]

Once back in New York, Giroux responded to Berryman on June 21, dealing more explicitly with the issues Berryman had raised; he did this to assure his friend that their contractual arrangement, in case Berryman might not read the fine print, would be clear from the start.[31] Giroux apologized for the mistake that Berryman had previously noted in his private journal:

It was sheer blindness on my part about the advance. I was thinking you would be five hundred dollars ahead of the Viking arrangement on signing our contract, and, so you are. But I overlooked their offer for further advances on delivery. In any event, we are upping the total advance to two thousand dollars.

As to the problem of signing with us before Viking's release, we have inserted a clause acknowledging that the cancellation of the Viking contracts is necessarily prior. This protects you from violating your present agreements and protects us against repayment of their advance without guarantee of getting your work. We have put everything into one document and I enclose two copies herewith.

As soon as you return one signed copy, I'll send you our check for fifteen hundred dollars, one thousand dollars of which you can forward to Viking. (A word of advice: Ask them not only for a letter of release, but an <u>exchange</u> of cancelled contracts. Write the word "Cancelled" on each page of each agreement in letters large enough to cover the printed text diagonally, but do not do this until they accept your check, which is tantamount in itself to a release.) . . . I note that you have reserved British publishing rights, and therefore I have followed that pattern here. I should tell you however that our English connections are excellent, particularly with Faber, and if when the time comes you want us to handle the matter for you on the usual basis we can arrange to do so by an exchange of letters.

I was sure you would want the SHAKESPEARE index [to be] your own responsibility; publishing practice invariably assigns this to the author. As to illustrations, our clause 4a (top of page 2) assigns this to the author also, but it means only the cost of supplying the material. In other words, we should have to pay for the cost of asking endpapers from those maps and plates from the illustrations you already have. If you mean permission costs, I doubt if there would be any since most of this would surely be in the public domain.

I am delighted that you are half way through the new first chapter and already see your way through the first three. More power to you.

To keep Berryman's imaginative momentum going, Giroux sent him *An Autobiography from the Jesuit Underground*, by William Weston, and Alfred Harbage's review of a book on Christopher Marlowe. Berryman replied, "This account [of Weston's life] helps my picture v much of all that underground, its extraordinary to find that he was the only Jesuit in England for 18 months."[32] Berryman's subsequent letter, dated June 25, revealed how delighted he was with the contract for both books, as he likewise expressed to his mother.[33]

Giroux sent Berryman the promised check and, in turn, received a signed contract; he agreed not to say anything publicly about the contract until he had received word of Berryman's release from Viking. For the Bradstreet poem, in addition to having illustrations done by Ben Shahn, an artist known for his figurative paintings, murals, and posters, he wanted the notes to be considered as an appendix, since they would make the poem longer and offer the type of pedantry critics all too often relish.[34] Berryman informed Giroux that the Viking contracts had been canceled and that he would contact Shahn, whose work he also admired, but he was not at all sure that Shahn would consent to doing the drawings.[35] He included some notes and asked Giroux's opinion of them, mentioning that he had not included any aesthetic or philosophical ones, leaving that to critics once they had read the book. He would send Giroux the galleys of the Bradstreet poem from its publication in the *Partisan Review*. Berryman wrote to his mother on July 9 that he had just received the canceled contract from Viking and that all the arrangements with Farrar, Straus were complete.[36]

In light of a forthcoming trip to England to meet with Victor Gollancz and the editors at Faber & Faber, Giroux worked hard behind the scenes to put everything in place.

Events move swiftly. We've already had a British offer for <u>Mistress Bradstreet.</u> It's from Victor Gollancz, a lively and enterprising publisher, and a good friend. Trouble is, he doesn't do much poetry; Faber, which does, really ought to have first look. Gollancz heard about it from Sheila Cudahy, now in London, and presumably he had read it in <u>PR</u> [*Partisan Review*]. I will be in London on September 20th and, if you like, can negotiate a contract at that time. Please let me know how you wish us to handle this. If Gollancz is enthusiastic, and Faber does not take it, it's worth a try. I don't, of course, know whether <u>The Dispossessed</u> had an English publisher or whether you have someone in mind for <u>Bradstreet.</u>

I have made up a manuscript from two copies of <u>PR</u>. "Slipshod" in stanza 39 has been corrected. I find the notes fascinating and think they should go in. Is the note of acknowledgement the prefatory note you mentioned in a previous letter? I've informed our designers there will be no dedication, and no epigraph. Is there any other front matter—your previously published books, for example?

Incidentally, would the parenthetical lines of biography which precede the <u>PR</u> text look better on a half-title page, so that the main text will begin with line one of stanza one?

I wish we could quote those phrases of [Allen] Tate, [Conrad] Aiken and [Jacques] Maritain on the jacket, just as they are. I suppose now that Ben Shahn has made the cover of <u>Time</u> (did you see his [André] Malraux?) he'll be more hardheaded than ever, and certainly more expensive. It would be great luck if he has made some drawings but, as you say, we had better proceed on the basis of no illustrations. We shall have specimen type pages for you in a few weeks. I plan to have the galley-proofs in time for my trip to England.[37]

Berryman replied on August 3 from Minneapolis, indicating that he was most willing to assist with the publication of his book. At this point, Berryman made an important decision: to follow through on contacting Shahn, whom he had once met at Princeton in the summer of 1947. His lengthy letter to Giroux had the organized, structured format that would please his editor's methodical sensibility.

I have been waiting to hear fr Big Ben [Shahn] but haven't; maybe he doesn't write letters, or is travelling, or prostrate. A number of people have died here fr the heat, and so many have collapsed in the laundries that it's hard to get clothes done. I can't say that my book has been moving like a jet plane. Yesterday however I bought one of these fast window-fans, apparently the last in the Twin Cities, and will now I trust be better. I thought it wd cost less than a funeral.

Various details abt the Bradstreet poem, but first thanks for Fr [Father John] Gerard's autobiography [*The Autobiography of a Hunted Priest*, written by an English Jesuit priest operating covertly in England during the Elizabethan period]. I don't know how I failed to hear abt this. I never read anything like it. It is much more remarkable in itself than Fr Weston's, and I'm grateful indeed. A trouble is that my sympathy with the regime is being impaired through all this; but it makes me watch Sh[akespeare] more carefully, to see if his ever was. The last paragraph of [Graham] Greene's introd[uction] is v[ery] interesting, by the way. A number of passages in my book go into this strange & unattractive moral smoothness of Shakespeare's, and I may quote Greene somewhere; I am not sure I ever saw the uneasiness (amounting almost to contempt) put better. Against it, in one corner, I shd put a passage of great strength in <u>Henry V</u> which I think I quoted to you once before—not <u>H.V</u>, where he acclaims Essex [Robert Devereux, the Earl of Essex] in a chorus, but the lines in <u>Much Ado</u> [<u>about Nothing</u>] about favourites,

Made proud by princes, that advance their pride
Against that power that bred it.

This is one of the most formidable immediate warnings anyone ever received. Essex paid no heed & did not live long. It is also to the point that, as [E. K.] Chambers says (who doubts the allusion, but I don't, given the v[ery] close dating & the linkage thro[ugh] [the third Earl of] Southampton), such an allusion wd be v dangerous for the playwright.

About Bradstreet poem:

1) Yes, the prefatory note I spoke of is just that note of acknowledgement. No other front matter except that as "By the same author." Two books might be listed, The Dispossessed and Stephen Crane. Yes, the parenthesis preceding the text might look better as you say on a half-title.

2) Mispr[int] in Notes: on 33.5 "grands" shd be feminine, "grandes" and in the next note maybe "or the hero" ought to be "or with the hero." If you think any of those notes ought to be deleted, or if anything remains signally (but only in detail I mean) unexplained, I wish you'd tell me. I can't judge.

3) Gollancz is a good publisher but I agree with you that Faber ought to have first look, if possible. No, The Disposs[essed]. was never publ'd [published] over there; it was reviewed in TLS [Times Literary Supplement], but is so rare that a Penguin anthologist complained to me several years ago not even the Brit[ish] Mus[eum] has a copy (please by the way do not let a copy of the Amer[ican] Bradstreet go to TLS but by the way I wd like review copies sent to Commonweal, Thought, and Jubilee); Eliot wrote [William] Sloane's agent abt it that he liked my work (huh) but when other Brit publ's [publications] were not sharing the obligation to make Amer[ican] poetry available, etc. If you can negotiate a contract over there for me, as you amiably offer, fine. You know more abt their practice than I do. Only I think I wd like whatever you arrange finally [to be] dependent on my signature, unless that's abnormal; mails don't take long, even if anyone were in a hurry. I had no one in mind except Faber, and I am not hypnotized by Faber.

4) Suppose Shahn's not done anything: there's a young artist in Iowa, Shirley Eliason, who says she wd like to make illustrations if he hasn't, and if there's time, both from your point of view (I don't know [your] schedule) and hers—she goes abroad in abt six weeks; she also wants to make a portrait, she writes, "an

overlay," whatever that is. She is rather good, especially at prints, though she paints too, and though only about 25 have won all sorts of prizes and has stuff in half a dozen big collections over the country. The stuff I've seen is bold and fine. What do you think, tentatively, about this? She knows the poem well & might do something interesting. How she cd do a portrait is not quite clear to me, unless we met in New York next month.

No, I knew about [Pope] Adrian IV. The names were pretty common. But I have deliberately put into the first chapter—or did I tell you this? It's so hot I can't remember my own name—a coincidence that will absolutely stand yr hair on end.[38]

When Giroux replied on August 5, he indicated that Shahn should be the one to do the illustrations, since he had the recognizable talent.[39] The illustration for the jacket, however, was another matter, and if Shahn had not already done one, perhaps Shirley Eliason would be willing to have her work used on the back panel of the jacket, provided the proposed sketch turned out well. In the long run, Giroux, trying to feel the visual impact of the finished book, preferred to stress typography—on the jacket as well as in text. Since he found the notes helpful, he had them retyped and requested that Berryman look carefully at the punctuation, italics, capitals, and brackets before returning the corrected version as soon as possible. He concluded by noting that "S[hakespeare]'s moral smoothness which worries Greene is expiated in the end. He lived a man of his times, but 'he dyed a Papist.'" Giroux found the Gerard biography superior to the Weston one, proof that he was mulling over his own projected work on Shakespeare and other Renaissance writers.

Berryman's next letter spells out in more detail his thinking about the design of the book:

Ben [Shahn] writes: "Yes I would like to make several drawings for Anne Bradstreet. Why don't you have your publisher, if they are agreeable to the idea, write me—all this of course if it's not too late" and the rest is about other things. He's at Roosevelt, New Jersey.

Expecting momentarily to hear from him, th[ough] not to this effect, and intensely busy, I've been slow writing. The awkwardness in that note on [Joshua] Sylvester & [Francis] Quarles that you point out is real, and it's my phrase too: the word "unfortunately" will fix it up. I wrote Shirley Eliason what you said. That "moral smoothness" I can give a better account of now; and it disappears in the final plays, if you ask me. I have only just noticed that you said (and very plainly too) that you want these notes back; I was misled by the carbon & hasty reading. I'll rush over them right now. Shirley writes that she may try something anyway, maybe a portrait (I think she must have a photograph; there are many, all atrocious, in print). She just sent me a stunning large print called The Funeral; she's very good at portraits. I'll be curious to see what Shahn does, if you & he work it out; I like his line-work of recent years exceedingly, and I imagine that's what he'll do.

[Peter] Beilenson [of Peter Pauper Press] put on his 7-league boots didn't he? I felt exactly as you did: astonished, and liking it better all the time. It's rather sumptuous, but austere also. I don't know that I ever liked a page better, and I wish you'd convey to him my admiration. I am touched, Bob, by yr saying you want a book of which I can be proud. Luckily the poem is damned well written or this production wd overwhelm it. I am against any more leading, myself, with all deference to Mr. [Hal] Vursell's view, and as to the one point smaller I think I wd leave the page as Beilenson has it unless he agrees with you & Vursell. Really remarkable page. And readable.[40]

As Berryman thought about his courses on Greek civilization and the authors for his modern literature course for the fall (Lenin, Eliot, Freud, Joyce, etc.), he received a specimen page for the Bradstreet book. Giroux told him that Gollancz had indeed offered to bring it out in England, but it might be better to wait for an offer from Faber & Faber.[41]

No doubt encouraged by having his future works published by Farrar, Straus, & Cudahy, Berryman continued composing the fragments and improvisational poems emanating from dream analyses that he would later call Dream Songs, the first of which was entitled "The Secret of the Wisdom." These poems, divided into three six-line rhyming stanzas using modified iambs, would eventually be divided into seven books comprising one lengthy, quasi-autobiographical poem, modeled to some extent on Whitman's great American epic, *Song of Myself*. In writing these Dream Songs, Berryman did not hesitate to rappel words from some inner abyss, all the while keenly aware that ordinary speech patterns never reveal the freshness and originality of an intended idea. These poems often embody private images that are sometimes linked to more objective flashes of known events. In a recorded interview, he said that one aspect of the "Dream Songs is to take an ordinary middle-aged American . . . and consult, deploy, his regular interests—supernatural, biological, friendly—and also take him to his limits . . . to find out what man can bear."[42] William Meredith, who first met Berryman at Princeton when both alternated in serving Blackmur as assistant in his creative writing courses, suggests that the Dream Songs give the impression of laughter in the face of humiliation, despair, and death—with a dose, one might add, of whimsy and wit that reinforces Berryman's self-indulgent, allusive, unconventional originality.[43] Something new was definitely happening in these Dream Songs, for Berryman's short phrases or sentences often rub up against one another, creating synergies that result in polysemantic subjectivity. Clearly, Berryman was entering into uncharted territory, the length and breadth of which he had still to determine. By mid-August 1955, he had composed approximately 650 pages of notes and poems.[44] When published, the Dream Songs embodied, according to Haffenden, "Berryman's own system of defense and aid against a threatening world; its efficacy is that of having held language to his trials. Thrilled and scared, Berryman observes and records one man's world: that man, Henry, himself. . . . To study and insinuate his destiny: that is Henry's design."[45]

Henry, a dominant—and dubious—figure in the Dream Songs, is sometimes depicted as a type of poète maudit, generally recognized as Berryman's alter ego. When once asked about Henry, Berryman replied, "Henry, eh? He is a very good friend of mine. I feel extremely sympathetic to him. He doesn't enjoy my advantages of super-vision; he has just vision. He's also simple-minded. He thinks that if something happens to him, it's forever; but I know better."[46] Given the subtlety of Berryman's imagination, other figures and personages for Henry also come to mind, such as Berryman's dentist, Henry Glickman; or "Negro masks," as suggested by Meredith; or Henry Fleming, the deserter-turned-hero in *The Red Badge of Courage*; or Frederic Henry in *A Farewell to Arms*; or Shakespeare's Henry V—or even, one might speculate, several of "Berryman's closest friends and most venomous enemies."[47] Coleman takes a more global appraisal of this figure by suggesting that Henry, "as a displaced figure for whom travel is a central aspect of his identity . . . reinforces the view that the work as a whole can be read as an extended meditation on the unstable nature of the American self considered in broad historical terms."[48] Publication of the Dream Songs, however, had to wait until Berryman was convinced they were more than exercises and that their form and content, as Van Doren stated in his 1936 review of Blackmur's *The Double Agent*, should "say something."

While in London in mid-September 1955, Giroux showed Faber & Faber the proofs of *Homage to Mistress Bradstreet*, which, if published in London, would require Berryman's signature. When Giroux returned to New York, he wrote to Berryman saying that he was "keen" to have Shahn make several drawings for the book, mentioning, too, that he was going ahead with the original typography done by Peter Beilenson.[49] With the Shahn illustrations and the designated typography, he was pleased to say that they would certainly have an original book. When Berryman saw the proofs in mid-September, he found them "beautiful," as he wrote his mother, still residing in the Chelsea Hotel.[50] No doubt inspired by Giroux's trip to London, Berryman wrote to his editor a letter, dated "Monday," indicating that he had been trying to get time to send some poems either to Eliot or directly to Faber & Faber. Furthermore, he sent Giroux a copy of *The Dispossessed*, which, alas, had sold only four hundred copies during the first week after its publication. Since he would be teaching courses during the next term that he had taught before, he felt his life might get back to some sense of normality, though he never wanted again to have such a demanding schedule.

Once back in his office, Giroux found, to his delight, both the Shahn illustrations and a letter from Faber & Faber, which he forwarded to Berryman on November 15.

We have now read and had a chance to think about John Berryman's HOMAGE TO MISTRESS BRADSTREET, about which you talked to me last month, and we are certainly most impressed by it. At the same time we feel—as I know you anticipated we would— that this poem by itself wouldn't perhaps be the best way to introduce Berryman to the English poetry-reading public; and we wonder if we could see some more of Berryman's work? What we would really like to consider—and about this we still haven't, of course, reached a final decision—is the possibility of doing here a selection from Berryman's poems with HOMAGE TO MISTRESS BRADSTREEET as the centrepiece. If you could, therefore, send me copies of any volumes that Berryman has published so far and perhaps, too, let me know something about unpublished poems, or poems published only in magazines, which could be included as well, I would be very grateful indeed.[51]

Giroux asked Berryman about his reaction to this letter, especially in light of the fact that Faber & Faber had accepted books by Lowell and Jarrell. If Berryman reacted favorably to their request, then Giroux would forward to them any poems Berryman thought they might consider. "Incidentally," he concluded, "Eliot mentioned two points about the Introductory Note. He wondered if the Arabella didn't cross in 1632 rather than 1630, and he thought that [John] Winthrop crossed not in the Arabella but on a previous ship, perhaps the Mayflower. This, mind you, was his recollection and he hadn't checked any sources." Uncharacteristically, Eliot's memory was faulty on these two points.

While in New York before Christmas, Berryman spent a brief amount of time with his mother and Simpson, though given the rush of the holiday season, most likely he did not see Giroux. At the beginning of 1956, Giroux informed Berryman, who had again spent Christmas by himself in Atlantic City, that the nine Shahn drawings he had received were marvelous; he would airmail photostats to Berryman and asked that they be returned soon.[52] Once back in Minneapolis, Berryman's exuberant reply of January 18 indicates his complete satisfaction with the Shahn drawings; he felt that they were "beautiful," rendering a whole and independent view of the world of Mistress Bradstreet and yet related to the poem in style by their conciseness and boldness, without being overbearing.[53] He wished he could see the originals, to get a sense of the gradations of the ink and the quality of the paper, especially of the two spare ones, the Small Houses and the Forest. The pedestalled Indian Cupid was unquestionably the most astonishing of them all. Berryman added that he felt as if he were coming back to life, and he subsequently wrote to Shahn expressing his satisfaction with the drawings. On January 20, Giroux telegrammed that the book would probably not be published before August because Beilenson worked slowly.[54] Now close to becoming a major published poet and feeling better about himself, Berryman acceded to the demands of the General Studies program, which wanted him to give three courses in the spring, each meeting every day, including one on Greek civilization and another on modern literature, which he had come to enjoy very much.[55]

Giroux sent a letter to Berryman on March 12, stating that Faber & Faber wanted to publish Berryman's *Selected Poems*.[56] He included a letter from Charles Monteith, a director at Faber & Faber, who had waited a while before replying due to the fact that T. S. Eliot had been in the London Clinic with bronchitis, followed by an attack of tachycardia that caused him to remain there for a month.

> T.S.E., I'm very happy to say, is now back with us and we've had a chance to talk over John Berryman. And I'm delighted to be able to let you know that he's very impressed with these poems and thinks them well worthy of inclusion in our poetry list. What we would like to do, I think, is a volume of selected poems with HOMAGE TO MISTRESS BRADSTREET as the centrepiece. We wouldn't, though, be able to bring it out for some time—late 1957 would be the earliest and indeed I rather think until sometime in 1958. I'm more sorry than I can say to have to forecast such a long delay. We do indeed look forward very much to bringing him out under our imprint here and very much hope that he won't be too disappointed by the prospect of what must look like a very long delay.[57]

For his part, Giroux was delighted with the news of the proposed volume and wanted, as he informed Berryman, to draw up a contract with Faber & Faber as soon as possible. "The publishing picture," he added, "often changes; books already committed for may not be delivered and yours may be advanced. BRADSTREET will soon be out here (I'm sorry that the illustrations are delaying us so). It is conceivable that the British collection may actually come out in the fall of the following year, despite what Monteith says."[58] Should the arrangement with Faber & Faber fall through, then they would approach Gollancz as a backup. "With Faber the book will be in print forever. The danger with Gollancz," Giroux cautioned, "is that when he sees the poem he might drop out. Then we have neither Gollancz nor Faber." Giroux wisely left the decision up to Berryman, though he wanted Berryman's permission for Beilenson's arrangement for Shahn's drawings, since they differed somewhat from the earlier order.

Berryman's reply, written from South Third Street, related his views on the layout of the book as well as his prospects of continuing in his academic post amid growing pressure to publish more. He liked the layout of the book very much, though, in addition to correcting a misprint, he suggested transposing stanzas 46 and 47 and the image of the Elder. "I am of one mind with you about Faber," he added. "Yes. Please go ahead contractually, with my thanks. I'm glad they want to. I think it ought to be called 'Homage to Mistress Bradstreet and other poems.' Certainly the delay is a bore, but if it can't be helped it can't."[59] With some reluctance, Berryman then spelled out what had been nagging him; the administration had waged a war against General Studies in the College of Arts and Letters, which might be dismantled and thus end his teaching career there. Moreover, he did not want to be saddled with debilitating, interminable committee work. Were his long poem to be published as soon as possible, he would have the academic stature he felt he needed. Recently, some courses had been canceled, and the tenure appointment he expected that spring would not be forthcoming until the situation stabilized. Given all this, he still expected to continue teaching for one more year at least. "The whole thing," he continued, "is almost purely a power-grab (budgetary) by the old-line departments, who are spurred on by envy (our courses are popular with the students and the programme is well-known nationally) & encouraged by a weak Dean. But it's been unbelievably damaging to morale and time. One week I actually had to spend more time defending my job in committee-meetings, etc. than I did doing it, and the same thing is even more true of some of my colleagues."[60] In Berryman's mind, it all narrowed down to "prestige." He had given one well-attended lecture on *The Tempest*, the best lecture he thought he had ever given, but otherwise it was "just more time-wasting & peanuts. Now all this bears like hell on Shakespeare." He concluded, "I hope everything is good with you. *Our book* is good anyway" (emphasis mine). Giroux briefly replied on March 28, giving some details concerning the layout of the book, but rather than enter into the "intramural skullduggery" of academia, he suggested that Berryman distract himself by reading the three books he enclosed: Nelson Algren's *A Walk on the Wild Side*, Sam Astrachan's *An End to Dying*, and Wilfred Watson's *Friday's Child.*[61]

At the end of the spring quarter, Berryman received a joint appointment in Interdisciplinary Studies and the English Department, promotion to associate professor, and a salary of $8,000. In mid-April, now forty-one years old, he lectured at the university on Eliot as poet and critic, no doubt prompted by the news of Eliot's forthcoming visit to Minneapolis. Giroux needed Berryman's authorization to act as his agent in drawing up the contract with Faber & Faber, since the publishing rights for all the poems in *The Dispossessed* had reverted to Berryman and were, in fact, in his control.[62] Giroux—now a vice president at Farrar, Straus & Cudahy and busy editing twenty-seven books for the fall catalog, including *Homage to Mistress Bradstreet*—assisted Eliot, who arrived in New York in late April on the *Queen Mary*.[63] While in New York, Eliot stayed with Giroux in his apartment. Almost immediately after his arrival in the United States, Eliot lectured on "The Frontiers of Criticism" at the University of Minnesota at Tate's invitation (undoubtedly Berryman would have been among the fourteen thousand attendees in the university stadium, though he seems not to have alluded to it). Eliot then traveled back to Washington, DC, to Boston, and finally, in May, to New York, from where he would return to England in early June.[64] Before leaving, Eliot dined with Giroux, Stafford, and Giroux's good friend Horgan, now a Pulitzer Prize winner, at the Carlton House restaurant in New York.[65]

Soon afterward, the unbound sheets of the Bradstreet book arrived from the Peter Pauper Press. Giroux was struck by the power and beauty of the book and sent Berryman the final proofs at the end of the month. After he received a blurb from Conrad Aiken ("It seems to me to be the finest poem ever written by an American, a classic right on the doorstep"), Giroux wrote to Berryman on June 19, saying that he felt the quote was so extraordinary that it deserved the whole front flap to itself.[66] Berryman's reply gave his editor a general update about his life and activities.

> I'm near the end of the Second Act of a play—I didn't want to waste time on the phone about it, but that's the current reason I haven't written. I wound up the academic year exhausted: Saul & Sondra Bellow arrived to spend several days with me the evening of the last day I lectured: after they left I was ill a few days, then I suddenly began to write very fast, and I have got to get this draft finished before I begin teaching week after next (a second-summer-session of five weeks, course in [Stephen] Crane & [William Dean] Howells). It's a prose comedy in three acts, laid in Washington DC right now, abt a State dept character etc, and so far it is the worst play ever

written, but by the time I finish I think it won't be. Present title: <u>A Tree, A Tree</u>.[67] Saul by the way thinks the Dream Songs are marvelous, which is a great relief. His new book, about half done, is a beauty; which is a great relief.[68]

Authorization enclosed. Thanks for advice abt [William] Morrow.[69] Directly I hear from them I'll let you know.

Anxious to see book. I hope the drawings print blacker than they do on these sheets; otherwise I am all admiration. . . . I'll have to write another time about Shakespeare. Thanks for Astrachan's novel (very interesting for the subject, but can't tell yet whether he'll be any good I think) and Wilfred Watson, who has a real gift—so far he relies wholly on Dylan Thomas and Yeats's final poems, so that the music is not his own, but the poems have a most agreeable music, nearly all of them. The biography of Southwell looks absorbing, as I said.[70] How fast all that area is filling in!

Very good to hear your voice, and Eileen's last night.[71] I feel utterly isolated out here. Wish me luck & dialogue.[72]

Copies of *Homage to Mistress Bradstreet* were due from the printers on July 3, with advance copies going to thirteen of Berryman's friends and acquaintances, including, as directed by Berryman, Louis MacNeice, Jacques Maritain, Ezra Pound, and Edmund Wilson. Though these copies were certainly meant as gifts from the author and editor, replies from the recipients might well be used, with proper permission, for publicity purposes.

An unforeseen conflict had unfortunately arisen. Criterion Books claimed that Berryman had given permission to Auden, whom Berryman had once met during his student days in England, and to Faber & Faber to include sixteen stanzas of *Homage of Mistress Bradstreet* in an American edition of a poetry anthology Criterion anticipated publishing in the fall (this anthology was never published).[73] Giroux was reluctant to agree to this because it would be in direct conflict with Farrar, Straus's publication of the Bradstreet poem. On the same day, Berryman wired that the permission had not been given to Auden directly, neither to Criterion, nor to Faber & Faber, but to Doubleday. Berryman saw no harm in accepting the new arrangement, though he left it to Giroux to decide what to tell Auden: "BUT I AUTHORIZE YOU TO DO WHATEVER YOU THINK BEST. HOW I AM COMMITTED TO AUDEN YOU

CAN NOW TELL BETTER THAN ME. FABER AUTHORIZA-
TION FOUND AND SENT YESTERDAY." Realizing that the telegram did not provide a proper explanation of events, Berryman immediately elaborated on his thoughts that same day:

> I tried to be explicit just now in the wire but actually this anthology
> situation is complicated. So far as I can see, four things are involved:
>
> 1) interference with your edition—in America, I take it; I don't
>   quite see this interference, from your wire; I shd have thought,
>   offhand, that it wd just be extra publicity—but you are certainly
>   a better judge than me;
> 2) the nature of my moral commitment to Auden, with whom I
>   never had any correspondence personally about this at all, but
>   whom I was glad liked the poem of course at a time when it was
>   almost completely unknown, and I shdn't like to offend so good
>   a poet anyway—as I once did by rejecting a bad poem he sent me
>   at The Nation;
> 3) the fee, which your wire doesn't mention (Doubleday offered
> $40, which I agreed to accept only because of Auden & because
>   I was horribly hard up);
> 4) my unwillingness, hereafter, to let parts of the poem be used at
>   all; I only did this, with [Paul] Engle, Auden, and Tate, because
>   of personal friendship & need of money & the poem's need of
>   attention; from now on, with your assent, I shd say that anybody
>   who wants the poem will have to take it all, and pay well for it,
>   in the neighbourhood of $150–$200.[74] But this present arrange-
>   ment, made years ago insofar as it was made at all, need not be
>   affected by that decision, for I did give permission for part of it
>   to be used: just what part, by the way, was never clear. They said
>   "16 stanzas" first, then St's [Stanzas] 42 thro' 54 (which is only 13
>   stanzas), and now your wire says "sixteen final stanzas." This wd
>   have to be clarified. Point is, I didn't like the look of part of the
>   poem in Engle's anthology, which is the only one of the 3 that's
>   come out; it didn't make sense.
>
> Now you know everything. . . . Odd, there's no colophon in
> Bradstreet. Copies ought to go to Auden, Delmore Schwartz, and
> Father [William] Lynch, though I certainly wish I cd inscribe these
> last two. A bad smudge under the Cupid's chin must be in my copy

only? Inking of the drawings is certainly well below all the other features of production: compare for blackness & clarity of line the trees above St. [Stanza] 16 with the trees opposite or indeed <u>any</u> other drawing. <u>Can I have some copies out here as soon as possible? better say 15</u>. All my thanks for everything. Maybe we got a pretty good book.

Giroux wasted no time in conscientiously sorting out the pertinent issues:

<u>Advance copies</u> [of *Homage to Mistress Bradstreet*]. I was delighted to have your note about the first copy. It <u>is</u> a handsome book, isn't it? We intend to enter it for the Fifty Books of the Year Award. Your ten author's copies were shipped to you yesterday; regular stock has just come in. Today I am putting five more copies in the mail (first-class); I have looked at these copies and they do not bear the smudge under the chin of the Cupid; this printing defect seems to have turned up only in some of the copies. (Incidentally, Professor Milton Halsey Thomas [of Columbia University] who is editing the SAMUEL SEWALL DIARIES for us, told me that he had seen the original of the Indian weather vane in Boston; I had thought it was entirely a product of Shahn's imagination! It's marvelously placed, isn't it?)

    <u>Auden Anthology</u>. Many thanks for your wire and the letter which followed. Apparently Auden, when the book fell through at Doubleday, considered that he was free to offer the rights to an English publisher—in this case Faber, who thereupon sold the American rights to Criterion. Legally speaking, they have no right to print the excerpt (which is 16 stanzas, down to the last line of the poem; Criterion has English proofs and read me the first and last lines), but morally speaking, Auden obviously acted in good faith and so did Faber and Criterion. However, we feel that the appearance of the anthology prior to or simultaneous with the publication of your book, containing nearly 30% of the poem, would be very bad indeed. If it had come out last year, or were to come out next year—but this fall! We have proposed a compromise solution, authorizing Criterion's use of the sixteen stanzas provided that (a) the American edition not appear prior to December 1, 1956, and (b) that the American publisher pay an additional permissions fee of $75.00 (I assume that although Doubleday agreed to pay you $40.00, this was on publication and you did not in fact receive the payment). Of course, Criterion

may decide to delete the excerpt, but at least we have offered them a compromise and face-saving solution and it would be foolish of them not to take it.

    <u>Authorization and Release</u>. Your authorization to proceed with Faber, signed conditionally, arrived yesterday. As I suggested in our phone talk, you should request a photostatic copy of the contract of THE DISPOSSESSED from William Morrow immediately. It may contain a "recapture" clause which would solve everything. If not, it may be that [William] Sloane's merger with Morrow provides the way out—unless you specifically authorized Morrow to acquire your contractual rights. In any event, I suggest that you forward the photostat of the contract to me for study by our legal advisors, as soon as you receive it; I can return it within a week. . . . We must get together on the matter of advance copies: if you want to inscribe copies for Delmore and Father Lynch, we ought not to duplicate them. Perhaps if you simply tell me which of your inscribed copies are being sent to pundits, this will eliminate duplications.

    Who is publishing Tate's anthology? And who published Paul Engle's? We ought to have this information for your permissions record. I agree with you that in the future we should agree to a reprint of the poem only in its entirety and for a big fee, and I am instructing our permissions department to this effect.[75]

In a telephone conversation with a representative from Criterion, Giroux consented to their publication date of November 15.

    Clearly relieved and trying to fill in the gaps in their recent communication, Berryman in his reply addressed Giroux familiarly by his middle names, Francis Xavier, a clear indication that he trusted his old friend. More than before, Berryman had to deal with the interlocking complexities of the publishing world, though he wanted his Bradstreet poem to have the singular spotlight he felt it deserved.

Thanks for good & clear letter. Glad the Auden business is arranged. You did that very well. What a nutty situation, however, it makes in England: where the last third of the poem will be visible or audible in Auden['s anthology], and the first third in Tate['s anthology], and the middle nowhere. You might gently intimate to Faber that they can remedy this ridiculous situation by bringing out their damned edition as quickly as possible. (Still not hearing from [William] Morrow, I have just written by air requesting a photostat of the contract and will let you have it immediately I get it; I can't think why I haven't heard from them, and intimated as much.) Tate's anthology is with Eyre & Spottiswoode over there, and I think Macmillan here—not sure—we ought to find out when that's being published here, too, eh? Tate is at Harvard right now. No, I never had a cent from Doubleday, and have not been paid by any of Tate's people. Engle's publisher I forget, some big Chicago house [Scott, Foresman & Company], they never sent me a copy, I only saw a friend's; Books in Print will tell you, under Paul Engle. Wd you do me a favour? Can we see, so far as possible, that copies of our edition do not go to England? And wd you be willing to write personally to the editor of TLS, Alan Pryce-Jones, explaining the above situation and requesting that, if a copy of our edition does fall in their hands, they not review it? You might add that in the summer of 1953 I submitted the poem to him for printing (it is rather long, but they had just been printing endless French poems) and never heard back, although later while staying with MacNeice in London [in 1953] I telephoned him repeatedly and could get nothing out of his secretary and he has never even returned the copy to me, and I have been wondering about this with indignation ever since, and if there is any explanation I will be glad to have it. I am accustomed to having my work either accepted or rejected, and this particular instance of British courtesy amazes me. The BBC did exactly the same thing with the poem, only there it was if possible even worse, for they had asked to see it; that was John Davenport's work, but then he got fired and I have no recourse.[76] You see I have some cause for resentment and caution overseas.

Query: How many copies are you printing?
Query: What date precisely in October?
Query: If any copies of the dust-wrapper remain to be printed, what do you think of saying, below Aiken's statement:
Extracts from this poem are currently appearing in anthologies edited by W. H. Auden, Paul Engle, and Allen Tate.

Or maybe leave Engle out [Engle and Berryman eventually drifted apart, reaching the point of despising one another], but this wd take the curse of solitary eminence off Aiken's opinion, which is certainly going to put some reviewers' backs up, if you ask me. I don't recommend this; I ask your view. Remember that I have been beating authors up, as a critic, for fifteen years and more, and some unfriends, like [Richard] Eberhart say, are bound to head for my book.[77]

The next day, Giroux relayed Lowell's enthusiastic endorsement of the book: "HOMAGE TO MISTRESS BRADSTREET is a scholarly, reckless poem and a very big achievement. For a long time I have been hearing the voice of the heroine alive and calling."[78]

On July 5, Berryman sent Giroux a poem that he would always cherish:

To Bob

—to whom the physical existence of
    this thing [*Homage to Mistress Bradstreet*] is due,
and after 20 years of unbroken
    friendship,
& more particularly: I was dying,
    not in brain but in heart &
    spirit, when you rescued me
    with this—so that I can
    hope to do some more—
        w admiration & affection

                John

Berryman and Giroux had now become as close as is possible for an author and an editor. This poem mirrors Berryman's inscription in Giroux's copy of *Homage to Mistress Bradstreet*: "It is easy to say how grateful I am to you for the existence of this thing as a book. It is impossible to say how much it owes to you as a poem—or part of me—for your championship of the Bradstreet poem: I could never have tried it twice in almost complete darkness." No matter the tensions that might develop between them, this short poem and inscription eloquently reveal a level of trust, especially on the part of Berryman, that he would never express again to anyone else.

But the nitty gritty of promoting Berryman's book properly still had to be done, especially in blocking any advance publicity that could be negative. For his part, Giroux was willing to write personally to Alan Pryce-Jones at the *Times Literary Supplement*, since he knew that they would review Berryman's book, though he also knew that no letter from him would ever stop them. "My feeling," he stated, "is that the reputation of Faber in England is the best 'stopper.' If they receive a literary note from Faber, announcing your book in advance of our edition, that should do it."[79] Giroux had already asked the opinion of Monteith, who subsequently informed him that he had written to Arthur Crook, the assistant editor of the *Times Literary Supplement*, asking him not to review the American edition, should it reach him.[80] It was anticipated that the initial American printing would be three thousand copies, published officially on October 1, perhaps with a jacket band featuring quotes by Lowell and Fitzgerald, and, if needed, a sheet inserted in all the review copies of the advance quotes from other notable authors.[81] Shahn had written Giroux his praise of the book, which Giroux included in his letter to Berryman. Giroux also shared with Berryman a highly laudatory assessment he had just received from Edmund Wilson, whom, as he noted, rarely gave quotes: "MISTRESS BRADSTREET SEEMS TO ME THE MOST DISTINGUISHED LONG POEM BY AN AMERICAN SINCE THE WASTE LAND."[82] Berryman had known Wilson from the time he stayed with the Tates in Connecticut after graduation and later when he and Simpson took a summer vacation in 1944 on Cape Cod. Bellow, who had been an assistant to Schwartz in the Princeton creative writing program in the fall of 1952 while Blackmur was away in the Middle East as a Fulbright lecturer, wrote to Berryman, "The *Bradstreet* is wonderful. I take nothing from it if I say that your more recent poems are written in something more like my tongue. I think *Bradstreet* is a triumph of modern poetry."[83] Unfortunately, this letter was private and could not be used for publicity. Tate wrote that the poem "adds a fourth to the three first-rate long poems by Americans in this century—the others being Pound (*Cantos*), Eliot (*Wasteland*), and (Hart) Crane (*The Bridge*)."[84] Van Doren kept his praise to a minimum, astonishingly so, given his previous support of Berryman during their Columbia days. In a letter to Giroux, Van Doren said that he had initially admired Berryman's poem when he first read it in the *Partisan Review*, but he admired it more in the "fine dress" that Giroux gave it.[85] While interest mounted and a handful of advance testimonials came his way, Berryman soon realized that the literary world hardly took notice of his important work, which proved to be a heart-breaking disappointment.

Berryman soon received some unexpected—and troubling—news: he found out in September 1956 that Ann Levine, who had spent the summer in New York, was pregnant with his child. Still married to Simpson, he wrote to her—then in Paris after visiting the Fitzgeralds in Genoa—asking for a divorce. If she granted it, the new marriage would have to take place outside of Minnesota because the state required six months between one marriage and another.

Although honored by receiving a *Partisan Review* Rockefeller Fellowship of $4,000 for 1957 and somewhat pleased by John Holmes's observation in a review for the *New York Times Book Review* (September 30, 1956) that while the Bradstreet poem requires much rereading it should be considered a landmark of American poetry, Berryman felt extremely disappointed that the *New York Times* had failed to mention his book in its year-end list. Reading the *Times* daily with extraordinary diligence, and even receiving advance notice of items pertaining to the firm, Giroux could barely control his fury. When he called Francis Brown, the editor of the *Times Book Review Section*, Brown could only say that it was an "oversight."[86] Berryman was, as he wrote to his mother, "pretty well resigned to the book's nearly-complete immediate failure."[87] It had been a rough year for Berryman, made lighter, no doubt, by the publication of a major poem, but it came to a sad conclusion when he and Simpson were divorced in December, as dramatized in her roman à clef *The Maze*. In addition to a heavy cold and dental and medical treatments, Berryman continued to fret about the lack of reviews (the book had sold only 940 copies as of the end of December 1956). His subsequent marriage to Ann after Christmas by a justice of the peace in Sioux Falls, South Dakota, undoubtedly meant a new start for him. Predictably, Simpson began distancing herself from John and some of his friends, though she remained in close contact with Giroux.

CHAPTER FIVE

From Anxiety to Reconciliation

The new year of 1957 did not bring unfettered consolation, as the prestigious Bollingen Prize in Poetry for 1956, announced in mid-January 1957, went to Tate rather than Berryman. Still and all, Berryman was pleased to continue teaching, at this time a course on the American character and one on medieval literature. Subsequent communication between Berryman and Giroux, as they tried not to address head-on the paucity of reviews for *Homage to Mistress Bradstreet*, caused them gradually to drift apart almost asymptotically. Would their friendship extend beyond this breach?

When Berryman next wrote to Giroux, on January 6 on letterhead from the Department of General Studies in the College of Science, Literature, and the Arts, he began by wishing his friend a belated merry Christmas and a happy new year. His unwillingness to go into detail with his editor about his divorce and remarriage seems to indicate that he had not thoroughly processed these important changes in his life. He avoided, too, bringing up any serious concerns about his future relationship with Giroux and the firm, seemingly suppressing the disquiet he felt at this time.

> Would you look over this contract [for *Plays of Shakespeare*, to be superseded in June 1958 by a proposal for *A Shakespeare Handbook*] for me, as you wanted to do, and if it looks OK pass it on to Jack Gallagher at [Thomas] Crowell [Company]?[1] If not, let me know what's unsatisfactory.

Thanks for sending various stuff about my book. I'm baffled by what has reached me of its reception. Some quite experienced people write to me congratulating me on its marvelous reception, other equally experienced people write to me wondering why it has hardly been reviewed at all—and I am more inclined to agree with the second group than the first; but what's your impression? I take it that there <u>must</u> have been more reviews than the half-dozen you sent, though I only <u>know</u> of one in the Chicago Sun-Times they sent me direct. Eileen says reviewers seem awed & nervous; but that the weeklies for instance shd ignore it completely truly surprizes me (I was once offered some 75 rev's [reviews] of The Dispos[sessed] & some 150 of the Crane [biography]. I suppose the thing has hardly sold at all?)

Tell me, what's with Faber?

Thanks abt the PR [*Partisan Review*] thing, piece of luck.

For his part, Giroux had little to share except to say in a telegram that the Crowell contract had been mailed to Jack Gallagher and that Faber & Faber had decided not to publish their book until after the release of Richard Wilbur's anthology (perhaps *Poems, 1943–1956*).[2] Giroux subsequently forwarded two recent reviews and a copy of a fairly obscure journal, the *Cambridge Magazine IE*. It is no wonder that when Berryman wrote Giroux on January 20, he repeated that his health had declined considerably, to the extent that his doctor had nearly "exterminated" him: "I'm now in my 5th day of withdrawal symptoms from cigarettes & drinking and ask myself whether the game is worth the candle and reply <u>No</u>!" After learning that he had come in second for the Bollingen Prize, he showed a glimmer of hope in this letter to Giroux: "This surprises me very much, partly because I've grown accustomed to regarding my book as a failure as things stand; but it suggests that notwithstanding the reception or irreception it may still have a shot at either the Pulitzer or the Natl Bk [National Book] award." He was aware that the sales of his book were poor and felt, nevertheless, that "it may go on selling for a while." Belatedly, the *Times Literary Supplement* (May 31, 1963) called the Bradstreet poem a "path-breaking masterpiece."[3]

Berryman's letter on February 12 indicates that he was still tracking the literary awards he might just possibly receive. Learning that Tate was one of the judges for the American Library Association's "creative" award of $5,000 gave him further hope. Giroux, at Berryman's suggestion, entered the book into competition for the National Book Award, but after seeing the names of the judges, Berryman knew he did not have a chance of winning: "Louise Bogan is committed to Wilbur, besides, not having even reviewed my book, and [Yvor] Winters beat up The Dispossessed; etc. [The other judges were Edward Davison, Horace Gregory, and Louis Simpson.] Thanks for the proof of the Times ad. The review in the little Cambridge magazine is the only serious one the book has had so far. I certainly wd be glad to hear yr opinion abt this curious reception & non-reception." Giroux's comments about various reviews could hardly have relieved Berryman's anxiety, especially when raising a false hope about the ALA's award:

> I enclose a copy of next Sunday's The New York Times Book Review containing a note by Harvey Breit about the National Book Awards in poetry. I really think that the poetry nominations, excepting Fitzgerald, Pound, [Marianne] Moore, and Wilbur are a disgrace, and it is nothing short of a scandal that MISTRESS BRAD-STREET is not among the titles. As soon as I saw the list, I called Breit and his column is a result of our conversation. Yvor Winters is batty, as we all know, but I would have expected Horace Gregory to behave better. As a matter of fact, I can't help thinking that there might be a mistake because Gregory phoned me for copies of your book. Anyway, we shall see what Breit's blast turns up. There is gossip but no confirmation of the award going to Wilbur.
>
> As I wired you yesterday, we had submitted the required number of copies to the A.L.A. last January in the category headed "Imaginative Literature." What a handsome award it is and how marvelous if Tate chooses BRADSTREET! Incidentally, the fifteen copies you requested were shipped yesterday.
>
> The review situation is also a scandal, but I'm damned if I know what to do about it. Frankly, the daily Times (Charles Poore) was more than I expected, but I'm left speechless by Irita Van Doren's failure to schedule a review in the Sunday Tribune.[4] She knows that Mark [Van Doren] admires the poem and would gladly review it, but even if she didn't want to ask him she certainly has plenty of other alternatives.

Incidentally, did you know that John Ciardi (who is now being clobbered for his unfavorable review of Anne Lindbergh's mush) nominated your book in the Saturday Review as among the best of the year? This and your Bollingen [Prize] news are two of the heartening signs we have had, along with those four stunning statements reproduced in our ad. I console myself by recalling that when the WASTE LAND appeared, it was not even reviewed in the New York Times. . . . I hope all goes well with you.[5]

Secretly, Giroux hoped that Breit's piece would shame at least one judge, particularly Tate, into making a defensive statement. "Technically, BRADSTREET may have been nominated. I had hope[d] Harvey's squib would elicit this much from the committee. It may still do so."[6] Later, Berryman reiterated that he was surprised by the degree of hostility toward him, and like Giroux he had been gathering information about the manner in which literary awards were given, but neither could predict accurately who the ALA recipients would be. When Berryman later learned that Wilbur was the recipient of both a Pulitzer Prize and the National Book Award for Poetry for *Things of This World*, he went into an emotional tailspin.

Although Berryman had moved into an apartment at 2900 James Avenue South with Ann and baby Paul as a way of trying to start his life afresh, he coped with lingering health issues, especially twice-weekly dental procedures that caused him considerable pain. He gave Giroux, nevertheless, a personal update about the Dream Songs, which allowed Giroux a chance to think about their possible publication.

Hello! after so long! I have been swampt w speaking engagements, and having a son (named Paul [born in Abbott Hospital in Minneapolis on March 5, 1957]), and Ann has been ill, and I've been writing—both serious things and most recently a poem abt [Richard] Eberhart that may endanger your life with laughter when I show it to you. Even now I can't write properly because I'm getting ready to preside over two things in Chicago and am dead-tired: I am going to arrange five days off late next week and get some rest. . . . Thanks for the proofs of [John] Ciardi's generous surprising & intelligent review [*Saturday Review* (March 23, 1957)]. Tate agrees w me that he never did anything like it before to our knowledge. I was sorry however to see <u>four</u> atrocious errors in the quotation from the childbirth passage. It was pleasant to see an important passage quoted & actually talkt about.

How are you? Is there any news? I thought the Trebizond book delightful (thanks) and my mouth watered. There is a possibility that I may go to India for the State Dept in June and my mouth waters. It looks as if my tenure appointment—delayed now for 18 ridiculous months—will go through very shortly, so that I can both plan and work. My dream-song sketching has been going beautifully, but I have not been able to get to Shakespeare yet and this is a <u>bore</u>. Here are three lines:

> The shadow of my father's shaming death
> lay over a youth.
> Phantoms suckt at my chances.[7]

He added a postscript: "I've written a short poem to the baby [that] Saul [Bellow] (who's here now) & Allen [Tate] think is stunning; I'll send you a copy when I make some."[8] While daydreaming about the endless possible variations to his Dream Songs, Berryman felt weighed down by having to lecture to more than one hundred eager students in his modern literature course, something that nevertheless pleased the department enormously. As expected, Giroux was delighted with Berryman's letter that was "full of marvels and amusements," especially about the birth of Paul and the prospects of a trip to India under the auspices of the United States Information Agency.[9] He later congratulated Berryman for having won the Harriet Monroe Poetry Prize of $500, though the communication between the two of them seemed at this point to come to an abrupt halt, in large part because Berryman, preoccupied with his travel plans, had made little progress with his Dream Songs.[10]

In 1957, Berryman started a lecture tour under the auspices of the U.S. Information Agency, stopping first in Tokyo and Kyoto in July and then giving more than two dozen lectures at fourteen colleges and universities in India, sometimes with Professor Howard Munford of Middlebury College in Vermont. That fall, with his infant son Paul and Ann, he met up with the Fitzgerald family in Levanto, Italy, and then toured Barcelona, Madrid, Salamanca, Seville, and Lisbon, where he had a terrible fight with Ann. From Avila he wrote to Tate, indicating that Robert

Fitzgerald had recently written and advised him to leave Ann and go to back to Eileen.[11] The three Berrymans sailed from Cadiz to New York on December 9. As at the end of his European trip with Simpson, Berryman and his wife now drifted further apart, though he wanted to remain close to Paul if possible. There is no record of Giroux meeting Berryman in New York before the travel-fatigued family flew to Minneapolis. What would have been the point of it, since they had so little to say to each other? Nor would Berryman see Giroux when he returned East in late February 1958 to give a reading at the Library of Congress.

Once back in Minneapolis, Berryman sadly learned that the university had abolished the Department of Interdisciplinary Studies, which meant that the Humanities section would have a lower profile at the university. He continued teaching with joint tenure in Humanities and English, though rarely in the latter, perhaps due to his increased alcoholism and a stay in Abbott Hospital in early April. Unstable, upset, and bored by teaching the same courses during the past three years, he manifested a calculated disdain toward certain members of the department, except for Bellow, Murray Krieger, and Leo Marx, who supported him in their own ways. His Dream Song 7 about invading rats (a reference to certain members of the faculty), entitled "'The Prisoner of Shark Island,' with Paul Muni," captured much of what he felt at this time ("For the rats / have moved in, mostly, and this is for real").[12] In mid-May, after a short trip with Ralph Ross to the Sagamore Resort on Lake George, New York, to speak to a group of college deans, he wrote to Giroux expressing his dissatisfaction that the Bradstreet volume was selling about eight copies a month. A few days later, however, he took a step forward, writing a preface for the British edition of *Homage to Mistress Bradstreet and Other Poems*, which he sent to Giroux, who forwarded it to Eliot. Though the preface failed to please Eliot and thus was removed by Berryman, the book was published in April 1959.[13]

During the middle of a five-week course on modern literature in mid-August 1958, Berryman returned to his research on Shakespeare. He had mentioned to his mother two months before that he had been spending ten to fifteen hours a day on this research project. He also said that the contractual arrangements with the Thomas Crowell Company for a handbook entitled *The Arts of Reading*, which he was coediting with Ross and Tate, was "working out" and that he felt more confident from a financial point of view.[14] Berryman chose most of the material in part 2,

"Imaginative Writing," which included fiction, plays, and poems; he selected such authors as Stephen Crane, Eliot, Hemingway, Joyce, Kafka, Shakespeare, Dylan Thomas, and Yeats, and Tate contributed analyses of the poetry of Marvell, Donne, Carew, and Ransom. The aim of the book, as stated in its introduction, is clear and straightforward: "To be fluent in thinking, reading, and writing, one must be fluent in all."[15] Later, discouraged by his relationship with Crowell and their ungenerous advance of $500, he put the demanding work aside. When he went to New York that September, he met with his publishers at Crowell to explain why the text was not finished. A follow-up phone call by Tate to Crowell did not ease the situation, and the resulting flare-up led Berryman to a stay in Regent Hospital in Manhattan. Berryman soon returned to Minneapolis, preparing to teach and lining up his thoughts for an address at the university convocation in late September focusing on a highly personal topic: poetry as a counterforce to whatever threatens to dehumanize people.[16]

Things, however, began to change for the better. By October, Berryman was proud of the work he had done on his Shakespeare biography and was well into composing *A Shakespeare Handbook*.[17] He wrote a long letter to Professor Samuel Monk and Dean E. W. McDiarmid at Minnesota in order to acquaint them more in detail with his background and the courses he was qualified to teach, explaining in part the work he had done over the years on Shakespeare. He noted, in particular, that for the last eight years he had been working on a critical biography of Shakespeare. His research would well qualify him to teach in the English Department. "The manuscript of the biography is about 250 pages, or half done; it is under contract to Farrar, Straus & Cudahy."[18] In addition, his collection of twelve poems, entitled *His Thought Made Pockets & The Plane Buckt*, dedicated to Ann, was published in mid-December in a limited edition of just over 500 copies by Claude Fredericks, a former student of his at Harvard.[19] Impelled by these publications, he set a goal to work three or four hours a day on writing his Dream Songs, though he recognized that some of the earlier ones lacked the creative impact he sought and some of the newer ones might have been written too hastily. At Christmastime he resorted to an earlier pattern, venturing alone to Atlantic City, where he worked on the Crowell handbook (Tate wrote only twelve pages), completing the task the following February.

Berryman's health deteriorated even more at the beginning of 1959, especially when Ann, feeling utterly despondent over her marriage, moved out with Paul. In mid-February, Berryman was hospitalized again for three and a half weeks in a closed ward at Glenwood Hills Hospital on the outskirts of Minneapolis for chronic alcoholism, tremors, and psychological problems, making forays by taxi to teach his classes. In his own way, Berryman was like the troubled man in Lowell's 1959 poem "Skunk Hour" who admits "I myself am hell; / nobody's here."[20] In commenting on this poem, Berryman reflected that "the poet [like the skunk] can be made helpless by what is part of his strength; his strangeness, mental and emotional; the helplessness of a man afraid of going mad is the analogue."[21] When released from Glenwood Hills, he moved to an apartment at 1917 South Fourth Street in the rundown Seven Corners section, across the Mississippi River from the main campus. He knew this area well—some said it had a reputation like New York's Bowery in the 1940s—since he had lived there two years before. The mixed critique he received on March 15 from Lowell of the Bradstreet poem and the first batch of the Dream Songs lacked detailed observation—and thus did not give him at this particular moment in time the encouragement to develop his surprisingly new technique: "I wonder if you need so much twisting, obscurity, archaisms, strange word orders, &-signs for *and* etc? I guess you do. Surely, here and in the *Bradstreet*, you have your voice. It vibrates and makes the heart ache."[22]

Already under incredible pressure, Berryman's ever-tightening world collapsed when the final divorce settlement came through on April 28, 1959, with Ann receiving custody of Paul, who had felt all along the impact of his parents' bickering. Ann had also terminated a second pregnancy once she realized that their relationship was irreparable. Berryman's compulsive drinking and womanizing had allowed little stability in their family life. He had little choice but to continue doing what he could do, researching material for his book on Shakespeare and teaching, first a two-week summer course at the University of Utah and then a course on modern literature and another on the works of Henry James back in Minneapolis. That summer he visited a university colleague, poet James Wright, at Glenwood Hills, where Wright was undergoing electroshock treatments for severe depression. Wright asked him, "Why are you coming to see me? I'm dead. Don't you understand, John?"[23] Because they had so much in common, particularly their illnesses, encyclopedic knowledge of poetry, and empathetic imagination, they remained good friends. Wright would later be refused tenure because of his alcoholism.

Tate voted against him in the tenure decision, considering him "damaged merchandise."

Berryman telephoned Lowell in late September 1959, despondent to the point of suicide as he thrashed about in his seedy apartment.[24] In a show of affection, Lowell wrote to Berryman on September 19, now praising effusively Berryman's accomplishments and how they had both

> gone through the same troubles, visiting the bottom of the world. I have wanted to stretch out a hand, and tell you that I have been there too, and how it all lightens and life swims back. And it's a sorrow to think of you alone, seeing your son and not being with him. I've thought of your dazzling brilliance, so astonishing to your friends. . . . Well what is there to say? The night is now passed, and I feel certain that your fire and loyalty, and all-outedness [will] carry you buoyantly on. The dark moment comes, it goes.[25]

Toward the end of the year, Berryman was again admitted to Glenwood Hills, feeling "nearly dead all the time."[26] He flew to New York to spend Christmas with his mother, longing for any support to prevent him from seeking refuge in alcohol, but collapsed when his mother decided to show him pictures of his father.

Berryman went to the University of California at Berkeley in February 1960, at the invitation of Anthony Ostroff, to spend four months teaching three courses as a visiting professor in the Department of Speech. He continued to feel alone and miserable, though he socialized on occasion with poets Thom Gunn, Carolyn Kizer, and others while giving a reading at Los Angeles State University. After his return to Minneapolis, where he taught two summer school courses while living alone in the Hotel Stone, his old rollercoaster habits returned. He summoned up enough strength, however, to continue his regular teaching duties.

Given the lack of communication from Berryman, Giroux continued his work with other authors whose writing needed close attention. To keep his equilibrium and relax after editing sixty-two books from the winter of 1959 through the spring of 1960, he and Charles Reilly headed to Europe for a six-week vacation in mid-July 1960, Giroux's first time abroad in five years. They dined with the Eliots at their Kensington Court Gardens home on July 16 before continuing on to the continent.[27] Giroux waited for Berryman to contact him, knowing that it would be untoward to bother the poet, especially since Berryman apparently did not have a finished manuscript in hand. The silence after May 20, 1957, when Giroux sent Berryman a telegram about the Harriet Monroe Prize, was most troubling for both parties, though neither one felt it necessary to reach out to the other.

As Berryman finished his teaching responsibilities in Minnesota in late spring 1961, Americans across the nation seemed to be basking in the early Camelot glow of the Kennedy administration. Berryman taught a six-week summer course, along with Robert Fitzgerald and Leslie Fiedler, at Indiana University's School of Letters in Bloomington. His life had changed, however, after meeting the previous spring twenty-one-year-old Kathleen "Kate" Donahue, who was half his age, Catholic, and the friend of another woman he had been seeing. By May 1961, he became a recluse in yet another apartment, this one at 415 Erie Street S.E., just south of the university. Trembling from the effects of alcohol, John married Kate in a civil ceremony on September 1, witnessed by Ralph and Alicia Ross and two other friends. Penniless but restored by the prospects of what this new married life might bring, he wrote fifty Dream Songs in a short time after his marriage. Naïvely, he thought that he might avoid paying $600 for child support to Ann, now a high school teacher, though before Christmas he sent Ann's lawyer part of the money he owed her. He was counting on a number of possible sources of extra income, in particular the hundred dollars that Meridian would pay him for a new preface to a paperback edition of his Crane biography. That fall, the university refused him permission to take time off to work on what he now called *Shakespeare's Friend*.

Berryman planned on sending, by mid-November, seventy-five Dream Songs to *both* Farrar, Straus & Cudahy and Faber & Faber, testing the waters to see if either would accept them as a single volume.[28] It would *not* have been a propitious moment, however, for Berryman to contact Giroux, who was preoccupied with planning for the return visit of T. S. Eliot, and his wife, Valerie, toward the end of November. Though Eliot had a full schedule, he wanted to spend Christmas 1961 with his sister in Cambridge, plus have readings at Boston College, Harvard, Yale, the Poetry Center at the 92nd Street Y, and Columbia.[29] After Christmas, Giroux spent time with them in Ocho Rios, Jamaica.[30] The Eliots then went briefly to San Juan and Saint Thomas, and then to Barbados, where Giroux and Reilly again joined them in late February 1962 at the Sandy

Lane Hotel. All four returned on the Grace Line *Santa Paula* to New York in early March, after which the Eliots returned to England. Giroux spent more time with Eliot than with any other of his authors, including Bishop, Horgan, Lowell, Malamud, Merton, O'Connor, Singer (whom Giroux accompanied to Stockholm to receive the 1978 Nobel Prize for Literature), and Stafford. As Eliot's American editor, he never even thought about changing a single word or a punctuation mark in the galleys of Eliot's texts once they arrived from London.

Berryman informed his mother, then living in Alexandria, Virginia, and quite poor, that he had sent fourteen Dream Songs in early March 1962 to the *New Yorker*, which, after they were rejected, he then sent to Giroux's former Harcourt, Brace colleague Catharine Carver, now at *New World Writing*. In a letter Lowell wrote to Bishop on April 14, he mentioned he had visited Tate and his wife, Isabella Gardner, at their home and there "also saw John Berryman, utterly spooky, teaching brilliant classes, spending weekends in the sanitarium, drinking, seedy a little bald, often drunk, married to a girl of twenty-one from a Catholic parochial college, white, innocent beyond belief, just pregnant."[31] He mentioned, too, that Berryman was going into the seventh year of writing his Dream Songs—most of them packed into a suitcase—which were "spooky, a maddening work of genius, or half genius, in John's later obscure, tortured, wandering style, full of parentheses, slang no one ever spoke, jagged haunting lyrical moments etc." Lowell also wrote to Berryman that same day,

> Just a note to say that I think the Henry poem is terrific. I'm guessing that the whole holds up to the short sections I read the other day, and no doubt adds immense momentum to those high spots. I think everyone who liked Anne Bradstreet will like this, and maybe much more, for it is more lyrical and a much longer sweep. Speaking in the dark about the whole, my guess is that some moderate length of a hundred pages or so, ought to be immediately shuffled together and gotten off to the publishers. . . . Glad to meet your lovely Kate. Do take care of yourselves. I think you should feel your seven years of labors are over and that now all you need to do is arrange, breathe and stop battering yourself. No, don't batter yourself, life's too good for that.[32]

Even for Lowell, who had not seen Berryman in ten years but was familiar with his life and poetry, these narcissistically exuberant Dream Songs now revealed new dimensions in Berryman's poetry.[33]

In June, the Berrymans drove to the Bread Loaf School in Middlebury, with side trips to visit Berryman's brother in New York, then to South Kent School, and finally to see Mark Van Doren in Connecticut. At Bread Loaf, Berryman met eighty-eight-year-old Robert Frost, whom he admired even though he thought he had been slandered by a comment by Frost on his womanizing (see Dream Song 37). He also met William Meredith, now an associate professor of English at the University of Connecticut, who also taught in the graduate program at Bread Loaf.[34] Meredith and Berryman deepened their friendship during the weeks they lived together under the same roof. "The fact that he and I drank gin at noon," Meredith recalled, "which had to be elaborately overlooked and was, when that was possible, may have thrown us together at first. But the lucid fact of Kate Berryman, during that summer as during the whole last decade of his life, translated what was difficult about John into terms that less extraordinary people could understand."[35] Revitalized at Bread Loaf especially by some of the best students of creative literature in the country, Berryman also grew in appreciation of Meredith's common-sense evaluations and words of understanding.

After this heavy academic and social schedule eased, Berryman assembled an assortment of 130 completed Dream Songs plus more than one hundred in draft form. One of Berryman's former students commented on these poems, "You get the voice of Shakespeare jamming up against Winnie the Pooh, coming up against a news announcer, coming up against a stage negro dialect, and all these things smashing into each other. I admire that, but I don't think I'd ever try to do it."[36] Would there be an audience for these seemingly simple incandescent fragments, which demanded the utmost attention on the part of the reader? Years afterward, Berryman articulated his poetic intentions in writing both *Homage to Mistress Bradstreet* and *77 Dream Songs* in his March 1969 acceptance speech for the National Book Award in Poetry. In a succinct and forthright manner—since he was never one to write long theoretical discourses on his own poetry—he thanked his wife and especially Saul Bellow and Robert Giroux, "who sustained and even endured me during the 13-year labour." His self-proclaimed "hostile" literary manifesto explained the novelty of his poetic efforts: "I set up the Bradstreet poems as an attack on The Waste Land: personality, and plot—no anthropology, no Tarot pack, no Wagner. I set up The Dream Songs as hostile to every visible tendency in both American and English poetry—in so far as the English have any poetry nowadays. The aim was the same in both poems: the reproduction or invention of the motions of a human personality, free and determined, in one case feminine, in the other masculine. Critics are divided as to the degree of my success in both cases. Long may they rave!"[37] To interpret these poems, readers need, he proclaimed, "gall, the outrageous, the intolerable—and they need it again and again." Ignominious failure haunted the greatest poets, such as Whitman, Eliot, and Pound, who served, he believed, not as models, but as antimodels. If anything, Berryman wanted to be included in this highly selective group.

Now promoted to full professor, Berryman accepted a post as writer in residence for the 1962–1963 academic year at Brown University in Providence, Rhode Island, where he and his wife moved into a house at 24 Congdon Street. He willingly took over the classes of Edwin Honig, founder of the graduate program in creative writing, who had temporarily moved elsewhere to provide a better environment for his wife, Charlotte, who was seriously ill with cancer. Nevertheless, the pressing question still remained: could the breach between Berryman and Giroux be broken, especially as Berryman was now thinking seriously about publishing his Dream Songs? He wanted to reduce his selection to seventy-five poems and organize them into appropriate categories. He proceeded cautiously because so much was at stake, writing again to Carver as the fall term began to request her help in reestablishing a rapport between himself and Giroux. "Three weeks ago, when we moved over here after a wild six weeks of two lectures a day and so much social life that I counted nine parties in one week, the thing was nothing but a seven-year mess filling a whole bag."[38] Carver replied that she had spoken to Giroux, who said that all Berryman had to do was to drop him a note.[39] (Bellow, who knew Carver well, oddly had a falling out with her over Berryman's alcoholism.)[40] After flying to Washington, DC, in late October to read at the National Poetry Festival at the Library of Congress, Berryman, now fortunate to be part of a group in Washington of some of the most distinguished poets and critics in the United States, including Frost, Jarrell, Lowell, Meredith, Schwartz, Tate, Wilbur, and Warren, gradually built up courage to contact Giroux. Later, after reading a number of his Dream Songs at Harvard in November (five of which were featured in *Poetry* that fall), Berryman grew more anxious, not only because their baby was due soon, but also because of his desire to have the Dream Songs published as a book. A day after he was released from McLean, a psychiatric hospital in Belmont, Massachusetts, Martha, named after Berryman's mother and grandmother, was born on December 2 at the Lying-In Hospital in Providence. A few days later, after drinking excessively, Berryman stepped out of a cab, which proceeded to back over his left foot, breaking his ankle.

January 1963, however, put Berryman back on familiar literary territory as he started teaching the short story, using the anthology *The House of Fiction* coedited by two old friends, Caroline Gordon and Allen Tate. Furthermore, when Amherst College in Massachusetts organized a memorial service for Frost on February 17, three weeks after his death in Boston in late January, Berryman had a chance to meet up with Eberhart, Meredith, Wilbur, Van Doren, and even Marshall Best of Viking. The question naturally arose in the minds of these influential men of letters as to who would replace Frost as America's preeminent poet. (It turned out to be Lowell, as evidenced by the fact that he filled Frost's place at the Academy of Arts and Letters.)[41] The decisive moment, nevertheless, had come; putting aside his pent-up feelings of discouragement, Berryman finally contacted Giroux.

After a total silence just short of four years, from April 1959, when Giroux had matter-of-factly telegrammed Berryman that he was sending him the British edition of *Homage to Mistress Bradstreet*, to February 1963, Berryman remained terribly annoyed that Farrar, Straus & Cudahy had remaindered *Homage to Mistress Bradstreet* without telling him. (He did not know that Roger Straus, *not* Giroux, was responsible for remaindering the book.) However, prompted by Carver's assistance, he attempted to reestablish old ties.[42] Berryman's long and straightforward letter of February 18, written from his residence at Congdon Street, is as chummy in parts as the first one that Giroux wrote him in October 1936.

I have a half-feeling that I've called you, or written before, but as I grow increasingly tired (I haven't taken a vacation from the poem for years—in June I damned well mean to) and keep on overworking (this month I did two sections the first weekend, three—on Frost [Dream Songs 37, 38, 39]—the next, and two more this last, besides running a full teaching schedule, writing reviews of both [Stephen]

Spender & Auden, and doing public jobs here & elsewhere) the actual world grows unreal to me and I can't remember or attend to it.

Let's make an end of the long estrangement. I have felt bad about it a thousand times. I wrote you a letter I should not have sent; but then you did not reply <u>at</u> <u>all</u>, and perhaps that was going too far, too. Moreover, soon after the letter, I think, while I was still burning with resentment and waiting to hear, I found you'd remaindered the Bradstreet [poem] (<u>without telling me</u>, this was the point), and the evil situation solidified. I am sorry. Of course I felt guilty too about the long-unfinished biography [of Shakespeare], harried about letting you down. That will yet be done.

Meanwhile let's wipe it out, both personally and professionally. Two more points, though. My gratefulness to you for bringing out the poem at all and so bringing the career of my work to a certainly new point has not ever diminished and it never will; still I feel puzzles and dissatisfactions about all that handling of it back there. And secondly, the lack of success I have had all my life in getting my books of verse published or attended to, in this country, has never and does not make it easy for me to believe in a continuing or serious publishing arrangement, in spite of more & more numerous signs of a likelihood that various influential people on both sides of the Atlantic take my stuff heavy. (Too heavy: the word "greatest" was aimed at me, and near me, both from Seattle and London last week; I ducked.)

So may we now together stand easy?

And how is your life proceeding, oldest (except for Halliday, whom I'm not sure you knew, he left & went to Ann Arbor, bk on Hemingway, now with Amer[ican] Heritage) friend?[43] I hear good things from Wm Meredith (whom Kate & I came to <u>love</u> in Vermont last summer), Cal, Catharine [Carver], others. I am re-re-married and have a daughter, Martha, who smiles at the air and sometimes us, and turns out to be the <u>twelfth</u> Martha in direct American line; we named her after Mother (who changed her name to Jill) and of course I knew Granny's name was Martha also, but Mother's dazzling information afterward was like hitting the jackpot. In all parts of the country, ancient acquaintance, loves, connections, come up after readings or lectures: but Paul Thomson!—no bishop, as Mark [Van Doren] (who did good at the Amherst jazz for Frost yesterday) and I predicted, but a mere teacher, like me.[44] Mark was reading Frost's stuff, after a choir and a bishop who tried to prove that F[rost] was like—man—a real Christian (scene a chapel) and the conning Pres[ident] of Amherst. He can't do, Mark, the singing some of Frost's poems need, but my god he read [Frost's poem] The Telephone wonderful. I walk around more than my broken ankle ever so far allow[s], or do now (in bed all day today). Cal [is] absent, also of course Conrad [Aiken]. In the men's room at the reception I pee next to Marshall Best and we chat gay, neither of us admitting or denying that either knows who the other is. I meet the excellent Wilbur's wife for the first time, love her, and she gives me fan-talk, going back as far as the Bradstr[eet] poem. Eberhart smiled like the love-baby he is. Thirty people explain how they love me.

A little of this is in the 2 songs in Partisan [Review], which 50 people have said or written to me about. (Snodgrass: 'Baby, you have dood it!'—only of course he had more to go on.) (Other adherents of the new poem: Fitzgerald, Ogden Nash!, Mark, many young people, Wilson.) PR [*Partisan Review*] were so imposs[ible] as not to send me copies, so I haven't seen [it]. I sent them a bitter card today. So I don't know whether they put on to the PRISONER OF SHARK ISLAND? with PAUL MUNI the dedication to you which I sent them many months ago. Anyway it is so dedicated, unless you object. It is a good one. Also I sent them various corrections in the two, with what result I don't yet know.

About 45 of The Dream Songs have appeared or are scheduled to do. Ramparts, a lay Catholic magazine on the Coast, gave their first prize to 15 of them; $700; private—only to be announced in May. They bombed the National Poetry Festival in Wash[ington] in October, and I recorded a dozen or so for the BBC later. [Alfred] Alvarez writes me that he's doing comments on two of them for The [London] Observer. There is more to go on, I think, than with the Bradstreet poem.

Now I am within a week or so—with luck, and if I don't break down, and if I quit writing new ones—of sending you & Monteith of Faber about 75 as a dry-run, which Cal advised, almost a year ago. I would want to hear quick: offer, and date of publication. Offer, from FSC [Farrar, Straus & Cudahy], independent of the Shakespeare account—which stands now at around $1,000, I think—an entirely inadequate advance for that book, as it goes on, but that's another matter. There is also <u>Shakespeare['s] Friend</u>, and <u>The Freedom of the Poet</u>, a book of essays Meridian are interested in, and many other things. Offers considered. Don't forget that I have never received one penny from either FSC or Faber for the Bradstreet poem, which took me five years to write.[45] Princeton yes ($200), L.C. [Library of Congress] (500), Loyola (300), Harvard (250) etc etc; but not from my publishers <u>anything</u>.

He enclosed some of his poems that he had written while in Vermont. If Giroux were to consider publishing the seventy-five Dream Songs—and perhaps more—then Berryman might even surpass his peers, including Lowell.

Since Giroux was about to take a vacation in Key West, Florida, on doctor's orders, after having a prolonged bout of the flu, he wanted to make sure Berryman knew what he thought about their relationship: "I don't want to leave without writing to tell you that we may indeed now together stand easy. I have never had any but the most affectionate feelings, arising from our most ancient and longstanding friendship, from the days of your white tie and tails, my hound-and-horns, and our common Mark."[46] He added that this was not the letter he wanted to write because that would take too long. But he would do it at a later date, when he had more energy to deal with the situation, and to show Berryman, from the record, how wrong he was about certain publishing facts. "Maybe they are just misunderstandings, but they need straightening out and that takes a great deal of time, especially when your heart is not wholly in it. I was deeply moved by your letter. Let us consider the long estrangement ended, though it never began for me. We want to be your publisher, we want to see 75 of <u>The Dream Songs</u>, we would like to make an offer." He thanked Berryman for dedicating the Shark Island poem to him. Furthermore, he liked Henry's postmortem religious poem, as well as the mention of Frost in the second of his three poems in the first issue of *New York Review of Books* (February 1, 1963). His offer to publish the Dream Songs was simple and direct, with no personal bravado about the other authors whose works he had edited in the interim.[47] As a sign of renewed friendship and seeking to achieve some normality, Giroux sent Berryman four books: Xavier Rynne's *Letters from Vatican City*; Gerald Brenan's autobiography *A Life of One's Own*; Dom Denys

Rutledge's *In Search of a Yogi*; and, "for laughs," Laura Huxley's *You Are Not the Target*.[48]

Berryman's reply clearly showed that he was overwhelmed by his contact with Giroux:

Oh this is luxurious: <u>thanks</u>, and I hope yr holiday went good. I am this minute, this evening, starting a desperately urgent one myself. I wound up my duties at Brown [University] last night, or rather today at 10 having been up all night w papers & 20 letters & reports. Slept like a dead [man] all day—and woke w[ith] nothing to read! Came downstairs, & and found these. One of my favourite characters [Gerald] Brenan vouched for too by the author of <u>The Spanish Temper</u>, one of my favourite countries India & fav. subjects [is] Hatha-Yoga (I too began in Poona & was later at Benares, tho' my yogic instr'r [instructor] was in Calcutta—fr.[formerly?] a banker), and a serious book [*Letters from Vatican City*] on the [Second Vatican] Council.[49] My God, I did really not know where to start, and my waves of gratitude must be reaching you in N.Y. But somehow I decided on, & am now in, Dom Denys [Rutledge's book]. Your copy of <u>Ramparts</u> [May 1963, containing fifteen prizewinning Dream Songs] wd have arrived days ago, if the 10 they promised me had come when expected; they ain't come YET. Grrr.[50]

He concluded by saying that Fitzgerald had recently arrived from Italy to be Martha's godfather on May 19 in a Catholic church in Providence.[51] Berryman liked *In Search of a Yogi* better after thirty pages than after two hundred, when he finally gave up, mainly because he found it chatty and unbelievably repetitious, and, unfortunately, the author was not really familiar with the sites he described.[52] On the other hand, he and his wife cried after reading Rynne's *Letters from Vatican City*, which Giroux had edited. Like others taken by Pope John XXIII's prophetic role in calling the Second Vatican Council, they praised this recently deceased pope. Giroux alerted Berryman to the issue of the *New Yorker* (June 15, 1963) that had a "marvelous piece" by Rynne on contemporary Catholicism.

After the death of Charlotte Honig in April 1963, the Berrymans felt they needed to vacate the Honig house because Edwin wanted to return to his residence. Once classes were over, they moved on June 10 to an old gristmill near Chepatchet, northwest of Providence, where they stayed for most of the summer. After learning that he had received a sabbatical from the University of Minnesota for the following academic year, Berryman knew that he could work uninterrupted on his various writing projects, though his subsequent, terribly fragmented, undated letter from Chepachet to Giroux might suggest that he lacked the organizational skills to accomplish what he wanted to do. Giroux replied in early July that he would like to read Berryman's "autobiography," as Berryman termed it, "since I've already been looking over your shoulder nigh these many years."[53]

By midsummer 1963, Giroux wanted very much to publish Berryman's volume of seventy-five Dream Songs or however many Berryman submitted. The trouble was that Stone Wall Press had offered to publish an edition of half of this number, which would take the bloom off a final publication. Would Berryman forego their offer of $150 in exchange for a contract with an advance of $500? Giroux hoped Berryman would want to do this, since he was eager to go ahead with publication for the spring of 1964. Highly motivated by this offer, Berryman gave a detailed update about his Dream Songs, his autobiography, and the possibility of publishing *The Freedom of the Poet*, a collection of critical essays and reviews written between 1936 and 1967.

Many thanks for letter & offer. Forgive delay, Mother was here for ten days and it wasn't possible to get much thinking or work done or even letters—I am getting amazingly (for me) up with my correspondence: I sent off 20 letters the day before she arrived, and then the day after she left, none between. . . . Oxford [University Press] by the way did use the whole critical chapter (penultimate) of my [biography of Stephen] Crane, maybe with Wm [William] Sloane Assoc[iate's] permission but not with mine and Sloane (so-called) kept as usual very quiet. [See JB, "Crane's Art." JB's essay was published with the permission of William Sloane Associates.]

I cannot decide what to do about the Dream Songs. Whether to sign with you, and give you 75 or whatever, or as many as 130, or 100 or so, or not to publish any now, I cannot decide. Of course I have not offered any to anyone else. It will just take more work and thought. But I'm anxious to get to work on an elaborate essay called "The Care and Feeding of Long Poems," and I'm also anxious to get back to scholarship; I don't know. Money is a problem too. And I want to go on with the autobiography, while remote from everyone (only Meredith dropped in the other evening, with a pitcher or bottle rather of Martinis and Jarrell's ex-wife, to our delight: if you ever want a day or so in a remote & ancient gristmill with a private waterfall let me know—we cd come get you in Providence if you don't drive).

Well, the problems with regard to the [Dream] Songs are enormous. I wonder how I ever sleep, and often I don't. There is a good deal of pressure from friends and strangers to publish a large number; and yet . . . Mark and Randall have lately voted for them—tastes as different, both being excellent, as I can easily conceive: Wilson is said to like [them], Snodgrass does, heavy, Allen [Tate] says he does; but . . . Spender, and Alvarez, and many other editors do, evidently; still . . . I am pretty clear that I won't take up the Stone Wall Press offer. Let me think. Maybe the thing to do is stop exacerbating, pretend to satisfy myself on some sort of Ms. (not the Poem of course), send it you, and come to NY for a chat. I want to talk with you abt Shakespeare anyway. [marginal note: "both books"[54]]—I have to select some Songs to be put into Italian, and I've promised groups to Poetry & Kenyon [Review] (special numbers of both magazines); that's trouble enough for one week. Some 60 or 70 will then be in print, here or abroad, and there seem to be perhaps some 230–250 of them?? Easy life, eh.

Of the 5 younger poets singled out in that TLS review of D[onald] Hall's Penguin [*Contemporary American Poetry* (1963)] you quote, 3 were students of mine [Merwin, Justice, and Snodgrass] and one of the other two a sort of disciple. I didn't teach them anything but I don't feel useless.

We have beds and are asking you to stay over.

How wd you like a book of poems for children by me?

How wd you like a book of essays called The Freedom of the Poet which I discussed w Meridian ([editor Aaron] Asher) as of a regular book first by somebody else, then a pb [paperback] by them. Abt 5/8 done, it is.

As ever (& you never said how yr vacation was).[55]

Writing on personal stationery on August 23 from Chepachet, Berryman sent Giroux sixty Dream Songs, having decided that one hundred of them were too many; he did not count on gaining any fame from them but would not be surprised if some of them "proved more or less immortal." Two of them were missing (Dream Songs 28 and 52) because he had given them in a batch of nine to *Poetry* for their special number in October. He would copy them from the *Poetry* proofs and forward them to Giroux. Unlike *Homage to Mistress Bradstreet*, Giroux did not want to include any notes in the published volume, a wise decision because he sensed that the sheer quantity needed would prove to be an overwhelming distraction.

The same day, Giroux wrote indicating that he would like to visit Berryman, but that his mother was very ill and he wanted to stay with her through Labor Day. He repeated his offer to publish Berryman's book the following spring, hoping to resolve any publishing issues as soon as possible, since their sales conference was scheduled for early December; unless all the aspects—jacket, dummy, etc.—were settled long before then, it would be impossible to do a first-rate publishing job. Giroux's main worry was that Berryman would be going back to Minnesota for the new term and thus get caught up with teaching. He hoped that Berryman would remain on the East Coast so that they could work together. No doubt sensing the benefits of proximity to his editor, Berryman wasted no time in spelling out in more detail his thoughts about the Dream Songs:

I am sorry for yr mother's illness—hope [all] come[s] out [well]. It seems to be a little monsterism we face at this time, old friend. My mother was regarded as dying of cancer for some recent years, in Fla. [Florida] & NY & a clinic outside Wash[ington] DC; now she's better. Was given up repeatedly. Not simple.

Our letters crossed.

SOCIAL: Come, in mid-Sept or later. I cannot form an idea of distinctness abt abroad or here till I hear from the Farfield people.[56] Half-salary will hardly do us: I am on sabbatical fr Minnesota, on half-salary.

PROFESSIONAL: It's very possible that my songs are no good; but damned unlikely. I am thinking of pushing the 60 I sent you up to 72. If I do, I'll do [it] quick. Besides you are off in Jersey. I NEED TO KNOW—: WHAT YOU THINK OF [THEM?]

The old blurb I would like to say as little as poss[ible] Abt This Poem, exc[ept] perh[aps] of its reception (in parts) by some of the most disting'd [distinguished] editors here & in England. On the Bradstr[eet] poem, TLS might be quoted—the remark you saw— and Fitzgerald's in The Roman Review ("He bided his time and made the poem of his generation"). Of me personally, nothing unless a photograph. My vague feeling is that photographs help sell books. Oh: some prizes are possible, as strictly public—the Harriet Monroe award 1957 [an award of $500 from the University of Chicago], a Brandeis [University] award 1960 (I think [actually in 1959]), Ramparts's first prize 1963—the first two were presumably, though to me, for the Bradstr[eet] poem, the last for 15 of these Songs, most of which are in the 60.

Finally, I need a legal opinion and a personal one. I suppose the firm has counsel better than my lawyer in Minneapolis: will you ask him whether the Robb business in "The Lay of Ike" [poem 23 in 77 Dream Songs, a satire directed at General Dwight D. Eisenhower] is actionable?[57] I read it, to a demonstration that may fairly be called riotous, at the Libr[ary] of Congress last Oct [marginal note: "also for BBC"], but I censored out that line or so; next month, at Harvard I [may] get carried away and read it all, with similar effect. But I have not printed it, because I figure Eisenhower has more powerful lawyers than I do, and I don't want to get screwed. The personal opinion is about "Baby Teddy": this too is very effective in reading—and it was in Ramparts—but tell me, is it any good? I enclose both these.

I hope you have an unmiserable week. I never met your family but my helpless good wishes to your mother.[58]

Thus, Berryman signaled to Giroux that he wanted to go ahead with the publication of his Dream Songs, in spite of thinking, at times, that they were possibly not worthy of publication. In his own convolutedly cryptic way, however, Berryman provided additional details about the Dream Songs, putting an onerous burden on Giroux to keep track of the order of these poems. On September 4, while working on a new draft of Shakespeare's Friend, Berryman informed his mother that he had just sent Giroux seventy-two Dream Songs, which represented eight years of work, about one third of what he considered an overall manuscript.[59] Somewhat irritated by not having as quick a response from Giroux as he had imagined, Berryman had to wait until his editor could decipher and sort out his seemingly impossible demands.

With assurance and composure, Giroux wrote to Berryman toward the end of September that he thought the manuscript was "terrific" and would like to retain it all.[60] He mentioned that he was getting legal advice, though his wish was that the firm would be able to publish all seventy-two Dream Songs. He was having a contract drawn up, along with a check for the advance, and both should arrive within a week. Once Giroux had gone through the material with greater care, he asked for more clarifications:

> May I clear up a few confusions? They are all mechanical, let me hasten to add. The more I read the poems, the more they grow. I am deeply moved by "Prisoner of Shark Island" (very well, Paul Muni [Warner Baxter starred in the film]) in which I feel a special proprietary interest, and I am delighted with the dedication (and with the fact that fate lists it first in the acknowledgements). The book has unity and surprise and variety and shock and music and it's so completely yours. Complimenti, mon vieux ["My compliments, old man"].
>
> Now the "confusions." Though by count I have 75 poems, I'm not sure which is to be the final one. "Henry's Confession" is 74. You left out "The Taxi makes the vegetables fly" from earlier contents; it that 75? It's awfully good (India), but "Confessions" seems better for the ending. Also one poem, "Henry's Meditation in the Kremlin" (57) is not with the manuscript. Then the insertion of "The Lay of Ike" as 23 displaces "Henry, edged," so where does that go? If it is a substitute for "Kremlin" the manuscript stays at 75 poems (and should it be transposed to Part III?); otherwise 76. . . . I enclose what I think is the table of contents. Do you need the whole manuscript back? We're getting up some specimen type pages, and looking for that Merrill type for heads. I need the manuscript until that is settled, O.K.?
>
> Contract before end of week.[61]

Although Berryman subsequently apologized for any confusion he had caused, he continued to communicate in a most enigmatic fashion, putting even more burden on Giroux to decode his slipshod, fragmented sentences. Berryman's reference in the following letter to Giroux about living underwater for eight years (emphasis mine) eerily prefigures his own death:

These confusions are all my fault. I keep tinkering, and just yesterday I put the Japanese one ("The taxi") through major repairs, installing it quietly between 71 ["]Spellbound["] and 73 ["]Henry hates["]—which must not come together. There are now 76. I enclose all the new front matter: dedication, note, epigraphs, table of contents.

But YES I must have the whole Ms. back as soon as possible[.] My Ms is not quite complete and in some cases your copies are superior to mine, as in others my copies are superior. [marginal note in RG's script: "I lack 61."] You say you don't have ["]H[enry]'s Meditation["]—here it is. "H sats" is now 5. "H edged" is 25.

Thanks for good words—"complimenti" much appreciated, as have been excessively depressed. . . . I'm reading in Boston on the ninth and have a tentative date with the Academy of Amer[ican] Poets for a NY reading on Oct 17, when I wd hope to see you & Cal, and my brother [Robert] and my son [Paul].

I am thinking of surfacing soon, *after only eight years underwater*, but first I must get every single damned stupidity out of the manuscript. I will be extremely grateful for any suggestions you are willing to make. I enclose, for instance, the new "taxi," now titled. I have just had to rip up the Kenyon [Review] proofs of their first one (57 here) so extensively that they are going to have to set it up afresh or kill it.

My next book is Shakespeare's Friend and I am desperately anxious to get it done and out as fast as possible. Can we switch the Sh[akespeare] contract for it, and put some more money in, and rush out the book for the 400th anniversary year? I have an idea it may sell. I also think of giving a version of it, when done, to Russell Lynes for Harpers. I have this year off, sabbatical (the first I ever had), but half-pay and am poor, poor. I can't wait to see how the unhappy bastards who are going to have to review 76 Dream Songs approach their task.[62]

Giroux enclosed the contract for *Dream Songs* in a letter he wrote Berryman on October 1, thanking him for the new front matter and corrected table of contents, which meant, in effect, that there would be seventy-six Dream Songs. He found the revisions of "The Taxi" a revelation: "I simply failed to dig it in the earlier version." Under separate cover, he sent Berryman the completed, retyped manuscript. Since Giroux wanted to get started with the sample type pages, he needed to have Berryman's reactions about the jacket design and general format.

Six days later, Berryman, clearly irritated by certain sections of the contract and by Giroux's silence about his proposed *Shakespeare's Friend*, replied in his now characteristic, muddled manner,

Saul [Bellow] has accepted the joint-dedication as "a great honour." I'm glad you like the revision of "Karesansui."[63] An interesting letter fr Wilbur [who] thinks the [substitution of] Strut for Roethke "awfully good"—"I begin to be confident with your abruptly strange grammar and your shifts of diction, which allow the poem to turn on a dime from one tone or stance to another." From a writer as conservative & elegant as Wilbur this is a little tribute, and I like it because I pretend to be conservative & elegant myself. Of course none of this is for quotation to anybody.

I am thinking, with all my shattered intensity, of changing the title of this version to

THE LAY OF HENRY
76 Dream Songs

I have had many titles, but essentially just the one, for all these years, and it hurts to think of changing. I don't know. Thoughts appreciated. This would not, by the way, be possible if "The Lay of Ike" is out—I wd require it to subordinate the sexual implications, wh must be sternly put down.

Thanks for the Ms back. Are you coming perhaps to hear Cal & me at the Guggenheim Museum over the 31st (new date)? Hope to see you. May be able to stay over, if I meet various little deadlines. I haven't been in the city, except for a few hours at a time—it seems to me incredible—for years. I don't know even the physical layout any more, much less "who's in, who's out," though I long since took on myself "the mystery of things." Isn't Mary [McCarthy] being the No. 1 fiction bestseller strange beyond ejaculation?[64] I hate to think of Jean [Stafford] gnashing her well-kept teeth—being long fond, as you know, of both.

I have to read in Boston day after tomorrow, and don't feel like it. Beside they are paying me $50, grocery-money. Which brings me at last to the contract.

Bugs me. I realize these things are more or less standard[;] that's what I don't like about them. Page 4 in general bugs me[.] Page 4 in particular, tho' looking again at this satanic prose I see 1. (b) about the title of the work, whose change requires 'mutual consent'; now we can't have that. I can have anyone involved decisively in the title of my poem?? <u>Please</u>. I wd never hang you up at the last minute, and I am seeking advice—Saul's [Bellow] and yours—but this contract is dated Sept 25th—we can't have that. P. 4 (f) is so vague that I wdn't dream of signing it; (e) seems to interfere with 4 [Dream] Songs I agreed to let Feltrinelli translate over a year ago; in terms of (g) it wd appear that I wd instantly owe you, for a mere $500, mysterious parts of my performing/copyright fees for the Boston & NY readings, $200 in all,—now we can't have that; (h) is <u>out</u>, unless it can be explained to me. British rights must be explained. 20 must be explained—esp[ecially] since you have replied to me nothing about <u>Shakespeare's Friend</u>. Nothing is contingent here for me.

Enlighten me, old friend.

After the Berrymans drove to Boston University, where John, still in very poor health, read some of his Dream Songs, Giroux replied almost immediately, not only giving Berryman candid advice about the book's title, but clarifying the nature of the contract.

Please don't change from 76 DREAM SONGS! It hurts me too to think of your changing, and THE LAY OF HENRY is too Walter Scottish and double-meaning for a whole book. It is perfect for Ike. It's just not good enough for the volume, too easily misinterpreted as a come-on, and just plain wrong. You mustn't do it to the book.

About the contract, clause 1(b) is intended to protect the <u>author</u>. Mutual consent means publisher cannot change unless author agrees. If author wants no change, he says no and that's that. Isn't that fair? You seem not to want the publisher even to think about a different title. For most books, fiction especially, titles can be important. Did you know Fitzgerald wanted to call THE GREAT GATSBY something like THE VEGETABLE, and Max Perkins dissuaded him? And Red [Sinclair] Lewis had it as SMITHERS or somesuch, not BABBITT, until Alfred Harcourt yapped. (I saw the letters myself.) If you mean it the other way, publisher can stop author from changing, we ain't agonna. If you really mean it to be THE LAY OF HENRY, that's it—but—don't do it![65]

Giroux further explained that he was willing to cover translation rights "with pesky foreign publishers," for which he would charge a fee of 20 percent. Furthermore, for a 10-percent fee, Giroux would handle U.S. first serial magazine rights, and the firm would be willing to have an option on Berryman's next book. "I hope to see you on the 31st at the reading," he concluded. "We can discuss <u>Shakespeare's Friend</u> when we meet. What do you think of A. L. Rowse, who has solved W. H. and everything else?"

Having brought up Rowse and explicitly admitted in his letter of July 3, 1963, that he had been looking over Berryman's shoulder since their time together at Columbia College, Giroux most likely started formulating plans at this time to enter a rarefied academic area that was, given all the pressures of his work as an editor, beyond his competence. Undoubtedly, he read as much as he could about current Shakespearean scholarship, but would he have the time to master such a difficult field, especially concerning one topic that preoccupied him: the identity of W. H., to whom Shakespeare's sonnets were dedicated? The biographical and historical evidence, including dates of composition of the sonnets and various puzzling textual questions, particularly as found in two of Shakespeare's letters and in Sonnet 26, as Giroux notes, led him to believe that W. H. should be identified as Henry Wriothesley, the third Earl of Southampton.

If anything, Berryman's renewed interest in Shakespeare brought Giroux back to their time together at Columbia. The first line of Giroux's preface to *Berryman's Shakespeare* states, "It started in the thirties, when John Berryman and I studied Shakespeare with poet Mark Van Doren at Columbia College."[66] Van Doren, in the introduction to his book on Shakespeare, which reflects the material presented in his classes, prefaces his remarks about the sonnets and plays by saying—incredibly for an academic of his stature and time—that in this book he has ignored the biography of Shakespeare, Renaissance history, the conventions of the theater during Shakespeare's day, and the plays and poems of Shakespeare's contemporaries. His sole methodological aim is explain how Shakespeare loved and understood the world so well that "he could make it over again into something so rich and clear."[67] Van Doren clearly states that he has not been preoccupied with the question of whether Shakespeare wrote the sonnets to one or more persons whom he loved: "Criticism in fact does not care greatly about these persons, because it is not to them or about them that the poetry of the sequence was composed."[68] In fact, he is more concerned about what interested Shakespeare, that is, what was lodged in the deep recesses of his creative imagination as he wrote sonnet after sonnet and what the better sonnets were saying to the reader. Sidestepping the question of the identity of W. H., Van Doren posits that "the recipient of [Shakespeare's] unworthy word" is "in fact his own poetry." In short, he continues, the sonnets are not, in the final analysis, love poems: "Their subject is the greatest possible subject, existence: beautiful or ugly, near or remote, celestial or domestic, and sometimes so awesome that its force can no more than be hinted at." Throughout his book, Van Doren's rhetorically eloquent voice can be heard as he shares his views about the sonnets; at the same time, he leaves much unsaid, thus opening a very wide door that Giroux walked through, taking careful, well-planned steps, precisely at the time he renewed his friendship with Berryman, most likely allowing his suppressed envy of him to rise consciously or unconsciously to the fore. Though Giroux, who still felt hurt by not having been given complete information about the Kellett Fellowship to Clare College, could not compete with Berryman as a poet, he might be able to outshine him in writing a book on Shakespeare.

Giroux's *The Book Known as Q: A Consideration of Shakespeare's Sonnets*, eventually published in 1982 and dedicated both to Berryman and Van Doren, shows that he accomplished his task in book form, something that Berryman failed to achieve. Giroux maintains that the collection of sonnets known as Q—a reference to its publication in quarto form by Thomas Thorpe in 1609—was published without Shakespeare's apparent consent because it was so poorly proofread.[69] In the undated essay, entitled "The *Sonnets*," Berryman gives his own general overview of Shakespeare's sonnets, Thorpe's publishing history, the date of publication of the sonnets, and possible interpretations of the wording of the dedication without elaborating in detail any of these topics, though elsewhere he probes certain dimensions of the sonnets. Giroux, on the other hand, kept a tight focus on the sonnets. In addition to Berryman's *Freedom of the Poet*, which Giroux would publish in 1976 after Berryman's death, Giroux read important works on Shakespeare's sonnets, as mentioned in the sources and notes to his book.[70] His thesis, which he supports with appropriate evidence available to him, is that Shakespeare (the *facts* of whose life, Giroux states, were little known) wrote approximately 150 sonnets over a period of three years, from 1592 to 1595. The first 126 are written to the young man, followed by those to the raven-haired mistress, plus two concluding "Bath" sonnets—each of which Giroux discusses in order as he deals with the dates of composition. In brief, Shakespeare was asked or hired to write a series of poems to persuade a young man of high station to become married. Giroux summarily dismisses the underpinnings of Van Doren's argument: "To eschew the biographical approach in favor of the antibiographical, in the hope of obtaining a purer or more accurate literary understanding of the sonnets, is an illusion."[71] Giroux's position is also in direct contrast to the views of noted critic Stephen Booth, who believed that the sonnets were solely literary efforts, devoid of biographical considerations. Thus, Giroux reacts favorably to Berryman's explanation of the antibiographical fallacy as found in *The Freedom of the Poet*: "One thing critics not themselves writers of poetry occasionally forget," Berryman wrote, "is that poetry is composed by actual human beings, and tracts [*sic*] of it are very closely about them. When Shakespeare wrote, 'Two loves I have,' reader, he was *not kidding*."[72]

Though Berryman does not deal with the complex problem of homosexuality in these sonnets, Giroux, as have countless other Shakespearean scholars, does. (Could this have been because of his relationship with Reilly?) He cites Sonnet 20 as the most explicitly homosexual of them all, adding that Sonnet 121 is Shakespeare's reproach for being homosexual, though, at age eighteen, Shakespeare married Anne Hathaway and subsequently became the father of three children. Giroux believes that suspicions of homosexuality hovered around Southampton, especially in his younger years.[73] Unfortunately, he does not establish with any precision the times when Southampton and Shakespeare were together; it might have been when John Florio, perhaps a colleague of Shakespeare, was in Southampton's service as an Italian language tutor. Giroux attempts to establish, however, that Thorpe knew Florio in late 1608 or early 1609, relying on the assumption—and it can only be called that—that the "Phaeton" sonnet in Florio's 1591 book *Second Fruits* was written by Shakespeare, thus linking Southampton to Shakespeare through Florio.[74] In addition, Florio's essay "Discourses upon Music and Love" in his 1578 *First Fruits*, in which he speaks of "labour lost to speak of love," is perhaps a reference to Shakespeare's *Love's Labour's Lost*, most likely first performed by the Chamberlain's Men at Christmas 1597 before Queen Elizabeth in her palace at Whitehall and then later in Southampton's manor during an entertainment for Queen Anne in January 1605.[75] But the manner of Giroux's argument is speculative at best.

In trying to answer the question of what kind of love is manifested in these poems, Giroux posits that Shakespeare went through a gradual process of self-discovery and eventually "experienced real love," even though the young man did not respond to the poet's advances.[76] After Shakespeare meets this youth, he is dazzled by his beauty, and having written seventeen poems that do not succeed in encouraging the youth to marry, he admits that he has fallen in love with him. Eventually dropping the marriage theme, Shakespeare promises to give the young man immortality through the sonnets he has written. In short, Shakespeare is not analyzing a complicated love relationship, just expressing it; his intention has not been to publish these poems, even though some of the sonnets were known to an inner circle of friends. Later, the young man, whose life Giroux carefully tracks, is charged with treason and given a death sentence on February 19, 1601, along with Robert Devereux, the Earl of Essex (who was beheaded six days later). After the youth's sentence was commuted to life imprisonment, he was released by King James I after the queen's death was announced on March 24, 1603. According to Giroux, Shakespeare may have been distressed by the publication of the sonnets because they seemed to have been received in almost total silence, perhaps even suppressed, though there is no direct evidence of this. They certainly were not reprinted during his lifetime.[77]

Berryman focuses less on the sonnets in order to explore the tremendous richness of certain Shakespearean plays. Yet, so expansive and comprehensive was his undertaking that he never could bring together in an orderly and readable fashion the totality of what he had studied and knew. He devoted months and months to carefully researching and writing about certain aspects of Shakespeare's life and works; as a student in England in February 1937, he had once remarked that it was silly "even to do anything but read Shakespeare—particularly when we have only one lifetime."[78] He added, almost unbelievably, that he seemed "to have been sort of untouched by Shakespeare," although he had thought of him often since he was twenty years old. As critic Peter Maber has written, "Shakespeare is behind some of Berryman's finest poetry. He is both a creative inspiration, and a direct influence, inextricably tied up with both Berryman's life and work."[79] No serious literary critic of Berryman would ever deny this. Since Berryman desired to publish a large, magisterial book on Shakespeare, Giroux opted to explore a limited topic, the identity of W. H., a topic that had once preoccupied Berryman.[80] Most likely in the fall of 1946, Berryman had told one of his students at Princeton, Frederick Buechner, that he was preparing to write a book that would deal with the identity of W. H. and the Dark Lady of the sonnets; in October 1952, he felt he had confirmed that W. H. was the actor William Haughton.[81]

Berryman wrote to Henry Allen Moe, the principal administrator of the John Simon Guggenheim Memorial Foundation, on January 23, 1953, sharing his views about the recipient of Shakespeare's affections in his sonnets: "I think it probable that the William Houghton, praised by John Weever in 1599 for his beauty, war-practice, and wit, is, like the other Houghtons praised by Weever, a Lancashire man, and is to be identified with the playwright William Haughton (the name being identical), whom I consider then, as connected with Shakespeare earlier in the Lancashire end and from 1597 in the London theatre, to be the best candidate ever proposed as the young man to whom most of Shakespeare's sonnets were addressed."[82] The question, explored in Berryman's essay "William Houghton," is rooted in a labyrinth of historical sources and conjectures, focusing on whether the two men, with variant spellings of their last names (Houghton / Haughton), were actually the same person.

In his essay "Shakespeare at Thirty," originally published in the *Hudson Review* (Summer 1953) and which, in all likelihood, Giroux had read, Berryman set the preliminary groundwork for identifying W. H., a topic that Van Doren undoubtedly would have raised, albeit minimally, in his classes as students studied the sonnets.[83] Giroux and Berryman dealt with the identity of this man for the very reason that Van Doren had opted not to pursue an in-depth discussion of him. Berryman begins by mentioning the dedication of *Venus and Adonis* to the "dazzling" Henry Wriothesley, the third Earl of Southampton, whom, at that point at least, Shakespeare seems not to have known very well. Shakespeare's second, longer poem, *The Rape of Lucrece*, is likewise dedicated to the same earl, though with a widely different tone.[84] While Berryman mentions briefly the fates of Devereux, who began his affair with Queen Elizabeth in 1587 when she was fifty-three years old, and Wriothesley, he passes over their intriguing military histories in Ireland, while Giroux details all of this. Berryman states in "Shakespeare at Thirty" that shortly after his thirtieth birthday in 1594, Shakespeare probably received a gift of one hundred

English pounds from Southampton to buy a share in the Chamberlain's Men acting company, something most likely that did not escape Giroux's purview.[85]

In his essay "William Houghton, William Haughton, *The Shrew*, and the *Sonnets*," Berryman explicitly treats the identity of W. H., but Giroux most likely did not see it before its publication in *Berryman's Shakespeare* in 1999. (Giroux would also not have seen the two letters of early 1953 written by Berryman to Moe, nor his 1953 letter to Professor Gerald Eades Bentley, all of which discuss Haughton / Houghton.)[86] Haffenden, in explaining the various threads of Berryman's argument, states that William Haughton and William Houghton were the same person. Thus Berryman considers this man "to be the best candidate ever proposed as the young man to whom most of Shakespeare's sonnets were addressed."[87] In his introduction to *Berryman's Shakespeare*, Haffenden provides the intricate historical background that leads to Berryman's con-clusion, indicating that the "slight difference in the spellings [of their names] presents little problem."[88] He maintains that William Haughton, whose works Shakespeare seems to have known, might also be considered a possible collaborator in writing *The Taming of the Shrew*, something Berryman believed up until nine months before he died. (These two men, Haffenden states, were "not, it is safe to say, the same person" as a third man, William Houghton, son of Thomas Haughton, of Lea in Lan-cashire.)[89] As he elaborated his argument, Berryman further worried, around mid-June 1955, that someone might catch on to his thesis about these two men. Frederick J. Pohl, for example, in an article published in December 1958, proposed that William Houghton, as summarized by Haffenden, was a "plausible candidate" for W. H.[90] Like a good detective, Berryman did not want someone else to receive the credit for his many years of careful sleuthing.

Though Berryman's interest in the sonnets, limited mostly to 94, 107 (about the "mortal moon"), 110, 111, 112, 123 (about the "pyramyds"), is pertinent to his discussion of the 1609 dedication to the "onlie begetter" of the sonnets, that is, W. H., he rejects both Wriothesley and William Herbert, Earl of Pembroke—the initials of the first are not W. H.— on the grounds that the dedication's date does not correspond to times when they were in proximity to one another.[91] Furthermore, when dis-cussing the relationship between Henry Willobie and Henry Willoughby (whom Berryman was not sure were the same man), Berryman concludes,

"Shakespeare's young friend of the sonnets was certainly named Will, and I see 'Will' in 'Willoughby,' and further, without evidence, we can hardly go [*sic*]."[92] By cavalierly dismissing Southampton in particular as the "onlie begetter" of the sonnets, Berryman opened the door for others to probe this issue more seriously, thus giving Giroux an opportunity to prove himself a better Shakespearean scholar than his friend.[93] The phrase "onlie begetter" can be interpreted in three ways: 1) as creator of the sonnets, 2) the procurer who obtained the sonnets, or 3) the inspirer of the sonnets, to whom they are addressed; Giroux preferred the latter interpretation.[94] The seed had been planted (the first paper Giroux wrote for Van Doren was on Shakespeare's sonnets), but would take years for Giroux to do the research and publish his findings.[95]

Giroux's argument is clear and orderly. He organized his book in a series of essays, each focused on one of six words beginning with the letter *p*: poems, patron, pedant, play, publishers, and poet, and concluded with a facsimile of the 1609 Q text. His ideas found concrete expression in two lectures: the first at Wesleyan University in Connecticut in 1978 and the second as the third Archibald Smith lecture, delivered in April 1981, at the Baylor School in Chattanooga, Tennessee.[96] It is worth noting that Giroux acknowledges in the preface to his own book that he is an amateur who has long studied Shakespeare: "After *forty years of intimacy with Shakespearean scholarship*, I can only regard with amusement those who profess the idea that one cannot interpret the sonnets as biography, and insist that they are 'pure' literature, whatever that is" (emphasis mine).[97] These words, alas, might be an exaggeration, given the time he spent in the U.S. Navy, but they do refer to the time just after he and Berryman had taken Van Doren's class together. What Giroux did not realize at this point was the width and depth of Berryman's research, as revealed in the posthumous *Berryman's Shakespeare*, which Giroux would edit. Yet, in that volume's perfunctory preface, Giroux never mentions his own book or his "forty years" delving into Shakespearean scholarship as a propaedeutic to determining the identity of W. H. Perhaps he was offended because Haffenden, who had edited the posthumous Berryman volume and written its erudite fifty-eight-page introduction, had entirely glossed over Giroux's book (with only two references to him, neither concerning the sonnets). Furthermore, Haffenden's biography of Berryman had been rejected by Giroux at Farrar, Straus & Giroux and also by Faber & Faber.[98] In Haffenden's notes to the text, however, there is a passing reference to Giroux's book.[99] Giroux wisely did not want to cause embarrassment for himself, since readers of his introduction to *Berryman's Shakespeare* might remember some of the negative critiques that overshadowed positive evaluations of his own book.[100]

In sum, both Giroux and Berryman discuss Shakespeare's sonnets, though Giroux approaches this topic in a more systematic way. Berryman, who had collected and read an enormous amount of material on Shakespeare, might have done better had he actually finished his projected book on Shakespeare. But that is sheer speculation. Giroux invested a good deal of time and energy into researching and writing his book, but in the end, he felt that his work had not been accepted the way he had hoped. It was one of the great disappointments of his life. Thus, the lives of Van Doren, Berryman, and Giroux intersected most significantly in the ways they dealt with these particular sonnets. Because their research and writings on the sonnets were not done simultaneously, especially Berryman's, none of the three commented directly on the views of the other two. One review of Berryman's Shakespeare volume noted,

> Yet no one seems likely to read *Berryman's Shakespeare* in order to inform themselves of the textual complexities of *King Lear*. This is a book about a great poet's struggle to fashion himself as a critic, and its strengths lie in the passion of the writer's engagement with his subject, the sharp intellect luxuriating in the beauties of the drama, and the sardonic humour. . . . There are points in the *Lear* commentary where you can smell Berryman's armpits, where his massive erudition becomes an end in itself, and the reek becomes almost unbearable when he insists that the complexities of bibliography are beyond the grasp of most readers. "The system of semi-research in modern education," he complains in his 'Textual Introduction' to *Lear*, "has produced so many pseudo-students, pseudo-critics, that it may be well to say that their assent or dissent in such matters as this is wholly without meaning." When Berryman reaches out to his readers, as in the lectures, he is a compelling and captivating writer. When he dismisses them, as here, he is a snob arguing from scanty evidence.[101]

It could be said that Giroux had the final say, since his book was published after Berryman's death, but in all fairness, Berryman's scholarship became public, for the most part, after Haffenden collected and edited what Berryman had previously written. Despite an unspoken rivalry over writing something definitive about Shakespeare, neither Giroux nor Berryman ever achieved the reputation he so desperately sought among a growing cadre of established Renaissance scholars.

Though Shakespeare seemed to be an ever-present preoccupation, Berryman needed the assurance that the anticipated publication of his Dream Songs had appeal and originality. When he wrote Meredith (who had previously nominated him, unsuccessfully, for a Ford Fellowship) in mid-October 1963, he said he had been ill and that his reading in Boston had gone all right, but he felt uncertain and "inventionless."[102] Before signing a contract that would irrevocably make his poems accessible to a large reading public, he asked Meredith to read the seventy-six Dream Songs and make an honest appraisal of them, which Meredith agreed to do. He again wrote to Meredith almost immediately, saying he was tired of waiting and could not make any plans since he was broke. "But my contract-difficulties w Giroux were solved day before yesterday."[103] Berryman also appreciated the clarity that Giroux brought to their relationship, noting that the number of the poems might be altered:

> A splendid letter, thanks, contract back signed & witnessed. I trust to your good honour for all the changes you agreed to: in my nothingly busyness I've mislaid your letter. Let's wish each other luck.
>
> Wow: do you believe Rowse's Southampton? I haven't seen the [New York] Times articles—you sound as if you had, or the book. Could I borrow? I thrash w excitement. I like Rowse—partly I suppose because fr his eminence he seems to like me. I never met him but he wrote me a fan letter and sent a book or so.
>
> Consent, consent, no change in title. I hated that new title, and Kate did—haven't heard fr Saul [Bellow]—I just tempted myself.
>
> Be lovely to see you on the 31st. My Boston reading was a honey, I believe, but I get not less tired but more and still have deadlines to make. I may go into Mass[achusetts] General [Hospital] for a bit. I'll take 76 DS [Dream Songs] with me and scrub them until clean. There are 2 brand new beauties, polished; alas.[104]

When Giroux sent Berryman a check for an advance, he said he was trying to locate an English copy of Rowse's recently published *Shakespeare*, which, once it arrived from London, he would be glad to share with Berryman.[105] Giroux wanted to have the design and sample pages of the new book of Dream Songs completed in time to show them to Berryman when they next met in New York. With the addition of two new poems, Giroux wondered if the title should be changed to *78 Dream Songs*. A week later, Berryman replied, "No! no: 76. There are hundreds, the new ones mean nothing."

At the end of October 1963, Berryman was pleased to join Lowell at the Guggenheim Museum for a poetry reading. In his brief introduction, Lowell noted that for several years Berryman "has been a kind of underground poet, the kind you hear digging, at work on a sequence that I can only describe as indescribable."[106] This unforgettable reading was the first public presentation and recording of Berryman's Dream Songs. Near the end of November, Giroux sent Berryman, care of the Chelsea Hotel, where he was staying with his wife and daughter, the design (typography and page dimensions) and layout by Guy Fleming for *76 Dream Songs*.[107] Berryman called Giroux and gave his final approval of the text. This conversation brought to a conclusion, or nearly so, a remarkable book of poetry that would not have been possible without Giroux's persistence and finesse.

The days following the assassination and funeral of President Kennedy took a toll on Berryman, as seen in his "Formal Elegy," a rare Berryman poem that deals explicitly with a critical moment in the public sphere. In this poem, Berryman again links death with water: "What in the end will be left of us is a stare, / underwater."[108] There was little for Berryman and his family to do but quietly wait and reflect in their room in the Chelsea. After spending six weeks in New York, all three Berrymans traveled to Washington, DC, to spend Christmas with John's mother, staying upstairs at her new apartment at 103 Second Street, N.E. One of Berryman's goals was to work on his Shakespeare book in the Folger Library, which he never seemed to do, though he did finish "The Elder Presences" (Dream Song 72), which would be included in the newly entitled *77 Dream Songs*.

On January 10, 1964, Giroux telegrammed Berryman, who by then had learned that the University of Minnesota had granted him a sabbatical for the full academic year, to say that he had mailed the manuscript to him. With the $4,000 award from the Ingram Merrill Foundation, established by the poet James Merrill, to work further on his Dream Songs and perhaps complete his biography of Shakespeare, Berryman was well placed to publish what he had planned.[109] He read his revised manuscript and returned it two days late because of an illness, though he considered it much improved, especially after having reworked thirty-nine of the poems.[110] "I'm low & battle-fatigued," he concluded. In late January, Giroux wrote to Berryman at the Washington address, letting him know that the manuscript had arrived; he was delighted with what Berryman had done to it, since it read better than ever, and added that he questioned the positioning of three of the Dream Songs. Giroux also wanted to know whether the dedication to Berryman's wife and Saul Bellow and the three epigraphs should be retained. Liking "The Elder Presences" very much, Giroux sent it to Alice Morris at *Harper's Bazaar*, since the *Saturday Evening Post* and *Show* had both declined its publication, perhaps because it dealt in a controversial way with segregation.[111]

Berryman reported in mid-February that he found the proofs very clean, though he had had approximately a dozen corrections to make.[112] Since he had corrected the *wrong* set of galleys, he returned both and indicated he wanted to see further page proofs as soon as possible, once Giroux had sorted out the corrections. In addition, he intended to submit some ideas for the jacket design and the table of contents page. "Rowse, bar his fan-letter to me," he added, "is a vulgar British self-lover." (Rowse would later write a highly negative review of Giroux's book on the sonnets.)[113] Giroux immediately informed Berryman in Washington that both sets of proofs had arrived and he was returning one of them.[114] All seemed in order, except for some queries and comments about the designer's layout. As was his wont, Giroux stayed with Berryman through the final stages of this book, though he reserved a good deal of time to meet with Eliot, whose *Knowledge and Experience in the Philosophy of F. H. Bradley* was listed in the current catalog along with Berryman's book. What Berryman would not have known was that Giroux had edited twenty-five other books for the spring 1964 catalog, including books (in translation) by Gabriel Marcel, Alberto Moravia, and Carlos Fuentes, plus *The Dark Dancer* by Frederic Prokosch; *Doings and Undoings: The Fifties and After in American Writing* by Norman Podhoretz; *The John F. Kennedys: A Family Album* by Mark Shaw; *Seed Money: The Guggenheim Story* by Milton Lomask; and *Selected Poems* by Derek Walcott.

When Berryman replied in late February from Washington, he dealt with Giroux's editorial concerns, adding that he had been having prepublication jitters and was not able to sleep normally, something clear in the style of his letter:

Many thanks for the proof-set back. I felt lonely. Besides I am doing a reading-swing in California shortly and needed them.

[Stephen] Spender took long ago for <u>Encounter</u>: 47, 25, 32. But has not printed them yet. 47 and 32 are heavily revised; could you send [to] him, at the Hotel Algonquin in New York, photo-copies of the final versions, <u>and</u> advise him in a note that he ought to print them at once if he wants [them] to be [published] before the book? He & I are very friendly, I saw him just a day or so ago, but not in circumstances that allowed business, and I've no facilities here for copying. I hope this is not an imposition, Bob. . . .

[Peter] Mayer at Avon [Books] has sent me an essay by someone named Cott at Columbia which suggests that I am the greatest poet of all time. I survived; but it was strange seeing all them passages quoted, and quoted wrong. I am now (meeting a deadline at the [New York] <u>Times</u>, the Voice of America, etc etc) writing an essay proposing Cott as the greatest poet of all time, if (I add, cautiously) he writes poetry. You wouldn't believe how people bug me. I can't sleep. Eighty times a day I withdraw from you the book, repaying the advance; eighty times I re-allow. They are going to kill us, you know. Jerks are waiting in the wings to destroy me. I don't know why we're doing it. I do feel no confidence that the stuff is any good. Cal seems to like some of it, Cal & Snodgrass & Wilson, and above all Saul; but it's so easy to be wrong.

Let the binding be utterly plain. Blue-black if poss[ible]. I'll be happy to send skin [*sic*] (see 16) if desired.[115]

Amazed gratitude for copies of the 2nd ptg [printing] of the Bradstreet. What is <u>this</u> in aid of (as the British say)?—esp[ecially] after yr remaindering of it, years past, which stood my hair on end and occasioned our rift.

The jacket is yours. Only I wd say (front flaps) one sentence about me, then <u>AB</u> [*American Bookman*], views of: Aiken, Alvarez, Fitzgerald, <u>TLS</u>, Wilson.[116]

He added a long, typically unrestrained postscript:

Can a corrected proof go as swiftly as poss[ible] to Ch[arles] Monteith at Faber? I don't want any review copies sent anywhere over there. With my compliments.

I am winding up a Voice of America broadcast on my ART which they are waiting for in Manila and 80 other countries.

Did you ever hear of such nonsense?

But they offered me 250 and conned [*sic*].

I am goint [*sic*] to Virginia & loaf.

Give me a boost, Marcel Proust! Last night I again gave up on the book so-called, and give up on the gave-up. . . . Whatever sentence you think up for me is up to you, but for God's sake put the firm's address on the jacket. Nobody knows where to reach me, exc[ept] thro the Intern'l [International] Who's Who (which we all read night & day), and that's troublesome as well as agreeable.

Fragment:
> The house-guest
> opened one eye and exposed one breast
> then.

Kate likes this—it comes from the conversation of a friend of ours here. I have abandoned the writing of verse forever. Revise it, yes. . . . Earlier & better version:

> The house-guest
> with one eye open and one breast out.

See why I'm giving up Poetry?

Aiken is on <u>AB</u> jacket, Wilson you prob[ably] have. TLS also, I forget Alvarez but presumably there was something to quote. Fitzgerald is from THE ROMAN REVIEW: "He bided his time and made the poem of his generation."

Bang.

Giroux subsequently sent Berryman, still in Washington, a courtesy set of proofs that he need not return because the book was already in the plating stage. He did have some additional small questions, which Berryman could answer by phone. To his credit, all of Berryman's emendations had been doubly checked by Giroux.

After four weeks in New York, the Eliots flew to Nassau for their winter vacation at the end of 1963. Giroux and Reilly joined them on

March 7.[117] While Giroux took a break from his daily grind, this was definitely not the case with Berryman. In mid-March, while on a reading tour in California, he was taken by ambulance to the Riverside Community Hospital, due east of Los Angeles, suffering from an ear infection, chronic exhaustion, and drinking excessively, as well as hallucinating.[118] After another short trip to Washington, DC, he flew back to Minneapolis. While again confined to Abbott Hospital, he wrote to Giroux that he was having chest problems and taking six drugs in all. In late March, Giroux shared with Berryman his delight about the *77 Dream Songs*, including the jacket and binding. "Book is lovely," Berryman replied. "I feel good abt it just now. Let's wish each other better luck. We'll need it. The Tates just sent me a tulip-pot. Allen is ill too. . . . Thanks. Yours as long as we last."[119] Berryman again wrote Giroux from the hospital, listing those who should receive gift copies of his book.[120] He knew the value of making influential writers and critics aware of his writings, even though he knew some of them only by reputation. After signing the Faber & Faber contract for *77 Dream Songs*, and having taken 150 milligrams of Thorazine, Berryman felt drowsy but somewhat better. "This is a long drag," he continued. He had tried to read the newspapers and two magazines, as well as ten pages of Günter Grass's *The Tin Drum* during his twelve days in the hospital. "But I've finished a new Song [Dream Song 93] (for Book V) which I hold to be a beauty—it begins with a court-martial at which is conferred on Henry 'the rare Order of Weak' and winds up with a lady hunched over her table-telephone, 'her white rear bare in the air'. . . . Tired now." He concluded, "I worked up several weeks ago a truly beautiful title for the next volume of the poem if we do one [eventually entitled *His Toy, His Dream, His Rest*]. I hear the [New York] Times announced the book, but [do] not [know] what they said." Writing poetry while under the influence of a strong antipsychotic medication might account for the high-voltage energy and the proliferation of shifting images that sometimes intersect at odd angles in Berryman's Dream Songs. In such a debilitated state, would Berryman be ready for reviews of his book—for better or for worse—written by professional poets and critics?

CHAPTER SIX

Working on *Another* Book of the Dream Songs

Although Berryman wanted very much to fly to New York for the book's official publication on April 27 (to be published in November by Faber & Faber), he could not bring himself to do it. Instead, he went on a two-day binge. From the hospital, he again wrote Giroux, apparently aware of the forthcoming Lowell review, "I am improving with the speed of the galaxy 4C . . . but I have a similar distance to traverse and probably won't make Monday."[1] He had hoped to have lunch with Giroux, Catharine Carver, whom he had previously inquired about, and Lowell—that is, if Lowell would be willing to "to break bread with a reviewee." Instead, he planned on attending a party in Minneapolis organized by six of his closest friends, which he looked forward to because he had "going-out privileges." He had written three new Dream Songs in the hospital—"General Fatigue," "Henry's Pencils," and "Henry of Donnybrook"—but did not send them to Giroux because he did not have the means for making copies. "Somebody observed recently," he added, "that the book is not at all like just a book of poems or a poem, much less part of a poem, but is like the lifework of a poet. Something in this." He expressed an interest in adding four blurbs that might be used, if, in fact, all the jackets had not already been printed:

> Quite simply, I am dazzled by these poems, and don't know what to say. . . . The wit, the resonance, the pity, the exuberance, the faultless, absolutely faultless ear.
> DUDLEY FITTS[2]

Extraordinary. . . . important. . . . new. . . . An authentic voice speaks; it is urgent and upsetting. It will be around for a while.

VIRGINIA KIRKUS³

I consider Dream Songs about the most moving and sensational poems since The Waste Land.

DAVID POSNER⁴

Baby, you have dood it!

W. D. SNODGRASS

In addition, he mentioned that Tate had visited him and "threatened" to write a long letter about the book. If Tate's or Lowell's comments were favorable, perhaps they could be used somewhere, he suggested, but he felt that the "quotes on the back of the jacket [might] look splendid. If only they were true." He added the names of two more possible reviewers: James Dickey and Ralph Ellison (and Giroux also sent one to poet James Merrill). "Friends are puzzled," Berryman concluded, "that there is no copy about me on the jacket, but when I tell them I askt that it be so, they track and like it." Four days later, Giroux expressed his delight in reading "General Fatigue," which he considered brilliant right down to the last line.⁵ "The quotes are all great," Giroux continued, adding that Elizabeth Hardwick had informed him that her husband, Lowell, had written a review ("excellent and detailed and long") for the forthcoming issue of the *New York Review of Books* (May 28, 1964). Once Giroux received an advance copy of this review, he would forward it to Minneapolis, along with a letter he had received from Conrad Aiken.

From the hospital, Berryman wrote on "D-Day plus one," most likely the day after the book's official publication, saying that he had come up with the title of his *next* volume:

> I'm delighted to hear from you, AT LAST, and to learn that Aiken does not feel that I have let him down and that you like General Fatigue. As in March I secured a death-grip on Book IV, so here I am hard into Bk V—seven done in hospital, five in the last six days, therefore I am on the heaviest drugging I have ever heard of: 400–800 mg of Thorazine a day plus phenobarb[ital] round the clock and other stuff. Of course I have more than a hundred finished [Dream]

Songs to compete for place also in V, and ditto in VI, for which I wrote a beauty yesterday. I enclose you the third, which please let me have directly back. Some people here think it a very high point in the whole work. I have conquered this machine to the extent of (usually now) one carbon. Next volume, then (have I told you this?—the drugs are destructive of memory):

His Toy, His Dream, His Rest: 84 Dream Songs

I can't wait. Or rather, I can wait. Though maybe in a year. Would you care to publish him [them]? My thanks to Mrs. [Dolly] Guinther for the firm's wire of best wishes.[6] Did you not receive the personal copy inscribed and sent to you, you don't mention it. Hurrah for [sending James] Merrill's address—his wrapt copy has been burning my pockets; it's his foundation's money I'm "living" on. For personal reasons I didn't suggest his or Tate's as professional copies, though I find you sent one of yours to Allen too. (He is coming in this afternoon, and I'll bet you nine first class lines that he has not indited no letter or will do [sic].) I keep exact count of all these copies, as I hope Mrs. Guinther does.

Berryman looked forward to receiving Lowell's review, though he could not imagine what he might have said. The "joke blurb-list" he had previously sent Giroux did not seem so funny once he had looked at it again, yet it might do for an ad in *Poetry*, provided permissions were attained from all parties involved. "My chief physician," Berryman continued, "tells me Jim Wright [who had tried to visit Berryman in the hospital but could not find him] has asked <u>Hudson</u> [<u>Review</u>] for the book (he won't get it, in my opinion—15 years ago they hired Yvor Winters to beat me up) in order to explain that it is 'unique' and I am 'unique.'" Berryman asked what critics had received review copies and was undoubtedly pleased when Giroux informed him that Meredith had ordered twenty copies for his seminar. "What a good book it is," Meredith wrote Giroux.[7] Two weeks later, Berryman wrote apologetically to Meredith, "I am still after a month in hospital at Mpls am too nervous to read."[8]

On May 1, Giroux sent Berryman, still in Abbott Hospital, an advance copy of Lowell's review. As Berryman tried to cope with his myriad problems, he felt angry and betrayed by Lowell's negative review, which was especially hurtful as it came from a friend of nearly twenty years. Lowell found the poems "puzzling, not quite intelligible—and beyond a doubt fun to read or hear. When they don't make you cry—these poems will make you laugh. And that is news. . . . As it stands, the main faults of this selection are the threat of mannerism, and worse—disintegration."[9] Lowell further believed that these particular Dream Songs were sloppy, "not quite intelligible," and indulgent, "with references to news items, world politics, travel, low life, and Negro music," though he could appreciate their cumulative power and worldly vigor, even if they could not be sung. "The voice of the man," he continued, "becomes one with the voice of the child here, as their combined rhythm sobs through remorse, wonder, and nightmare. It's as if two widely separated parts of a man's life had somehow fused." Furthermore, he wrote, at first "the brain aches and freezes at so much darkness, disorder, and oddness. After a while, the repeated situations and their racy jabber become more and more enjoyable, although even now I wouldn't trust myself to paraphrase accurately at least half the sections." Upon further reflection, Lowell modified his views, admitting that "the *77 Songs* may speak clearest, almost John's whole truth. I misjudged them, and was rattled by their mannerisms."[10] For Lowell's biographer, Paul Mariani, the "Dream Songs were nothing less than a new planet swimming into view in the near ether, and instinctively Lowell knew that they had caused a fundamental disturbance in the universe of American poetry."[11] Critic Norma Procopiow noted that, in retrospect, Lowell "identified with Berryman as a kind of victim-hero, whose *Dream Songs* had been something of a model for his own later volumes. . . . Lowell realized that domestic trivia, random conversations, private anecdotes could be contained in a text which gives the illusion of structure. But was suicide the price one had to pay in order to reproduce life's haphazard flow in writing?"[12]

Berryman's Dream Song 177, about essayist and poet Joseph Addison, could well serve as a disguised riposte to Lowell ("I would not war with Addison. I love him / and Addison so loves me back / me backsides, I may perish in his grins / & grip. I would he liked me less, less grim. / But he has helpt me, slack / & sick & hopeful"[13]). If Lowell found an extreme mannerism in these Dream Songs, balanced, however, by a fine sensibility and attention to language, what he wrote to Jarrell reflected his more personal thoughts about his review: "I've always felt he threw all he had into writing, and more and more as time went on, though his top, I think is Bradstreet. As I wrote, I tossed in all my larger more enthusiastic impressions, though he'll probably feel I've hemmed him in with barbs."[14] Lowell further nuanced his views in his letter to Meredith:

> My Berryman piece is perhaps of some value as a record of a man's struggle with the text, a climbing of the barriers. In this book, he really is a new poet, one whose humor and wildness make other new poets seem tame. I read him with uncertainty and distress and quite likely envy, which is a kind of tribute. I think it's only here and there that I read him with the all-out enjoying amazement that I feel for Bishop, Plath, Larkin and much of Roethke. A handful of songs now seem part of which we are proudest of.[15]

As before, John found the hospital stay was most upsetting, especially when answering long-distance calls from Kate, who had remained in Washington since December so that her mother-in-law could help her care for Martha.

Giroux soon had good news for his friend, reflecting, no doubt, his own research on Shakespeare's sonnets: "Would I care to publish the next volume of Dream Songs? Well, who else? We are the original and onlie begetter of these here Dream Songs even if our name ain't Thomas Thorpe."[16] Review copies of 77 Dream Songs had gone out *"everywhere,"* particularly to Tate, Fitts, Posner, Wright, and the *Kirkus Bulletin*, he told Berryman. Sales to date: 703 copies sold of the 3,000 in print. Giroux was "flabbergasted," as he wrote in the same letter, that Berryman had so much of the new volume ready and suggested, for strategic reasons, that they bring it out in a year. It would eventually be called *His Toy, His Dream, His Rest: 308 Dream Songs*, with more songs than either of them could then have imagined. In a letter to Giroux written on May 6, Berryman indicated that he hoped to return to Washington after being released from the hospital and then head to New York on May 19. He was grateful to Giroux for spotting Lowell's "incredible blunder." (In a subsequent issue of the *New York Review of Books*, Lowell wrote a letter to the editor in which he made a correction: "Mr. Bones is not 'one of the characters,' but the main character, Henry.")[17] In his letter, Berryman noted that Lowell had called "to say he'd changed that 'detail,' as he calls it—not knowing, that is, <u>who the poem is about</u>. The review is still a disaster but will mislead <u>less</u>. Remains to see if it will kill the book. I think not. In view of this, I may expand the 'Note' for a second printing if possible. If one gets imminent, do let me know." In a postscript, he added, "I thought of the next volume for next year, too. Certainly wouldn't be ready till late Fall if then." Berryman was so discouraged by Lowell's evaluation that he hardly could think of his new project. He included a most remarkable comment sent to him by Wright: "Almost blood-curdling, truly magnificent." Wright had once said of Berryman, "Berryman's greatness included of course his utter mastery of the craft of the language. But he also was demonstrating that poetry is not simply an ornament, that poetry has some deep-rooted relation to life itself, the way we go on living."[18]

After being released from the hospital on May 8, Berryman flew to the East Coast and stayed with his wife and daughter in Washington, where he wasted no time in contacting Giroux about his proposed trip to visit him. He was still preoccupied by Lowell's review:

> Still on strict hospital routine for several months, three drugs round the clock plus double night—sedation and Mycebrine-T [Myrcene], but out & back, and better. Unquestionably. Certainly NY for the 20th unless unforeseen setback.
>
> Book Week is a nice vicious one. Possibly the whole [Dream] Songs Cal quotes and this man quotes may offset a little, for some readers, the effect of their reviews. Kate points out that Cal's review is reasonable until he reaches the book; thereafter it degenerates into a series of charges of violent eccentricity and massive obscurity. A difference between the public and the private reception of my book begins to be perceptible. But both these notices were written too soon, it is hardly a book to be gulped, "like a whale ingesting a whole school of fish at once" as [Theodore] Morrison wrote me yesterday: "I like to make acquaintance with them and renew acquaintance one by one or a few at a time."[19]

As his family joined him on May 20 in New York, Berryman received the National Institute of Arts and Letters' Loines Award of $1,000 from Lowell, in the presence of James Baldwin, Truman Capote, Ralph Ellison, Bernard Malamud, William Meredith, Ben Shahn, John Updike, and, of course, Robert Giroux. Berryman's son, Paul, whom he had not seen in five years, also attended the ceremony. Given Berryman's feelings about what Lowell had written, he must have negotiated a minefield of conflicting feelings as he stepped forward to receive his prize. Berryman appeared professorial in his pressed suit and bow tie. It could well have been one of the most difficult, unscripted, unsettling, public moments of his life, but if he could summon up an innate sense of *politesse*, as he had expressed in some of his letters to Giroux, then he and Lowell might become even closer friends, especially since each was aware of how the other had suffered and, at the same time, continued writing remarkable poetry.

Once the ceremony was finished and the Berrymans had returned to Washington, Kate and young Martha drove to Minneapolis in a car purchased for the trip. After a week's vacation in Maine, Giroux sent Berryman, now residing in an apartment at 3209 Lyndale Avenue South in Minneapolis, a rave review in the Sunday *New York Times* by John Malcolm Brinnin, poet and biographer of Dylan Thomas.[20] However, a relapse was inevitable. By mid-August, Berryman was back in Abbott for another two-week period of observation and recuperation, though not without composing more poems for *His Toy, His Dream, His Rest*. This particular stay depleted him in a number of ways, and he decided not to teach his two summer school courses.

Once Giroux had become a partner in the fall of 1964, the firm underwent another change of name, from Farrar, Straus & Company to Farrar, Straus & Giroux. The most important title under this new imprint, as Giroux mentioned to me, was Lowell's *For the Union Dead*, listed in the fall 1964 catalog.[21]

By October the Berrymans had moved again, this time to a two-story house at 33 Arthur Avenue S.E. in the Prospect Park area. Berryman's physician friend A. Boyd Thomes mailed to Berryman approximately fifty boxes of books, largely Berryman's Shakespeare collection, that had been in storage for over ten years, thus giving him an impetus to continue with the Shakespeare project, despite the incredible amount of scholarly work he had already done on the Bard.[22] Berryman taught a regularly scheduled course beginning in the fall, even lending a hand by teaching classes for two friends and colleagues, Ralph Ross and Jim Wright. Though Berryman learned in January 1965 that he had been nominated to become a member of the National Institute of Arts and Letters, along with Howard Nemerov and eleven others, thus raising his literary stature, the deaths of T. S. Eliot (January 4) and Richard Blackmur (February 2) undoubtedly made him reflect on his own mortality. Likewise deeply disturbed by Eliot's death at age seventy-six, Giroux did not dwell on it as he tried to set a timetable for Berryman's next volume:

> I've just got back from London. The [funeral] services for the Old Possum [T. S. Eliot] at Westminster Abbey were marvelous, and everyone turned out. The most impressive presence was that of Ezra Pound, white-bearded and shrunken, and looking like the ghost of Lear. He arrived from Venice and presumably he had not been in London since 1922! He refused to meet the press or indeed anyone, and did not once open his mouth. When I greeted him, he bowed very formally. The silence, after all the years of over-talk, was crushing.
>
> We would like to get on with the collected edition of your poems, other than the Dream Songs, that we discussed on the phone some time back. Do you have a table of contents, and copies of the books from which setting can be done? I'd like to get it all in hand so that we can have some production estimates made, and draw up a contract. At this point I wonder whether FORMAL ELEGY AND OTHER POEMS is right for the title. Wouldn't it be better to call it Poems: 19xx-19xx, or something like that, making it quite clear that it is a collection of work over an extended period? Perhaps you will want to divide it by sub-heads, and "Formal Elegy" [in honor of President John F. Kennedy] could lead off the final section. At any rate, I would like to see the book ready for late 1965 or early 1966, and the sooner we can get started on the mechanics (which always take longer than one calculates), the better.[23]

In May 1965, Berryman learned that he had received a Pulitzer Prize for *77 Dream Songs*. The accompanying $9,500 Guggenheim Fellowship for the 1966–1967 academic year seemed to be the fulfilment of two goals desperately desired. Fitzgerald wrote to Giroux, "Ain't it grand about John's Pulitzer."[24] Unfortunately, the high point of Berryman's career coincided with a very low point in his life.

Giroux's correspondence with Berryman during his hospital stays, which encourages him to continue writing and gives him a realistic appraisal of when his next book could be published, reveals a deep reverence that he manifested for all his authors: he encouraged them to continue to be the best they could possibly be.[25] The letters and the attention from newspapers across the country, however, were too much for Berryman to absorb. From Abbott Hospital, where he was suffering from alcoholic withdrawal, he wrote Giroux in mid-July,

> You were right abt the Pulitzer and I was wrong: it doesn't matter a straw—I've had much larger & more important awards—but believe me people think it does. We had reporters & photographers in & out of the house like flies—there was a vast picture of Kate & me on the front page of the main paper—Time commissioned a story and I gave an interview & was photographed, then they rescheduled the story and have now obviously killed it, as too late (to the morgue for my next book—even Time must be getting uneasy that they have never reviewed any of my five American bks of verse, though they've twice lately had to refer to me in their columns). Publicity is a bore. The correspondence! the articles! the wires! the phone calls! all meaning nothing. Real fame must be intolerable. But one of the best shots of me ever taken is in a local magazine wh I'll send you when we get copies—the article is good too—I think we ought to use the photo as the whole back of the jacket of His Toy. . . . I drafted & revised the preface the other day; it's good; I have also written 7 beautiful new [Dream] Songs in hospital—I sent 3 to the Atlantic, whom I hate, this is their last chance. I hear of reviews of the 77 in Poetry and The Reporter but have not seen them: did they not send you copies?[26]

Giroux later wrote Berryman with good news about reprinting *77 Dream Songs* in light of the Pulitzer Prize:

> It is good to hear from you, and I must gently disagree with you about the Pulitzer Prize. It does matter a straw, in the material sense, because the sales of 77 DREAM SONGS shot up instantly, and we had to reprint! It is now in [its] third printing, and total sales are now 4,041 copies, which is a lot more than they were before the prize. I was delighted to notice that last week's sales were 129 copies, while [Lowell's] FOR THE UNION DEAD sold 128. There has been a little action with MISTRESS BRADSTREET too, no doubt due to the Pulitzer Prize.
>
> The enclosed ad will appear in the August 5th issue of the New York Review of Books. This is a very rough proof, of course. The ad

will appear on the inside front cover and I think that in its final form it will be a most handsome job. So you see, I ain't a-down-gradin' the Pulitzer Prize. At least, not in <u>this</u> case.[27]

Berryman apparently did not reply to this letter, though he summoned up the strength to teach during the summer. Exhausted from that experience, he was forced to return to Abbott for another two-week stay and then another soon after that. In late August 1965, Giroux and Reilly took a tour of Greece, and thus Giroux and Berryman did not communicate during that time.[28]

Though Berryman had reached international recognition, he was still in poor health and thus asked to teach only one course during the fall term. He read some of his poems in mid-November at the Plutzik Reading Series at the University of Rochester in upstate New York, and after that at Bennington College. Giroux apologized to Berryman for not being able to attend the December 6 reading at Columbia University due to an in-house, all-day semiannual sales conference.[29] Most likely, given his instability, Berryman did not accept Giroux's invitation to attend the opera *Arabella* two days later.

Committed to teach at Minnesota for the 1965–1966 academic year, Berryman started the new year in 1966 impaired by a broken left arm and the unsteadiness that he experienced after another ten-day stay in the hospital. One could well wonder if Giroux was pushing Berryman to publish too much too often, all the while sensing that it was to Berryman's advantage to continue writing—and publishing—even under great duress. Whatever Giroux was thinking, he decided not to impede Berryman's productivity in any way. He was quite aware, as he told me, that Merton wrote and published too much. At the same time, he would leave it to future generations to determine what was of value in Merton's writings, something that could not be determined until one had seen the entirety of his spiritual and literary corpus. Would the same be true for Berryman? It did not take long for Giroux to show his hand.

Giroux thanked Berryman on January 6 for sending two new Dream Songs—two of his best, he thought—bringing the total to 161. He indicated that it was not too early to think about "another volume" for the fall; fortunately, this occurred as the university freed Berryman up during the winter term to work on his Dream Songs. "I think it would be a great advantage to follow 77 DREAM SONGS with DREAM SONGS 78 to 100 or so, if there's *to be just one more group*, 84 DREAM SONGS or

LAST DREAM SONGS, or whatever, during the latter part of this year [emphasis mine]. Is this conceivable and desirable from your point of view? Please let me know what you wish to do."

Berryman read at Harvard in late February and then at Yale for the memorial service for Randall Jarrell, whom he had known since 1946.[30] To fortify himself for reading in front of this distinguished group, which included Lowell and Meredith as well as Richard Eberhart, John Hollander, Stanley Kunitz, Adrienne Rich, Peter Taylor, Robert Penn Warren, and Richard Wilbur, Berryman, looking extremely tired and aged, and filled with visible angst, predictably had too much to drink. Yet, his booming voice astonished his auditors as they listened to some of his new Dream Songs. As Berryman recuperated again in Abbott Hospital, Lowell wrote to him on March 8 to express his great fraternal concern and overwhelming affection: "This is really just to say that I love you, and wonder at you, and want you to take care. . . . You must be physically fragile. If anything happened to you, I'd feel the heart of the scene had gone."[31] Whatever had happened in the aftermath of the Loines Award program, especially in light of Lowell's own psychological struggles, seems not to have mattered now. Lowell—often sad, remorseful, turbulent, and bewildered—had stayed at the Institute of Living in Hartford, Connecticut, as a patient for the second time from December 1963 until mid-January 1964. His bouts of mania and depression remained constant. In early December 1965, he was admitted for the third time to McLean Hospital, as he seemed incapable of extricating himself from the tangled web that had enveloped him.

In the months before the publication of the next volume of Dream Songs, Berryman instinctively knew, perhaps after evaluating Lowell's debilitating psychic journey, that he needed to write at the highest and most imaginative level possible. He wrote Van Doren on July 4, saying that after weeks of "dazzling work I have the ms. of the second (final) volume of my poems ready to take abroad, for a year in Dublin—it's 259 Songs, to be cut to 84—I know I can't do it but I plan to try."[32] As Berryman was about to leave for Ireland on his Guggenheim, his letter to Giroux showed an exuberance Giroux instinctively knew could not continue:

Hello. Various topics. I have just got the ms ready to take abroad (I have a Guggenheim wh I'm spending in Dublin) after weeks of dazzling work: it's 259 finished [Dream] songs (15 brand new) of which

only ten have been printed, and 35 unfinished and scores of fragments: the second (final) volume of 84 to be made up out of this
corpus. I hope to have it for you by March. I need money for travel:
can you advance me 500 [dollars] or more against the book?

The German Bradstreet, by a woman finally, is good, in sample.
I also answered her four sheets of enquiries. Will be glad to see the
Italian version, my Italian being much better than my 1937 Heidel-
berg German.

This man <u>Stephen Berg</u> of the free-verse anthology says you
want to charge $1,500 for 20 Songs.[33] Somebody is insane. Let him
have them as cheaply as possible, Bob: this is a <u>critical</u> anthology as
against a general or text anthology, and comes to free publicity. As of
a general or text anthology I believe in charging whatever the traffic
will bear, but this is more like quotations in criticism for which
<u>nothing</u> is charged, rightly; 20 Songs there—I admit it's a hell of a
lot, good for them—can only sell more copies of the book. His selection by the way is interesting and I am going to do him a prose piece
(explaining that I do NOT write free verse) once the obstacle with
you is cleared.[34]

Giroux wasted no time in providing details about the publication of
a new volume of Berryman's poetry, as he had intimated earlier, explaining
not only the finer points of granting permission to reprint Berryman's
works but detailing his modus operandi in an attempt to ward off fiscal
mismanagement that might harm Berryman in the long run.

It's good to hear from you, and wonderful news that you are going to
Dublin. We'd like to draw up a contract for the new poems, paying
an advance of one thousand dollars, which we can break up $750 on
signing and the rest on delivery, or half and half (whatever is most
convenient for you), with the other terms the same as for 77 DREAM
SONGS. Let me know if this is all right, and I'll get the contract and
check to you as fast as possible. Sorry but I keep forgetting the title;
let me have it again for the contract.

I enclose a photo of Stephen Berg's original letter. Does it sound
like a "<u>critical</u> anthology"? It sounds to me very much like a general
anthology with possible textbook use. (He sent us exactly the same
letter—a form—for Lowell's poems.) The fee may be high but it is

not insane when you analyze it. Our flat permission fee for a "Dream Song" is $25 (that is, $1.50 per line averaging 18 lines). Berg wants to use 18 Songs. For all but two (73 and 74, which are the longest) we charge $25, and for those two $30—making a total of $460. For hardcover general anthology rights, the rule of thumb is either to ask for a share of royalties (which we dislike because of bookkeeping problems), or to double the original fee. That makes it $920. But Berg also wants <u>paperback</u> general anthology rights, and in that case we triple the fee, making it $1,380, which he hyperbolized into $1,500. The fact that 77 DREAM SONGS won the Pulitzer Prize makes it commercially desirable to anthologists, and we are only asking standard rates which we ask consistently. (Cal's fees come to $990 for half the number of lines.) . . . What are your dates, leaving for Europe and returning, and when will I see you in New York? Did you know that Katy Carver seems to have worked it out for England?[35]

Berryman taught a summer course on "Humanities and the Modern World" from July 18 to August 20 to ensure that he had enough money on hand for his voyage. What Berryman did not know then was that fifty-two-year-old Delmore Schwartz had died a terrible death on July 11 when trying to put out the garbage from his sleazy New York hotel room, and his body lay in morgue for two days before being identified. When Berryman learned of Schwartz's death, he wrote to Van Doren, saying that he was suffering "half-paralyzing grief."[36] In Dream Song 153, he further expressed his sorrow for his poetic companions who had died:

> I'm cross with god who has wrecked this generation.
> First he seized Ted [Roethke], then Richard [Blackmur], Randall,
>   and now Delmore.
> In between he gorged on Sylvia Plath.
> That was a first rate haul. He left alive
> fools I could number like a kitchen knife
> but Lowell he did not touch.[37]

The tragic deaths of his friends never seemed to leave him.

After a phone conversation, Giroux sent Berryman the contract on July 29 for the new volume, to be entitled *His Toy, His Dream, His Rest*, he offered both an advance and a better royalty than previously mentioned. When Berryman returned the contract, he mentioned that he had found the 114-sonnet sequence that he had written in 1947 to his paramour Lise.[38] He intended to seek Meredith's advice on whether it should be published at once, as a way of softening up his audience, as he put it, for the second volume of Dream Songs. Berryman hoped that the book of sonnets would appear the following spring and *His Toy, His Dream, His Rest* later in the fall—though he was most conscious that he might suffer from "overexposure." When Giroux replied on August 11, he suggested they wait until Meredith had reacted one way or another: "Two books of verse in twelve months is unusual, of course, but 1967 is also our twenty-first anniversary (founded in 1946) and we intend it to be a banner year, so at least the timing is right for both. We'll see."

Berryman and his wife sailed from Montreal on the *Carmania* on August 26, 1966.[39] Giroux followed through with his commitment to publish Berryman's sonnets, especially as Meredith thought them "remarkable."[40] His next letter to Berryman, care of 55 Lansdowne Park, Ballsbridge, Dublin, contained a royalty check for $306.92, part of which Berryman used to continue drinking, sometimes heavily, which caused depression and feelings of insecurity. By September, however, he had written thirty or forty more Dream Songs.[41] On a train ride to a vacation at Avon-by-the-Sea on the Jersey shore, Giroux wrote in this letter of September 28 that he had read all 111 [*sic*] of the sonnets written by Berryman in a white heat in a relatively short time, and he was especially pleased that certain days and months of 1946 were mentioned. Giroux wished to contract for the sonnets, with the same advance as for the new Dream Songs, but paying $500 on signing and $500 on publication. The royalty would be 10% to 2,500 sales and 15% thereafter—the same as for *His Toy, His Dream, His Rest.* "The only point I have not yet been able to make up my mind about is timing. I can think of good reasons for waiting until HIS TOY, etc. comes out first; on the other hand, does it matter as long as we make it quite clear that this book is not in lieu of the expected Dream Songs (some rats might try to imply this)? I must really be guided by your own thoughts, but I'm inclined to doing the sonnets in mid-1967, with HIS TOY in 1968, provided we announce the latter on the dust-jacket of the former. Let me know what you think about this. . . . I am honored by and gratefully accept the dedication. I never expected to be an onlie begetter." In light of the news about the dedication, Giroux was absolutely delighted to receive the following handwritten poem from Dublin:

Old friend, he swore, I have sent you one
of my 14 unpublished books & you have not replied.
Now that was not well done.
[I]f it comes to a decision, spring to my side:
damn the trustees: down w. business meetings:
up the adventure of art.

Which we were born for, now so long ago:
your poem abt Proust still sticks in my head
& yr good-humoured editing.
Between us, we ran the place, a small place,
Columbia, but worth the running: our first scene.
Now that _was_ long ago.

But I remember later scenes, two grand,
our weddings, when you wd have had my hand
but you were in the Pacific, on the Essex,
so Mark [Van Doren] did, in the Lady Chapel in St. Patrick's,
in Naval Air Intelligence you were,
concerned w. winning a different war.[42]

Meredith's response, in forwarding the sonnets to Giroux, confirmed the editor's views: "I regarded my responsibility as this—to decide whether it would serve John's reputation well to publish it now," Meredith wrote. "The answer came back yes." Giroux interpreted this simply as "marvelous"—and perhaps risk-taking since it would raise the question in the minds of some as to Lise's identity, in spite of the fact that the sonnets were written approximately twenty years before. After Jill Berryman thanked her son for sending a copy of the book in late June 1967, she wrote, "I have read them with great interest and, again that word, astonishment. How little any of us know of another, much less of oneself. They must have been enormously private for you never mentioned them during the years of and after their writing when you did still speak of your work to me."[43]

In his reply from Dublin, Berryman, now looking haggard under an overflowing full mustache and beard, showed how involved he wanted to be in the publication of both books.

I'm glad you like the sonnets[;] they are good. The terms are v satisfactory. About [the] Timing: I feel that nothing should interfere with the fall 1967 publication of His Toy (which unfortunately, owing to my incessant production of new ones—some 40 in the last month alone—I feel less & less confident of controlling at 84). But I don't see how a spring 67 edition of the Sonnets can interfere, since of course they have a prefatory Note reading: "These sonnets, which were written many years ago, have nothing to do, of course, with my long poem in progress, The Dream Songs. Sonnet 25 appeared in the 40th anniversary number of Poetry; the others are unprinted. J.B." And announce as forthcoming His Toy..[.]either on the jacket of the Sonnets or on the "Also by John Berryman" page, or both. Give me your thoughts about this. I wd, in short, like the Sonnets out as soon as possible, but not to the detriment of the long poem.

Two pieces of good news. Book IV I fired instantly when finished to Meredith and to the London Times, which has taken either eight or nine—a whole page, they say, and I don't ever remember in the last thirty years their ever doing this before. And from Meredith I haven't heard yet, the baboon-bottomed bastard, but he must have shown IV to Cal because Cal with great generosity cabled me last Friday "Your posthumous poems are a tremendous & living triumph." Book IV is very strange—Henry is dead all through its 13 Songs—and I have been wildly doubtful abt it, all during the 3 years of its composition; so that this immediate high recognition by the chief American and English authorities is reassuring. I am now working on Book VII, which is hell, because, for instance, day before yesterday I wrote 3 new Songs.

We had to decline an invitation to the White House which came two weeks late!!! and Mrs. [Lyndon] Johnson wrote me a letter at any rate.[44]

Such praise from Meredith (via Giroux) and Lowell clearly energized Berryman, as he anticipated seeing more of his Dream Songs in print. The first three books, or sections, of the larger work *The Dream Songs* had appeared in *77 Dream Songs*. Books IV through VII, with 308 Dream Songs, would make up *His Toy, His Dream, His Rest* (which would receive the National Book Award for 1968).[45] After having lunch in New York with Charles Monteith, Giroux sent the contract to Berryman in Dublin and informed him that Monteith would like to publish both of Berryman's forthcoming books.[46]

On November 4, Giroux, now fifty-two years old, wrote to Berryman asking if he had received the contracts he had sent, since he could not proceed with his publishing plans without them in hand. Berryman replied from Dublin,

> Good: let's do the sonnets first. The contracts came all right but I was disturbed about the difference betw[een] our feelings on timing, also incredibly busy with Bk VII—which to my horror Kate counted the other day at 74 (that is, revised, accepted by me, and located), with 12 or 15 more to go that have always been intended to serve as its end & the end of the whole work. I have a phantastic [*sic*] amount of work to do, and only 3-odd months to do it in. Well, it's what I was made for, and no one else could do it. I reckon a month each for V and VI, then a month for the whole Ms.
>
> Anyway, let's do the sonnets in the spring and argue abt His Toy later, supposing I do get it done by March. I like BERRYMAN'S SONNETS rather than Sonnets as a title: there is the dedication to you: there is the prefatory note I wrote out in my last letter; we ought to use the photograph by Rohn Engh that appeared in the Twin Citian [published in Minneapolis] which I think I had sent to you, and it ought to take up the whole of the back of the jacket—I am convinced that poets' pictures sell their books, since books <u>are</u> sold and there's no question of the text doing it.[47]

Berryman was pleased to inform Giroux that he had been offered $1,000 to give two readings in Manhattan at the Guggenheim Museum, sponsored by the Academy of American Poets. As he mentioned in his reply of November 16, sent to Dublin, Giroux was glad to have received the contract. In turn, he sent Berryman the advance. Giroux wanted to know if he should expect the three additional sonnets Berryman had indicated previously that he wanted included in the book. "The only thing is, will they disrupt the numbering of the present sequence? In other words, we cannot set the book until we have them unless they come at the very end. Will you let me know about this right away?" Otherwise, all was in order to publish the book.

Berryman later sent Giroux from Dublin four, not three, sonnets, writing, "I do not love them: I wrote them months ago just after turning up the <u>Sonnets</u>, as a sort of self-dare to see whether after 11 yrs of Dream Songs I cd still write Petrarchan Sonnets. I found I could; but does it matter? Use them or kill them, as you like—I wd say <u>use</u> them, since they exist, and make a better end to the sequence than the existing ones. In any event, coming all at the end, they don't affect the numbering."[48] He enclosed Sonnet 107, in case Giroux did not have it. "I finisht the poem the other day, w a terror called 'Henry's Guilt.' Now the heavy job is simply editorial & administrative; living or dead I expect to make the March deadline." Five days before Christmas, Giroux informed Berryman that he had not included any the four sonnets, nor Sonnet 107; although the manuscript had gone to the printer, they could still insert these poems into the galleys. He complimented Berryman on the "marvelous group of Posthumous Dream Songs" in the *Times Literary Supplement*, as well as the ones in the *New York Review of Books*: "It's your year, John, and next year will be an even greater one with the two books, and the [American] Academy [of Poets] award [of $5,000]."[49] Lowell cabled Berryman in mid-December that he considered Book IV "a tremendous & living triumph."[50]

From Dublin on January 1, 1967, Berryman, injured in a fall due most likely to the effects of Thorazine, informed Giroux that a BBC television station would interview him for a half-hour film. Two days later, Giroux airmailed the galley proofs of *Berryman's Sonnets* to Dublin, with the request that Berryman send them back in less than two weeks' time in order to meet an April publication deadline. Giroux mailed the printed jacket for the book of sonnets on January 13, commenting that the blurb spoke of 111 sonnets, rather than the 115 he had in his office.[51] He thought it would not make any difference, and with Berryman's approval he would add the four additional sonnets. He also asked Berryman to airmail to him the corrections on the proofs, since it took longer to publish a book than before. John had injured his right side in the fall, so Kate returned the corrected proofs (and Giroux found a few typos himself).[52] By February 3, the final page proofs, with Berryman's corrections—especially the crucial one of "Lise" for "Lies"—had been sent to Dublin. At the same time, Berryman proudly informed his mother that he had finished Book V.[53]

Giroux provided even more details on Berryman's upcoming publications:

I phoned our printer the moment your letter with the two new sonnets arrived, but unfortunately the pages were already off press and it was too late to make the change. You see, if we are to make April publication we must have finished books in March—and we'll just about make it, as is. It was also too late of course for the index of first lines. I'm happy to say that there was time to do the binding and spine in the same style as 77 DREAM SONGS, so all was not lost. The book now contains 115 sonnets (our jacket has the right number). Bill Meredith tells me he has been asked to do the Times review![54]

During your forthcoming visit to New York, I had intended to bring up our proposal to reissue THE DISPOSSESSED and HIS THOUGHT MADE POCKETS in one volume, both in cloth and in Noonday [Press], but surely it will be more intelligent to get things sorted out before your arrival so that we can show you designs, etc. The trouble is I have never had a copy of HIS THOUGHT MADE POCKETS, nor can I find it listed anywhere by title or publisher to obtain an o.p. [out of print] copy. I do know that some of the poems are in the Faber book, which I have. What do you think of this proposal? Would you rather make a revised collection out of the two books, along the lines of the Faber edition; or have us reproduce them in toto? We ourselves would rather do the latter, especially because the paperback edition would be of great use in the colleges and may as well be complete. If you agree, can you tell me who published HIS THOUGHT MADE POCKETS? I know (from Faber's text) it came out in 1958, but it is literally unrecorded in any Cumulative Index of published books. I hope that at least it was copyrighted. Is the [William] Sloane edition of THE DISPOSSESSED OK to reproduce as is, or do you want to change it in any way? I do think a new brief preface or note for the combined volume is in order, and it will prolong your copyright as well. If you say yes to all this, we'd like to draw up a contract on the same royalty terms as BERRYMAN'S SONNETS with an advance of five hundred dollars.

The reissue, the Sonnets and HIS TOY, HIS DREAM, HIS REST will make this indeed a Berryman year. I'm delighted to hear that you've finished Book V! Our next project (fall, 1968?) is of course a Collected Edition.[55]

Dealing with all the publishing variables and the proposal added more strain to Berryman's life. At the end of January, he was admitted to Saint Brendan's Hospital, a psychiatric facility located in the north Dublin suburb of Grangegorman Lower.

As Berryman's health problems continued, the same was true for Lowell; they seemed to have formed an inseparable, brotherly bond, made deeper, perhaps, because they could rely on communal memories about their friends and colleagues and the successes and setbacks of their publishing careers. Berryman informed Giroux that he was sorry to learn of Lowell's stay at the McLean Hospital (December 24, 1966, to March 8, 1967) due to a diagnosis of manic-depressive psychosis.[56] "Tell him I love him," he added, "and he must do exactly what the bloody doctors say & get out as quick as possible and his new book is splendid—until I finish Bk VI I can't read it properly." In addition to enjoying his time with the BBC TV crew, Berryman liked all of Giroux's proposals, and agreed especially "in toto" about The Dispossessed and His Thought Made Pockets. He concluded in an understated way, "I have been very ill myself."

By mid-February, Berryman, now released from the hospital, attempted to keep his focus on his publishing prospects in the States. Giroux informed him that he and Reilly would be away from April 8 to April 26, on vacation in the Virgin Islands, though he would be back in New York to listen to Berryman read on April 27 at the Guggenheim Museum, another event sponsored by the Academy of American Poets, but not in time for the official publication of Berryman's Sonnets on April 24 (also published a year later by Faber & Faber).[57] As planned, Berryman returned to New York for the launching of Sonnets. Introduced by Lowell, Berryman was accompanied by journalist Jane Howard and one of his former students at the University of Minnesota, Janet Groth, whom he had been seeing on and off for a while. Howard's article in Life (July 21, 1967) had a picture of a full-bearded Berryman scowling by the seaside, which, according to Giroux, made Berryman look like Lear.[58] Most likely, it was at this time that Berryman, "drunk and shirtsleeved and rambling," had lunch with Groth at Giroux's apartment.[59] Later, Isabella Gardner (who had divorced Tate in 1966) and Elizabeth Kray went to visit Berryman at the Chelsea Hotel and found him vomiting profusely; they knew a doctor in the hotel, who rushed Berryman to the French Hospital on West Thirtieth Street for alcoholism, exhaustion, and malnutrition. There Lowell and Meredith visited him before he returned to Dublin in mid-May.

As Giroux drew up a contract in early June for the collected volume, initially entitled (with some reservations on Giroux's part) *Formal Elegy*, he was still having difficulty locating a copy of *His Thought Made Pockets*; this was rectified when Berryman sent him the name of the book's publisher, Claude Fredericks/Banyan. Since the galley proofs for *Short Poems* (a single volume containing both *The Dispossessed* and *His Thought Made Pockets*) were expected toward the end of June or the beginning of July and since everything in the book had been previously published, Giroux offered to have it proofread in-house, though he thoughtfully sent Berryman a courtesy set of proofs. As the Berrymans set off for Paris, Venice, and Athens, Giroux wrote to Kate, wanting her to know that a check should arrive in Athens about the middle of July.[60] John read at two international festivals (first at Spoleto, Italy, and then backtracking to London), and he also sent Giroux a batch of poems that he could publish anywhere he wanted, evidence that he could write about Henry even while on the road.[61]

When Kate subsequently wrote Giroux, she mentioned that the $500 check for *Short Poems* had arrived (c/o Mrs. Eugenie Foster in Athens) and that John was still in London, though he was expected any day in Greece, where they would stay until September 1, before returning to Minneapolis.[62] Giroux wrote to the Berrymans in Athens on July 19,

> The 57—count 'em, 57—Dream Songs for periodical publication arrived safely, and Lila Karpf [of the subsidiary rights department] and I are conspiring to find the most interesting and lucrative way to have them printed, lavishly and in large batches. Don't be surprised if you turn up in <u>McCall's</u> and <u>Playboy</u>. After all, the world is revolving faster now and <u>Partisan Review</u> ain't what it used to be and never paid much anyway—though I suppose that some of the 57 will end up there too, as well as in <u>The Nation, The New Republic</u>, and other loyal standbys. I'll keep you posted as things develop; and you keep me posted on your movements, Kate!

He mentioned, too, that a recent *Time* article referred to *Homage to Mistress Bradstreet* as "one of the best long poems to appear in America since <u>Four Quartets</u>." Giroux, clearly wanting to keep the publishing momentum going, continued with a summary of his publishing plans: "Give John my love and tell him to start writing down a table of contents for BERRYMAN'S PROSE—essays, criticism, and fiction. Does he agree that it should be the book to follow SHORT POEMS?"[63] After the three Berrymans cut short their time in Athens because of John's health problems, they flew to Liverpool, took a ship to Montreal, and then flew to Minneapolis in early September. Giroux sent a telegram to Berryman on September 19: "ALL THREE HUNDRED AND SEVEN DREAM SONGS SAFELY RECEIVED. BRAVO AND FELICITATIONS!" What Giroux did not know was that Berryman had been confined to his room on board ship for three days while vomiting and enduring delirium tremens. On his arrival in Minneapolis, he was again admitted to Abbott Hospital.

Now serving more and more as John's secretary, Kate wrote to Giroux on October 4, saying that her husband wanted a Dream Song she was enclosing to be entered fourth from last in the manuscript, since John would remain in Abbott until he left for Trinity College, in Hartford, Connecticut, for a reading, introduced by Meredith, of some of his poems. He would also lecture on *The Tempest*.[64] Unable to attend this event, Giroux sent Berryman a telegram on October 13 that contained good news: "TOY DREAM REST IS SUPERB. YOUR GREATEST BOOK AND THAT IS SAYING A LOT. WRITING YOU MINNESOTA. SUGGESTED CHANGES BOOKS SIX AND SEVEN. BOOKS FOUR AND FIVE ARE PERFECT." Giroux's subsequent, detailed letter provided specific criticism; most likely he did this because he knew that Berryman's mental and physical condition would not permit him to focus on the important editorial and legal problems that needed to be resolved in order to produce a book worthy of such a renowned poet.

> Now that I sit down to write you suggestions for the book, I realize that I do so with some misgivings and only because you asked me to. Who am I to suggest deletions? You have lived the poem, you have put it together, you are "Lazarus with a plan, a stratagem no newsman will unravel." Well, no doubt you are prepared for the fact that many readers will be amazed (and some critics will carp) at the number of Dream Songs—308! Four times 77; four times as big a book; 308 times 18 or 5,544 lines plus of course 1,386 lines from the earlier part—nearly 7,000 lines! What was it Pound wrote, when he was operating on <u>The Waste Land</u>—"let's say the longest new poem in the English langwidge"? Well, why not? There are virtues in length, God knows. It is merely that the level of the songs is so high that the

slightest falling-off becomes apparent. I had an eye out for strategic points, and that's why I suggest the following:

Author's note. You do not say anywhere how long HIS TOY took to write. My impression is that some of the poems are as early as any Dream Songs, and are only now appearing. You gave a hint in 77 Dream Songs where you say "its working title, since 1955," but you say nothing here about dates. It's important to make clear how long the whole work has absorbed your energies. Some of the later poems—the series aboard ship, sailing to Ireland—must clearly be of recent date. I think it of strategic importance to make it impossible for snipers to say that you tossed off this big book since 77, unless of course you did. . . . I have the impression there are too many Dublin poems, good though they are, perhaps because the book seems to become at this point a diary instead of a recorded dream. I may be wrong, but I feel that cutting here would strengthen the poem as a whole. Song 373 brought tears to my eyes, especially the last lines, but the facts in middle and part of beginning are wrong. The last ten or so songs are perfect—a strong and memorable ending. All the father poems are great.

I am well aware that repetition is part of the character of the poem. Let me put it this way: I think the book is the best work you have done, just as it is, and I would be prepared to set it up in type as is, without cuts. If you like, we can send proofs to Mark [Van Doren] and Bill Meredith, with the understanding that if after hearing from them you decided to make any deletions, you would be perfectly free to do so. We will pull just a very limited number of proofs for private consideration. You can have months to put them aside and consider them. As long as you release them by April or May, we can publish in the autumn of 1968, which seems to me the right time. If you decide a few hours after you see them that they are right, that will also be fine with me. So let me know what you think of this proposal. The design has been established by 77 Dream Songs. It should be possible to pull say seven sets of proofs by November. Is that OK?[65]

Giroux also wrote to Van Doren, relaying the message that he had received from Berryman: he would like Van Doren to read the manuscript and give him "heavy criticism" of *His Toy, His Dream, His Rest*.[66] Nor did Giroux forget, as indicated in a telegram on October 25, Berryman's birthday. He concluded affectionately with "Love," a word he rarely used in my presence.

Giroux further informed Berryman, still suffering from the effects of alcoholism and nervous exhaustion, about the magazine submissions he had facilitated.[67] After receiving two highly laudatory letters (one from Aiken on *Short Poems* and the second from Fitzgerald on the forthcoming *His Toy, His Dream, His Rest*), Giroux congratulated Berryman upon receiving a $10,000 Senior Fellowship grant from the National Endowment for the Arts (Van Doren was one of the referees) for research he anticipated doing at the Folger Shakespeare Library in Washington, DC, and at the Huntington Library in San Marino, California.[68] Unfortunately, this moment was overshadowed by another relapse that forced Berryman to return just after Thanksgiving to the mental health unit at Abbott Hospital.

Giroux couched his next letter most positively: "Good news continues to come in. The Atlantic have taken the following four Dream Songs: 'Them lady poets,' 'Scarlatti spurts his wit,' 'Draw on your resources,' and 'I don't know one damn butterfly.' A total of $200."[69] Giroux inquired whether Berryman had heard anything from Meredith. No doubt sensing more his own mortality after so many hospital stays, and clearly wishing to rush things, Berryman contacted Meredith at the end of the year: "I was so delighted to hear from you the other night that I totally forgot to say that Giroux & I are burning to know what Dream Songs you do not like. I killed about fifty in Greece, Bob was dubious about six, of which I killed four, Mark put one down and I threw it out, now we are waiting for you. . . . Crucify them, kid."[70] Berryman knew that his dear friend would give him an honest evaluation. When he thanked Van Doren on December 27 for his praise of the recent Dream Songs, he said that he believed he "may have received more encouraging and more welcomed letters in my life, but I honestly cannot remember them."[71]

CHAPTER SEVEN

The Final Years of Collaboration

Waiting to hear from William Meredith was almost more than Berryman could bear. Nevertheless, he felt impelled to write Giroux in March 1968, trying to give final shape to *His Toy, His Dream, His Rest.*

I'm going crazy waiting over Meredith, let's get the show on the road, let's put the book into galleys. Whatever he may suggest can be corrected there. This is my fault, I never should have saddled him with the job, over-conscientious & self-overworked as he is. I am in very bad shape myself, in & out of hospital like a yoyo all winter. But a month ago exactly I began to write again, very reluctantly, having resisted the daily or hourly impulse for months, and I have about a dozen new Songs, some bad, some good, which I'm using to plug the gaps left by you & Mark [Van Doren] & me. I am superstitious about the numeration, which cost me such hell for years to effect. Let's protect that.

Now this is in response to your admirable letter of October, which I now fully answer.

I have killed, and substituted for, 193 (which Mark didn't like, nor do I), 247, 255, 285 and 286 as well as 284 (I took yr suggestion of amalgamation, which to my great surprise worked), 288. On my own I have killed 320 and substituted for it, and transposed 302 and 304. 327, first line, shd read "some wrong" for "all wrong," and this change made also in the table of contents, some pages of which I enclose, and please return them directly you have made the relevant changes in the master. . . . One of the new ones, a beauty, which I enclose, we <u>might</u> put between 301 and 302, making 305 in all. What do you feel about this? I can't make up my mind.

I have a devilish week coming up week after next, in & around New York. Cd we have lunch on the Monday, a week from tomorrow, or meet some evening when I will have been performing at Queens [College] during the day?[1] "At Henry's bier" this is.

I hope all is better with you than with me.[2]

While there is no indication that Berryman and Giroux met for lunch, their subsequent letters certainly give the impression that poetry and its publication, not socialization, were the main focus of their attention. Whatever views preoccupied the rest of the country—the North Vietnamese Tet Offensive against the United States and South Vietnam or the assassination in April of Dr. Martin Luther King Jr. and in June of Robert Kennedy—Giroux continued to write to Berryman about editorial problems only, not wanting Berryman to dissipate his creative energies on questions about his political views. Likewise, as the Berrymans were meeting with a psychiatrist in order to resolve the tensions in their marriage brought about by John's acute alcoholism, Giroux chose not to relate his own marital troubles. In all their years of communication, Giroux had never mentioned in writing to Berryman his marriage in August 1952 to Doña Carmen Natica de Arango y del Valle, known informally as Carmen de Arango. The daughter of a Cuban aristocrat, Don Francisco de Arango, the third Marquis de la Gratitud, and his wife, the former Doña Petronila del Valle, she became the fifth Marquise de la Gratitud after the death of her sister Mercedes. An alumna of Manhattanville College of the Sacred Heart with an M.A. in English from Columbia, she most likely met Giroux through a connection at their shared alma mater. On several occasions during our conversations, Giroux referred obliquely to his marriage, his long estrangement from Doña Carmen, the canonical dissolution of their marriage on October 25, 1968, and their divorce a year later.

Despite the upheaval in his personal life, Giroux made the deletions, substitutions, and corrections that Berryman requested to the collection of more than 300 Dream Songs. On April 9 he wrote Berryman to inform him that the printer was in the process of setting up the book and the proofs should be ready by the end of the month.[3] Berryman replied in mid-April, focusing on the unavailability of his latest book and his travel plans: "Am stumbling forward: a reading in So[uthern] Calif[ornia] next week, plus one 3 days later (w my double lecture here in between) in Chicago. I'm never again going to be victimized this way. Here's to one job only!"[4] Berryman summoned up enough strength, while still waging war with alcohol and prescribed medications, to give additional readings at the Guggenheim in New York in late April and then at the State University of New York at Binghamton.

Moving forward with great speed, Giroux handled the editorial details as needed. He sent a telegram to Berryman, care of the English Department at San Fernando Valley State College in Northridge, California, congratulating him on winning the *Virginia Quarterly*'s Emily Clark Balch Prize of $500 for a group of eleven Dream Songs, including ten he had written to honor Delmore Schwartz.[5] Giroux made some final emendations on the galley proofs after receiving Dream Song 149, and, as was his habit, paying careful attention to each poem, he queried some lines in Dream Songs 167, 211, 277, 308. After sending the final page proofs to Minneapolis on June 25, Giroux rechecked the master copy against the manuscript and the corrected galleys and then saw the book through production during the summer months. When Lowell read an advance copy, he wrote to Berryman praising the poems for being "perfectly clear": "Either they are really so, or I am much more at home with your idiom."[6] In a letter to Berryman dated September 22, Lowell further wrote, "I've read most of the poems, my admiration still rolling up. I'm dumbfounded at how many of the same things we have: rough iambic lines, often pentameter (for me mostly), short sections that are not stanzas; wife, wives, child, old flames, new ones, sex, love, loves, portraits of writers (I have Frost, Jarrell and Williams too), landscape (I have more of this), portraits of the dead, full middle age, humor, death, etc."[7]

On his return from the Frankfurt Book Fair in Germany, Giroux informed Berryman of his contractual arrangements in England.

Let me quote what Charles Monteith of Faber has written about HIS TOY, HIS DREAM, HIS REST: "I was absolutely delighted to find a copy of HIS TOY, HIS DREAM, HIS REST waiting for me when I got back to the office this morning after a few days in Frankfurt—though I had in fact seen a copy on the Farrar, Straus stand there and I had a long and pleasant talk with Roger Straus. What a superb book it is. It will be years before I've really read it properly; but I've been through the set of proofs you sent me a week or two ago and already I'm immensely impressed by it. We would of course be delighted to make a contract with you for it straight away. . . . If that's all right I'd be most grateful if you could let me have a formal agreement."

The only trouble is that he's forgotten we do not handle British rights. If you'd like, we'd be glad to handle them for you, provided you agree that we ask for more than one hundred pounds advance (approximately $240). Our commission for handling these rights, collecting royalties, reporting to you and so on would be fifteen per cent. If you want to continue yourself, as before, write to Monteith directly but I hope you will ask for a higher advance at this stage for your longest book.

All is readying itself for the luncheon party [at Lüchow's restaurant in New York, which JB attended] on October 25th [JB's birthday and publication date of *His Toy, His Dream, His Rest*, published in England by Faber & Faber in May 1969]. Martha McDowell, Elizabeth Kray and Jean Stafford have accepted. I'm waiting to hear from Mark [he did attend]. Jane Howard will be in California and can't come—has she written you?[8]

Cal Lowell phoned today to say what a fine book he thinks it is. The Harvard Advocate asked for copies for their Berryman issue. Good, good.[9]

Giroux informed Berryman on November 11 of Lowell's touching tribute, which would appear in the *Harvard Advocate*: "I have had no leisure of ideas for a critical piece on John Berryman. Instead, I must substitute my brief praise. I think Dream Songs, now completed, is one of the glories of the age, the single most heroic work in English poetry since the War, since Ezra Pound's Pisan Cantos. Berryman handles the language as if he made it. He makes me feel better about our poetry, better about being a poet, better about. . . . But what can I add?"[10] In addition, Lowell, who had just finished his *Notebook 1967–68: Poems*, which Giroux edited, wrote that the Irish poems made Berryman "the best Irish poet since Yeats."[11] After the Lüchow's gathering, Berryman went to Brandeis University, outside

Boston, and then to Harvard. He then finished up two seminars at Minnesota, "The American Character" and "The Meaning of Life," bringing the year—an annus mirablis—to a productive conclusion.

As 1969 began, Giroux congratulated Berryman on sharing the Bollingen Prize in Poetry of $10,000 with poet Karl Shapiro, who likewise highly praised the new volume of Dream Songs, which the committee cited as having "volatile excitement."[12] Given such an accolade, it was decided that *His Toy, His Dream, His Rest* would go into a second printing. Berryman wrote to Giroux on February 6, thanking him for his article on silent film director and producer Mack Sennett and mentioning he was in low spirits and ill health—now a characteristic letdown after the publication of a book. He had recently spent three days at Skidmore College in Saratoga Springs, New York, giving a reading and signing books, as he had done once before. Giroux sent Berryman a letter of agreement on February 20 to cover the combined edition, entitled *The Dream Songs*, which they had discussed by phone. Publication would be in November, and the edition would be a selection of the Literary Guild with a minimum guarantee of $5,000, which they would share equally. He asked two questions: Would Berryman want to write a short note or preface to the combined edition to replace the front matter for the separate editions? And would he want an index of first lines at the back? On the same date, Giroux wrote in detail about the contractual details of publishing this one-volume edition. There would be an advance of $1,000. In hindsight, this letter signaled that Berryman was moving toward the apogee of his career as a poet. Could he ever surpass a volume of his collected poems and the awards his poetry had garnered?

On March 12, Berryman gave a surprising acceptance speech in New York for the National Book Award in Poetry for *His Toy, His Dream, His Rest* that revealed an edginess not expected from a great poet who was making a genuine contribution to poetic language.

> Thank you very much, sir. And my thanks to the benevolent Committee, as also to my wife and several friends, especially Saul Bellow and Bob Giroux, who sustained and even endured me during the 13-year labor.
>
> I remember that a predecessor of mine in this award, Mr. W. H. Auden, expressed surprise that poetry should figure at all in these awards, where actual money, sales-money, is at stake. I share that

surprise, in an increased degree, since the award this time is for that abomination of bookseller and book reader alike, a *long* poem—or at any rate the second volume of one. Worse still, the award is made to a person not perfectly respectable, myself, whose first long poem, called *Homage to Mistress Bradstreet*, was accused by a certain eminent critic of lacking "inherent imaginative grandeur." Think of that! I wonder if I dared ever lift my head and trouble the public again. "You lack inherent imaginative grandeur," I said severely to myself over my Grape Nuts: "down with you!"

Needless to say, I attended with rigor the next poetry reading given in my vicinity by this eminent critic, wondering if he too (who so glibly accused me) might lack inherent imaginative grandeur. To my astonishment the question never came up. His tidy little poems followed each other tidily into silence. Nothing large or continuous—much less grand—was ever attempted. He had no gall. He couldn't succeed, on any serious scale, because he couldn't fail.

Both the writer and the reader of long poems need gall, the outrageous, the intolerable—and they need it again and again. The prospect of ignominious failure must haunt them continually. Whitman, our greatest poet, had all this. Eliot, next, perhaps even greater than Whitman, had it too. Pound makes a marvelous if frail third here. All three dazzlingly original, you notice, and very hostile, both Pound and Eliot, to Whitman. It is no good looking for models. We want anti-models.[13]

Berryman continued on his rollercoaster ride, especially when away from familiar surroundings. He gave a less-than-coherent reading at the University of Notre Dame in early April, another at Michigan State in East Lansing, and still a third scheduled for the University of Illinois on May 19. When his plane was delayed at O'Hare Airport (leading to a quick retreat to a bar), the latter reading was finally held before a small group of students in a private home.[14] Afterward, he went to Wayne State University (which had been renamed in 1956), where he appeared slumped and disorganized, though on occasion he soared to great heights. This was followed by yet another reading at the University of Washington in late May, where he rallied triumphantly for the prestigious sixth annual Theodore Roethke Memorial Poetry Reading in spite of being drunk the night before. He would not have been surprised by the news from Giroux that his mother was preparing the index of first lines for *The Dream Songs*.[15]

For his friend's sake, Giroux needed to move forward steadily with the new volume, even though Berryman lacked the will to stay on course with him. His greatest gift now to Berryman would be freedom. He sent Berryman in early June a copy of the new jacket, explaining that he had combined the two prefaces into a single note for the omnibus edition.[16] He would need to have the proofs back no later than June 16, at which point he would add the index of first lines and titles. Fortunately, this was done expeditiously; Berryman had injured a nerve in his neck, which occasioned a prolonged stay in the hospital followed by a routine of daily therapy, causing him during the summer months to lose approximately thirty-five pounds. Berryman tried to be helpful in his own way, though his physical fragility allowed only a minimum of communication. In his reply to Giroux, he cryptically noted, "Very ill & in great pain fr a nerve injury—10 days in hospital have hardly helped. These proofs look all right exc[ept] for some errors in the index. The dust-jacket looks fine, only why is the back blank?"[17] Giroux wrote him on July 15, saying that Monteith had asked if it would be possible to do a volume of Berryman's *Selected Poems* in their paperback series, one that was more up to date than the *Homage to Mistress Bradstreet* collection. He also suggested that if a selection were to be made of any of Berryman's work, covering the early and middle poems up through the *Sonnets* and *The Dream Songs*, Berryman ought to make the selection himself.

When classes resumed in the early fall of 1969, Berryman had not fully recovered from his neck injury. During the October convocation ceremony, he was appointed Regents Professor of Humanities, for which he would receive an annual stipend of $5,000 plus a royalty check of $8,000.[18] He could not, however, break the pathological patterns that were tearing him apart. That November, after receiving an advance copy of *The Dream Songs* with 385 poems, he felt he had not lived up to his potential. Again, he was faced with a dilemma of whether to continue writing or not. Furthermore, he felt despondent that, after eight years of married life, he had not advanced as a husband and father as he had expected. Under the influence of drugs and alcohol, he fell in his bathroom, bruising parts of his body, and thus was admitted for a six-week stay at the Hazelden Foundation, a rehabilitation facility in Center City, Minnesota. While there, he attended talks by the staff three times a day, went to group therapy twice a week, and talked to his unit manager, psychologist, and particularly his counselor, James Jensen, who helped him gain some understanding of being self-sufficient. His five-hour interview with the Reverend Hector LaChapelle, a La Salette Missionary Catholic priest, gave him an insight into the value of having, however belatedly, an interior spiritual life, reinforced by reading books on the twelve steps of Alcoholics Anonymous and doing daily chores, such as vacuuming the TV room and a small lounge. During the first four days at Hazelden, he felt weak from sweating profusely and shaking uncontrollably. Fortunately, the chairman of his department at the university found two replacements to teach temporarily his classes on Montaigne and Pascal and someone from the Spanish Department to take over his class on *Don Quixote*. During moments of clarity, Berryman realized that he was indeed an alcoholic and at times still dependent on his cocktail of drugs: Phenobarbital, Haldol, Tuinal, Serax, Librium, Thorazine, and Nembutal. He returned home from the hospital on December 19, feeling that the various forms of therapy he had undergone had been of enormous help, especially the encouragement given him by fellow alcoholics.[19]

As Berryman entered into the new year of 1970, he prepared a seminar on *Hamlet* for the coming term, the first regularly scheduled course he would teach in the English Department. ("No wonder he obsessed over *Hamlet*'s play within a play, in which the death of Hamlet's father is rehearsed on stage before his mother and her new husband, the usurper king," Mariani once observed.)[20] Berryman wanted, yet once again, to write a book on Shakespeare's life and works.[21] Unfortunately, he so alienated a number of his students with his ranting and unprofessional behavior that some faculty members turned their backs on him. As he was thinking about organizing essays and unpublished stories to be included in a future volume, *The Freedom of the Poet*, he accepted an invitation that had triggered problems in the past: a reading far away from home—this time, in late February, at New Jersey's Fairleigh Dickinson University. Depleted after this trip, he again entered Abbott Hospital for a ten-day stay after another drinking binge, only to return in March and again soon after for another stay, trying, as before, to cope with delirium tremens. Could anything be done to reverse this situation, or was it already too late? No doubt he was cheered by the wonderfully human, considerate letter he received from Meredith:

Now that we've talked, glancingly, twice about the poems you sent me two weeks ago, I still feel the vagueness of my misgivings. This is partly because on the other occasions when you've asked my opinion, the opinion was so easy: the Dream Songs, early and late, and the Sonnets are so obviously successful that all one could possibly speak of was an occasional unclarity or a personal obtuseness, the way one would say of a Woodrow Wilson candidate, Miss O'Flaherty has dandruff, to show that she was not perfect. The new poems do not please me as much as the poems of yours I've gotten used to seeing. I find the story line, as they say, unsophisticated, and even when what is made of it is serious. I find the concern with autobiography lacking in the transfiguring imaginative process of the Dream Songs, diary-raiding than fantasy. . . . As a loving friend, I am bothered at your wanting either criticism or praise, at this point with this urgency, from them named above [Elizabeth Bishop and Richard Wilbur] or from Mark [Van Doren] or me. An insecure Berryman is a contra-diction in the adjective. . . . The only thing in your brilliant life I don't envy is the hard way you have gone about being a great poet. But even that perverse and roundabout way is inextricable from the man and the work I love.[22]

In early April, Berryman sent three chapters of his Shakespearean biography to Meredith, who continued to reply with supportive, con-soling words rather than with a point-by-point critique.[23] Unfortunately, Berryman was admitted to the hospital that month for another three-day stay, and just when he seemed, yet again, at his lowest point, he rallied, writing blunt, tragic, and sometimes shocking and funny poems for a new volume, *Love & Fame*, which he had modeled to a degree on the poetry of Emily Dickinson.[24] He expressed great pride to Giroux in his latest achievement, believing that this was "one of the beautiful, original & powerful works of the age."[25] He gave a reading at Vassar College in Poughkeepsie, New York, in mid-April and then before an enthusiastic audience of six hundred at the International Poetry Forum in Pittsburgh, with predictable results. From early May until mid-June 1970, he was in the Intensive Alcoholic Treatment Center at Saint Mary's Hospital in Minneapolis, enduring pain far more radical than he had experienced in his previous alcoholic bouts.[26]

Berryman's life, at this point, seemed to take an odd turn, perhaps stemming from a congeries of factors that contributed to a general sense of malaise and the need to reevaluate his life. He told Peter Stitt later that year that he "came back . . . into the notion of a God who, at certain moments, definitely and personally intervenes in individual lives, one of which is mine."[27] His counselor, James Zosel, an Episcopalian priest and a recovering alcoholic, advised him strongly not to go back into the classroom because he was shaking so much. Father Zosel also taught a class for Berryman on Saint John's Gospel, since he had the necessary background in theology. During his second week at the treatment center, Berryman underwent some type of religious conversion, giving him the energy to make considerable progress on his Shakespeare biography. Furthermore, he wrote approximately fifty lyrical poems in a five- or six-week period, in addition to eleven explicitly religious poems. These wonderfully lucid, Hopkinsesque tributes to God, entitled "Eleven Addresses to the Lord," reflect a type of religious conversion that Berryman wanted to add, as part 4, to *Love & Fame*. Lowell commented forthrightly on this prayer sequence: "The prayers are a Roman Catholic unbeliever's, seesawing from sin to piety, from blasphemous affirmation to devoted anguish."[28] On a more personal note, Lowell wrote to Berryman, "I've read your marvelous prayer . . . and can hardly find words to praise it. Though cunning in its skepticism, it feels like a Catholic prayer to a personal God. . . . Along with your posthumous poems, to my mind, the crown of your work."[29] Gradually, Berryman began to express his belief that the God who rescued the abandoned did exist: "He saves men from their situations, off and on during life's pilgrimage, and in the end," he said to Stitt. "I completely bought it, and that's been my position since."

While reading more about theology and the Catholic Church, Berryman became deeply interested in Christ, though he did not pray to him. "He certainly was the most remarkable man who ever lived," he told Stitt. "But I don't consider myself a Christian. I do consider myself a Catholic, but I'd just as soon go to an Episcopalian church as a Catholic church. I do go to Mass every Sunday." This conversion, however one might describe it, was one of the most remarkable events in Berryman's life. The "Sixth Address" reflects a fresh, highly confessional, religious sensibility that emerges to a great extent from the twelve-step program of Alcoholics Anonymous:

Under new management, Your Majesty:
Thine. I have solo'd mine since childhood, since
my father's suicide when I was twelve
blew out my most bright candle faith, and look at me. . . .

Then my poor father frantic. Confusions & afflictions
followed my days. Wives left me.
Bankrupt I closed my doors. You pierced the roof
twice & again. Finally you opened my eyes.[30]

At one point, Berryman reacted with "rage and contempt" at being labeled as a confessional poet, for he considered the confessional to be a place where a penitent sacramentally reveals to a priest his or her sins.[31] Sessions at Alcoholics Anonymous and transactional analysis following his extended stay at Saint Mary's Hospital were helpful, but Berryman's life problems were so deep-seated that he was not sure he could surmount them, though his literary efforts continued unabated. He was pleased to learn that the *Saturday Review* would publish the first five of his religious poems.

In May 1970, Giroux sent Berryman a tentative jacket sketch for *Love & Fame*, which, in Giroux's mind, showed Berryman at his best, even if there were to be a delay in publishing it. Giroux did not want to discourage his friend with less than a most positive critique.

From my conversation with Kate last week, I assume that you will not have the setting copy of LOVE & FAME ready for fall publication. Nevertheless our fall catalogue has gone to press with the enclosed description of the book. As you will note, it is down for September, but I have explained to Howard Moss at The New Yorker that this is merely a tentative date. He said he could not use the poems unless we publish next spring, so the postponement of the book should solve his problem. Kate also told me that you like the jacket design, and I was happy to hear this.

The more I've been reading the manuscript, John, the more I am convinced that it is far and away your best book. The Columbia section involves so much of my own past that I realize I'm a less objective critic than ordinarily; nevertheless, I think this section is superb. The book has design, movement, shape. The final section is

like a symphonic coda. It's a grand book and my hat is off to you. . . .
I very much look forward to seeing the new poems that I understand
you are inserting just before the last section. If I've misunderstood
your own wishes with regard to the timing of the book, we can still
go ahead with fall publication. To spell this out, if you get a setting
copy of the manuscript to us by June 30th, we can still publish LOVE
& FAME in the fall. In fact, I would favor this unless you feel that
you need more time for the book and unless you feel that The New
Yorker problem is crucial.

Everything considered, I think that New Yorker publication
could be helpful, but I hardly look on it as crucial. In any event we
are announcing the book in our fall catalogue, and even if we may
not publish in the fall this kind of advance notice is always helpful.
Whether we publish in the fall or next spring it will be a great publishing event.[32]

Giroux remained the consummate editor, laying everything out clearly so
that Berryman would not blur details during one of his debilitating hospital stays. Discharged on June 12, Berryman wrote Giroux a few days
later, saying he was just out of the hospital after a long stay—prostrate, as
he mentioned, after five or six weeks of work on his poetry. His doctors
said it would be a year before he would be back to normal. He enclosed
a new table of contents that included the sequence of eleven religious
poems written in the hospital after his "sort of conversion experience."[33]
In a draft preface for his unfinished *Life of Christ*, Berryman states that
Christ "is the most important human personality, and [had] the most
important career, of which we have knowledge; and it befits us to try to
understand them."[34] He wanted a copy of the manuscript sent to Bellow,
care of the Committee on Social Thought at the University of Chicago,
since Bellow had been enthusiastic about some of the poems that Berryman read to him over the phone. Berryman wrote Giroux again the same
day, "*Enfin, mon vieux!* Put it ['Death Ballad'?] into the revised & en-
larged master Xerox. Isn't it a beauty? & how do you like 'The Home
Ballad?'" Giroux responded immediately,

The manuscript arrived today, and your letter. I read the new poems
at once, and I think they are marvelous. The "Eleven Addresses to
the Lord" moved me very much. What an ending for a great book!

I will go over the whole manuscript now and correct the titles and the other items. I'll try to get from Howard Moss your corrected proof of "Death Ballad." We do have a manuscript version starting, "Tyson & Jo, Tyson & Jo / became convinced it was no go." Isn't that the right poem? I'll assume it is OK to set and that you will change it in proof.

The contract is now being drawn up and will soon be mailed to you.

I'm not sure we can duplicate the typography of the Shakespeare sonnet [that Berryman had sent Giroux]. It's an English font in monotype, which we don't have in the U.S.—only linotype. It's a difference in machines, one of those mysteries. We had a designer working on the text. Let me at least send you a sample of his work, so you can see if you like it. I'm sorry about the monotype. . . . I'll send Saul Bellow a xerox copy, with a new table of contents, and new titles. This will take two days or so.

Sorry to hear of your long hospital stay, and glad to hear that you are out. I'm off to France at the end of July, to stay at St. Tropez with my cousin Claude Giroux and his five daughters, Nicole, Monique, Pascale, Jocelyn, and Marie-Claude. Isn't that a lovely constellation of names?[35]

Two days later, Giroux wrote again, thanking Berryman for the copy of "Death Ballad," which he had belatedly received and which had a profound effect on Bellow (Berryman had dedicated *77 Dream Songs* to his wife and Bellow).[36] "It is of course the poem I already had," Giroux mentioned, "one of the best in the book, I think."

Giroux immediately returned one copy of the signed contract and a check for the advance, and he would soon have type pages ready to send Berryman.[37] He noted that an October publication date would rule out publication of "Death Ballad" in the *New Yorker*, but if Berryman thought there were other possible publications, such as *Atlantic*, *Life*, or *Harper's*, he should inform Giroux. Berryman's quick response on July 1 supplied information about the progress of still another book:

No, damn it, I did not know The New Yorker wouldn't have room for Death Ballad; I had even returned proof; I'm disappointed. Life is a good idea for it, which wouldn't have occurred to me; yes, try them—

though aren't they more likely to take several poems on roughly the same themes than just one? Unfortunately the others such are at Locations, Saul [Bellow]'s new review in Texas, I'll let you know when I hear from them. Kate reminded me the other day that you & I had agreed that you'd send my stuff out to periodicals; I had forgotten this and have been sending things myself, not that it matters does it?

Thanks for noticing the iteration of "scientific & philosophical": let's just delete the phrase from Message. And change "Toltec," in Of Suicide, to "Olmec."

I have been very busy in a relaxed sort of way, about a quarter of my next book of verse is written [most likely incorporating the "Opus Dei" ("Work of God") section of Delusions, etc.] What progress have your people made with the prose-collection? We ought to be able to bring that out next year, no?

On the back of the jacket of Love & Fame I'd like the arms-outspread photograph Life blew up for their article four years ago [taken by Terence Spencer]. It's theatrical but very good.

Hot as hell here, we just bought a vast new air-conditioner that arrives day after tomorrow. I am reading 20 books simultaneously, all excellent, the best being Exodus, next-best Eve Curie's biography of her astounding mother which I'm teaching to a pro-seminar this Fall.

The next day, he again wrote Giroux, suggesting, almost unbelievably, still another volume:

A new project—as if I hadn't enough already. This morning I suddenly got fed up with all existing anthologies, for the hundredth time, and decided to make one of my own. It is going to be a beauty. In a few hours I have ripped out fifty poems from half a dozen anthologies in my vast collection, and am well under way. Maybe a few weeks or months will see it done. It's called A Verse Anthology with comments (Mark [Van Doren] on Emerson's Brahma, me on Wordsworth's Resolution & Independence, etc etc), running from the Iliad to Wilbur's "Waking to Sleep," maybe six hundred pages. Are you interested, I hope? Can you suggest a better title?

Giroux replied on July 17, noting that the galley proofs for Love & Fame would be ready in early August; Berryman finished revising the galleys on August 14, but he still hoped to make changes.

Giroux and Reilly set sail on the *Raffaello* to visit London for the first time in five years and then continued on for the planned stay with Giroux's cousin Claude in the south of France. When Giroux met with Monteith of Faber & Faber in London, they agreed on terms for publishing *Love & Fame* in England.[38] Giroux and Straus were delighted with the proposed anthology, now tentatively entitled *The Blue Book of Poetry*. Once it had been assembled, they could estimate the permission costs. Louis Untermeyer and Oscar Williams, Giroux had earlier mentioned, "made fortunes with their lousy anthologies. Berryman will do so with an elegant and highly personalized one."[39] Before Giroux returned on August 24, his assistant mailed Berryman two sets of proofs of *Love & Fame* to be corrected and returned.[40] All three Berrymans then took a vacation to Mexico City toward the end of August, staying at the Hotel Majestic and then visiting Taxco and the Tula Toltec pre-Columbian ruins at Teotihuacán.

In early October, at the invitation of poet William Heyen at the State University of New York at Brockport, Berryman participated in a televised reading and interview, during which his slurred, incoherent speech visibly dismayed his two interviewers.[41] Returning by plane to New York on October 9, he met with Giroux and Michael di Capua in a restaurant near the Chelsea Hotel.[42] Berryman's mental and physical condition would have been clear to them; they sensed immediately that nothing should be done to provoke further anxiety. Once back in Minneapolis, Berryman flared up again, causing great pain to his wife and to himself, so much so that he was taken by ambulance to Saint Mary's Hospital. He sent Giroux a postcard from the hospital's locked ward, asking for a copy of *Love & Fame* once it was printed. He also requested that copies be sent to the Pulitzer Prize committee at Columbia University.[43] This was followed by another postcard from the hospital, dated "Fri": "<u>This is important</u>. I have decided to kill 'The Amer. Hero.' I want the printer just to leave that page <u>blank</u>. That won't hold up production, will it? It may look a trifle odd, & the title in table of contents, but who cares? My reasons are both literary & political, and are strong. Treatment is going well again, after a setback. Wish me luck. I am working at present mostly on mysteries connected w his [Berryman's father's] death—esp[ecially]. Why I attach no affect to three of the (<u>only</u>) four memories I have of his death. My history emotionally is even weirder than I've always supposed." During his stay in the hospital, Berryman considered converting to Judaism (he had tried to learn Hebrew in 1954 under the tutelage of

Frederick Bargebuhr), but finally decided against it. Giroux wrote him on October 29, care of the Extended Care Unit, focusing entirely on the production of Berryman's new book. Tactfully, he did not ask about Berryman's health, nor about the death of Berryman's father, but instead expressed a desire to have the book published by November 30, the deadline for the National Book Award and Pulitzer Prize.

A letter from Berryman's mother, written over a two-day period at Thanksgiving in response to Berryman's urgent request to know more about his days at South Kent and the manner of his father's death, further disturbed Berryman, who was still undergoing treatment at Saint Mary's Hospital. Why would a mother want to dredge up layers and layers of anguish and present them to a son who was clearly sinking into a whirlpool of amnesiac guilt? Wouldn't sidestepping these issues, in a loving, maternal way, have shown her son the soothing compassion that might help him endure better his current agonizing crisis? Her long letter reads more like a disinterested police report.

> It must have been very hard for John Angus to endure, I realize now. But all that time I did not know nor do I now believe that Allyn knew the gun was loaded when he pulled the trigger—to carry it around, empty, still, so the doctors said, it might be the thing that made him feel strong and powerful and all agreed that it should not be taken from him, it was an assertion of self and was an affirmation of strength and every responsibility that he, alone of the men around, had a gun. I buried the bullets way down the beach, and when Allyn asked about them I said what the doctors told me to say: they (the bullets) were old and probably no good, and that when we went to Tampa again we could get some if he wanted them; that the gun was enough to frighten any thieves or rascals away, and that was all he wanted it for, wasn't it? and he agreed. He always kept the gun on an empty bullet space, for safety, and it is possible that he, in clicking the trigger, as he often did, if he had put that bullet in the gun, it would have come around to it. None of the five bullets I buried was missing and whenever I had a chance I looked to see if there was a bullet in the gun but there never was, so the only possible solution is that Allyn did put the sixth bullet in and forgot it, and when clicked often enough would bring that sixth bullet into the firing chamber. He must have hidden that bullet somewhere outside, as I searched the apartment every day, and the car, too. I did not believe then and do

not now that Allyn intended to end his life. John, he did not care enough about life to take it.[44]

Berryman had regrets about bringing up such sensitive family topics: "It simply is *not* God's will that I shd at present—or possibly ever—find out any more abt those mysterious subjects."[45] Rather, he would turn his attention to writing a book about his experiences and treatment in the hospital. His mother's subsequent, babbling letter—smothering him with information about giving birth to him (and later to his brother by Caesarian section), apparently meant to reveal that she was gloriously free of guilt toward her son—could not have come at a worse time.

Berryman, upset that he had not received any copies of *Love & Fame* and that *The Nation* (November 30, 1970) had published a long, hostile review by Hayden Carruth (the poems were "a splotchy muddlement of crude desires"), impelled him to send off another missive to Giroux.

> Waiting. Waiting. Calling down strange true curses on that printer.
>
> Writing new poems constantly (but not "like a madman")—3 or 4 yest'y [yesterday] or Friday, 2 of them v. witty. Trips [to the Interior, his new projected volume] won't be as ambitious maybe as L. & F. [*Love & Fame*] but I hope excellent.
>
> I am intoxicated by a ravishing raven-haired tall large-eyed full-hipped folksinger who came up to me after Thanksgiving Mass (I'd read some of my Addresses, she'd sung) and embraced & kissed me (50 people, incl[uding]. Kate, her boyfriend, the Priest, standing around)—saying when you'd finished yr. poems, I just said to myself "Yes." Well!
>
> Send me 6 pb [paperback] Homage & Other Poems, and 6 pb 77 D.S. [*Dream Songs*]. Now.
>
> How abt tickets to Home [starring John Gielgud and Ralph Richardson at the Morosco Theater, for which RG sent JB tickets] & the new Beckett evening [*MacGowran on the Works of Beckett* at the Public Theater], around Xmas, for Kate & me? (6th row, bec[ause]. of my hearing loss) I hear my letter is in The Nation.[46] Expect word of his suicide.[47]

While two of Berryman's friends, Adrienne Rich and Richard Wilbur, had minor reservations about the book, poet Robert Phillips, literary executor of the estate of Delmore Schwartz, wrote an unpleasant review:

"John Simon once titled a review of Philip Booth's *Letter from a Distant Land*, 'Postcard from Around the Corner.' Perhaps this review of *Love & Fame* should be captioned, 'Lust & Notoriety.' In any event, in this latest of Berryman's books of confessional poetry he doesn't confess, he merely gossips about himself."[48]

After his release from the hospital in late November, vowing not to touch another drop of alcohol, Berryman was required to undergo out-patient treatment for the next two years. In mid-December he flew to New York and stayed at the Chelsea, where he started drinking again; Kate, now pregnant, did not accompany him. When he met with Giroux about forthcoming projects, he received the first copy of the limited edition of *Love & Fame*. On December 14, he sent Giroux a short, but heart-felt note: "Old friend, your belief in my work has been a help in this hard place—I pray for yr happiness. You [are a] good man."[49]

Berryman also caught up with Lowell, then about to fly to England, in what proved to be their last meeting. Asked when they would meet again, Berryman replied, "Cal, I was thinking through lunch that I'll never see you again."[50] Two days after Christmas, Lowell wrote from London to Berryman, expressing his admiration for *Love & Fame* and adding that he was completely overwhelmed by the sequence "Eleven Addresses to the Lord": "It's one of the great poems of the age, a puzzle and triumph to anyone who wants a personal devotional poem."[51] Berryman could not have had a better tribute, coming as it did from an internationally recognized poet and friend who had negatively critiqued him at a most vulnerable time in his life. It had taken years for Lowell to admire the allusively semantic nature of Berryman's poems, realizing that Berryman's willful indirectness and dizzying virtuosity created a radical rupture from the poetry of his peers. Only by reading Berryman's poetry with sympathetic attentiveness over the years could Lowell finally admire Berryman's esthetic paradigm.

On January 4, 1971, Giroux wrote Berryman at his Arthur Avenue address saying that he had a note from Monteith asking for a setting copy of *Love & Fame*. (Giroux had previously informed Monteith that Berryman was working on revisions and that he must wait for the second edition before proceeding, which meant that they would not be able to publish the British edition until November.) Berryman replied by asking for nine copies of the limited edition, since only a dozen of the regular thirty copies had arrived. He was most concerned that noted writers and critics receive copies.[52] He added a postscript: "The Blue Bk [of Poetry] is marching, marching. . . . I am still writing 2 or 3 poems a week, v much against my will; but am otherwise relaxing somewhat—no drink since I came back—my lectures (Xtian) better even than usual." Berryman wanted his editor to know he was still active and going through an important period of sobriety. Giroux wrote to Berryman in mid-January with an update on his publishing situation: "The copies of the limited edition are now being mailed to you. I gave you No. 1 in New York and the rest of the 250 are now all numbered and ready. . . . There are no paperback copies of LOVE & FAME and it will not be available in Noonday for at least a year, as is our custom. However regular copies are going to all the people you've listed. Monteith writes another letter, begging for the corrections. Relieve his angst, old friend."[53] Giroux felt upset about the paucity and assessment of reviews, though he knew that the *New York Times Book Review* would soon evaluate the book. He shared a less-than-positive note: "Oh well, as Arnold Bennett used to say, 'Don't read your reviews; measure them.'"[54]

As time went on, Tate found Berryman's behavior to be so weird that they gradually grew apart.[55] (Earlier, Berryman had chastised Tate, saying that Tate's lack of consideration for other people was so scandalously notorious that he requested that Tate communicate with him in the future only by letter).[56] Berryman was most upset by a venomous, dismissive letter from Tate, thanking him for a copy of *Love & Fame* but adding, "I don't like it at all. I can't find any love in any of the poems, and to talk about fame as you do would be childish [for] a man of twenty-five, vulgar in a man of fifty-five."[57] What Berryman did not know was that Tate had previously written but not sent him a letter in which he also negatively commented on Lowell's *Notebook: 1968–69:* "What is the matter with you boys? Self-indulgence and exhibitionism have overwhelmed you. You are *not* famous; if you were, you would not refer to it. I can't find *love* anywhere in the book: merely an adolescent boast of sexual prowess. If you are concerned with love, where in the 'poems' is your first wife, who fed, supported, and nursed you *in love?*"[58] As expected, Berryman started drinking again to assuage the inner pain caused by someone he had long admired. He wrote to his former wife, Eileen Simpson, saying that he was so upset he drank for forty hours: "Tate used his hatred of *Love & Fame* as a springboard for reading me out of not only the pantheon of art but the Book of Life; he accused me of every known immaturity . . . and took it upon himself to explain my life-failure as an artist."[59] That his former mentor and current colleague had turned against him added to his mounting sense of self-defeat. He waited well into the new year before sending a card to Tate in Sewanee, Tennessee, from, as he noted on the envelope, one Regents Professor to a Regents Professor Emeritus, with three words already imprinted on the card: "You hurt me."[60] In his own handwriting, Tate added to the card, "This was my intention"—a phrase that Berryman, fortunately, never saw. It is no wonder that when Bellow described Berryman's unfortunate visit to give the annual William Vaughan Moody Lecture at the University of Chicago on January 27, 1971, he wrote, "He had arrived during a sub-zero wave to give a reading in Chicago. High-shouldered in his thin coat and big Homburg, bearded, he coughed up phlegm. He looked decayed and had been drinking. The reading was a disaster. His Princeton mutter, once an affectation, had become a vice."[61] Berryman had failed completely at such a prestigious university; sadly, this was the last time Berryman and Bellow saw each other. Once back in Minneapolis, Berryman's condition, particularly his difficulty with walking, forced another hospital stay, prompting a renewed effort to return to his Alcoholics Anonymous group.

For the moment, Berryman's rage subsided, though he seemed at sixes and sevens in dealing with his various publishing preoccupations, even the second edition of *Love & Fame*. Near the end of January he wrote to Giroux,

> I hope to Christ the first edition sells out quickly and you can reprint: here is the preface (tell me what you think of it) and I want deleted six poems—pp. 48, 51-2, 60-1-2-3—and I'll send you—phone you if necessary—the very few corrections in the text. Too much Italics, no? Will you study this for me? I can't decide. There's one bad misprint, "ball" for "bull" in the (p. 23 top) football passage, and a little rewriting of "Heaven," that's about it. The setting-copy I airmailed to Monteith[;] he has acknowledged but is not certain they can do this spring, transatlantic proofing being the problem, with the current mail embargo no help either.
>
> Please airmail me a copy of either His Toy . . . or the combined Dream Songs volume, whichever you have there in the office. I am unaccountably out of both, while re-studying the whole poem with

two aims: revision of the representation in the <u>Selected Poems '38–68</u> I sent Monteith last year, and revision for possible reprinting by you of either of those two volumes [marginal note: "<u>and</u> the <u>77 D.S.</u>" (Dream Songs)]. I am killing Songs and substituting. I may also do some stylistic & even thematic revision.

The Times reviewer is a cold fish, I agree. He did not hear at all <u>either</u> the suffering or the exaltation in the best poems. On the other hand he didn't really let his distaste loose either (only nailing me as overbearing and cruel—both charges true—WHY did I <u>name</u> [Robert] Creeley & [Professor Emery] Neff??? Initials are not only just as good but better—you might have caught this, Bob, yourself— or maybe you did and I was resistant, in my delusion—anyway, change to initials now . . .) and he did give us one sentence to quote:

> <u>Love & Fame</u> "combines strength and ease with great expertness that is never less than immensely readable, and feels highly reas- suring to one worried about the difficulty of Modernist writing."

Modernist, eh. Where did this professor surface from, anyway—I haven't seen that word for decades.

Frank[lin] Reeve has sent me a carbon of the stunning review he's done for <u>Book World</u>, and it is certainly the most remarkable ac- count of my work written so far.

What stage is the prose-selection in (<u>The Freedom of the Poet</u>)?? Let's get this book out. I am about to start revising that piece by piece, and I could do with a schedule, because I am unbelievably busy with other things—I wrote five poems this week (the book is now called <u>Delusions</u> abt 50 poems written at present and it may be ready by Easter <u>or</u> it may not be ready till Christmas) and the anthology (let's call it <u>A BLUE BOOK OF POETRY</u>) pushes on daily, as I think I told you. Draw up contracts, will you, for some of these books. I am going to need provision for a secretary as of the <u>Blue Book</u>— heavy copying. Of course there is <u>no</u> estimating yet of permission fees. I think I'll send you in a month or so a partial table of contents which might make an estimate feasible. Unfortunately a great bulk of the translations is copyright (Mark [Van Doren] 40 years ago could rely largely on very old translations but that is absolutely no longer possible, the last two decades have revolutionized the availability in English of world poetry ancient medieval & modern).

Two deeply engaging new scale-poems under way. One 9-poem sequence (3 done) called <u>Opus Dei</u> and a large poem on Che Guevara. I owe you for the theatre tickets [see letters dated "Sun. morning" (December 1970)].[62]

Because of the manner in which Berryman submitted revisions to his books, they were sometimes difficult to track. He needed all the strength he could muster to continue working on his anthology, *The Blue Book of Poetry*, as well as his next poetry book, *Delusions, etc.*, which would include the "Opus Dei" poems, reminiscent of Auden's *Horae Canonicae*, that recall the fixed canonical hours of prayer that the Church prays throughout the day.

Giroux replied in his typical, systematic fashion on February 4, precisely so that Berryman might understand even better certain controversial editorial positions, as well as plans for future publications:

Are you sure you want to kill those [six] poems? To put it another way, can you? They've been printed, and whether or not they appear in the second edition, they will always be available for quoting and comment. In fact, if you take them out you draw attention to them, as the opening sentence of your *scholia* does. I also wonder if there's any point now in changing [Emery] Neff to N and [Robert] Creeley to C, when everyone now knows who N and C are. I did suggest using initials throughout, when you first sent the script, but you wanted Van Doren and others spelt out and I assumed you had good reason for these two "enemies" being known. (Most of the names are initials).

The situation is this: we printed 6,000 copies in the first edition of LOVE & FAME plus 250 copies in the limited edition. It is already down to 1,000 copies; when the regular edition gets to 500 we have to order a second printing. That will probably come in late February or early March. So if these changes are to be made—and I'm preparing copy for the printer—we shall have to move ahead. So you decide; call me collect, with a red light or green.

My feelings about the *scholia* are mixed. What does it achieve (brilliantly written though it is) that the poems themselves do not say? If you insist on its going in, let me delete all the italics, except "unreal" and "unchanged" in 4, and of course <u>The Romantic</u>. Also, let it be added at the end rather than in the front matter, no?

A further thought. Wouldn't it be better to wait for the paperback edition of LOVE & FAME in, say, the spring or fall of 1972 to do this revised edition? There really seems more point to it at that stage than in what is, after all, just the second printing. Also: more time to get perspective on it. You've asked me for my thoughts and I've taken some days to brood, and them's my sentiments, pal.

I want to get off this now, and I'll write separately about contracts for THE FREEDOM OF THE POET and A BLUE BOOK OF POETRY and other matters. . . . The theatre tickets were charged by Pat [Irving] to your royalty account last December.

When the second, revised edition of *Love & Fame* was published in New York on November 15, 1972, Giroux assumed that the revisions for the Faber & Faber edition done in March and June 1971 were the same as those Berryman had previously made for Farrar, Straus & Giroux the preceding January. "In any event," as Thornbury wrote in his commentary, "it is clear that Berryman's last revisions were in the FF [Faber & Faber] edition."[63]

Giroux soon sent Berryman two copies of a contract for *The Freedom of the Poet*; though the delivery date was given as September, it could easily be changed because Giroux had a good deal of the contents in hand.[64] Some details needed attention, however, such as assembling all the essays and determining copyright assignments, especially those related to the *Kenyon Review*, which had ceased publication in 1969 (though it would be revived ten years later). As soon as Giroux had a complete manuscript and could get manufacturing estimates, he would write to Monteith and get a Faber & Faber contract too. He added a postscript: "I've forgotten about the poetry anthology. The contract for that, as I'm sure you realize, is tied in with the permission problem, and therefore must await your final or semi-final table of contents." Absorbed with the editorial details of *The Freedom of the Poet*, Giroux could never have predicted the next three projects Berryman was contemplating—a life of Christ, *Delusions, etc.*, and a novel. He wrote to Berryman,

What a marvelous letter from an author. The most exciting item for me was the life of Christ you're doing for Martha [Berryman's daughter]. This is unexpected and intriguing news; tell me more. How long a book do you think it will be? Do you intend it for children primarily? Using illustrations by great painters could be quite a feature. I'd like to talk to the others about it, with your permission, and I'd appreciate further details, including the deadline you have in mind. I think it's a great idea.

Let me brood some more about a better title for THE FREE-DOM OF THE POET. I enclose your copy of the contract and the check for the advance. DELUSIONS & as you described it on the phone is really exciting. If it turns out to be ready for the fall of next year (and it sounds as if it will), I'd be delighted. And the news of the novel [*Recovery*] caught me completely by surprise. When I come out in July, a prospective godfather, I want to hear all about it.[65]

Two questions needed to be asked: was there any real hope of bringing these works to a satisfactory conclusion, especially as Berryman was experiencing a deeper sense of his own mortality? Would they be so rushed that they would lessen Berryman's reputation as an award-winning poet?

After receiving an honorary degree (his first) in May at Drake University in Des Moines, Iowa, Berryman met Meredith at the airport in Hartford, Connecticut, so they could travel to a poetry festival at Goddard College in northern Vermont. While on the way, they stayed in Woodstock, Vermont, where late in the evening Meredith witnessed Berryman composing the inscription for his tombstone: "John Berryman, 1914–19—('There's no particular hurry about that last date'), and then, very loud: 'Fantastic! Fantastic! Thank Thee, Dear Lord.'"[66] Amid a gathering of poets at the Goddard festival, including Louise Glück, Galway Kinnell, Charles Simic, and James Tate, Berryman, taking many unwarranted and unscheduled verbal detours, took ninety minutes to read five Dream Songs. On their flight to Boston, he slipped Tate the draft of the poem "How Do You Do, Dr Berryman, Sir?," including the ominous phrase *"he'd just as soon be dead / (on the Promise of—I know it sounds incredible— / if can he muster penitence enough— / he can't though— / glory)"* (emphasis mine).[67]

More than any other poem, Berryman's "The Facts & Issues" is the most searing pronouncement of his impending death:

Let me be clear about this. It is plain to me
Christ underwent man & treachery & socks
& lashes, thirst, exhaustion, the bit, for my pathetic & disgusting
    vices,
to make this filthy fact of particular, long-after,
faraway, five-foot-ten & moribund
human being happy. Well, he has!
I am so happy I could scream!
It's *enough*! I can't BEAR ANY MORE.
Let this be it. I've *had* it. I can't wait.[68]

After heading home by way of Washington, DC, where he visited his mentally failing, seventy-six-year-old mother, Berryman finished his teaching obligations and reflected further on the new novel. He hoped, too, that he might receive a grant from the National Endowment for the Humanities to work on his long-simmering Shakespeare book.

Berryman wrote Giroux that he had found the contract for *The Freedom of the Poet* and was open to suggestions for a new title, since he agreed that *Selected Essays* had little impact. Their recent telephone conversation, he noted, had helped him in organizing his future plans:

Present plan:

1)   vol. essays / stories—Spr. '72
2)   *Delusions, etc.*—Fall '72
3)   *Recovery* (the novel)—'73?
4)   *Shakespeare's Reality*—74?
5)   *The Blue Book of Poetry* (ed.)
6?) I am also doing a *Life of Christ* for Martha: illustrated—e.g. Titian's great 'Scourging' in the Pinakothek [der Moderne in Munich].[69]

He enclosed the syllabus of one of his present seminars: readings from the New Testament, *The Tempest*, Whitman's poems, Freud's *Civilization and Its Discontents*, *The Meaning of Death* edited by Herman Feifel, *The World of the Child* edited by Toby Talbot, and Tolstoy's *Master and Man*. This letter amazed Giroux with its ambition and succinctness, though he realized at the same time there was something inexplicably disturbing about it, since he knew how depressed Berryman was over some of the reactions to *Love & Fame*. Giroux said in a letter dated May 19 that he would be delighted if *Delusions, etc.* were ready by the fall of the following year, though, in fact, the typescript was finished by late summer.[70] Giroux also wanted to include in *The Freedom of the Poet* what he considered one of Berryman's best stories, "Wash Far Away," as well as "The Ritual of W. B. Yeats," a general review and analysis of six plays from *The Collected Plays of William Butler Yeats*, which was first published by Berryman in the *Columbia Review* (May–June 1936). In reviewing the final table of contents, Berryman put the stories last but never veered from his five-fold plan.[71] Once Berryman had finished teaching his last seminar, for which he asked Van Doren, Meredith, and Ross to fill out forms evaluating his competence as an academic, he worked four hours a day on *Recovery*, his novel about the "real world, people, events, [and] history," and hoped to finish seven sections by Christmas.[72]

Kate gave birth on June 13 to Sarah Rebecca, their second daughter. John's mother arrived shortly beforehand and moved into a new apartment at 26 Arthur Avenue S.E. Soon afterward, Giroux flew to Minneapolis to participate in the baptismal ceremony as Sarah's godfather at the university's Newman Center. He found Berryman more confident and serene than he had been in years, having apparently conquered his addiction to alcohol.[73] Having his editor in town provided a psychological boost to Berryman, who showed Giroux twenty-five pages of his novel to prove that he was making progress. He told Giroux, "It will have the greatest number of technical details about alcoholism ever to appear in a book. I *know*, I'm an expert!"[74] Giroux especially enjoyed the moment he spotted Martha, the Berrymans' older daughter, at her father's typewriter. For the time being, however, Berryman put aside assembling the essays for *The Freedom of the Poet* and leapfrogged ahead to thoughts of another book of essays, tentatively called *Sacrifices*—a title that might reflect his inner thoughts about going through enormous struggles, with perhaps a Christian hint of something about survival afterward. When Berryman showed Giroux a sheaf of notes about this book, Giroux copied down some unexpected, optimistic observations: "An entirely new kind of freedom manifested in several ways, in retirement, in death, but invariably in a special retirement or death that contains as one of its chief meanings a repudiation of the earlier 'freedom.' There is a *conversion*, in short, if we can employ the term without either religious or psychoanalytic overtones. Someone is changed, simply, into someone else."[75] Later, on July 8, Giroux sent Berryman the contract for *Recovery*; the one for *Delusions, etc.* would follow shortly. In a follow-up letter the next day, he mentioned that they were aiming to publish the second book in late March or early April. (*Delusions, etc.* would in fact be published posthumously in New York in April 1972 and in England in December 1972, both with a dedication "TO MARTHA B / passion & awe.") However, facing age as well as his addictions, Berryman felt increasingly pressed in and even, at times, totally defeated and dejected. Thus he took Martha and Paul (who had come for a visit after not seeing his father for twelve years) on a short vacation in Colorado in mid-July.

After an anonymous, condescending, and dismissive review of Allen Tate's *The Swimmers and Other Selected Poems* and *Essays of Four Decades* appeared in the *Times Literary Supplement* (March 19, 1971), stating that "few poems entice one to a second reading," Conrad Aiken wrote to the *TLS* that he considered the review "barbarous" (April 9, 1971). Berryman wanted to add his own personal commentary. In a letter to the editor, he acknowledged, in a seeming volte-face, that "without Mr. Tate's assistance at several points, my career, such as it is, would not have been what it is" (July 30, 1971). His public view of Tate, however, did not coincide with his private feelings about this former mentor, who wrote "half a dozen lyrics to his credit" and whose "Ode to the Confederate Dead" was overblown and inflated.[76]

After receiving a pin from AA for being sober for seven months, Berryman flew to the Berkeley Faculty Club in California in late July to try to get some work done, hoping to have 250 pages of *Recovery* written by Labor Day.[77] Outlining writing projects proved easy for him to do, but the execution of each demanded more discipline than he could muster. That fall, as he resumed teaching and put *Delusions, etc.* into final form— one that, unfortunately, lacked a visible structure and cohesion—he continued going to AA meetings while feeling that his efforts were inadequate. Indeed, his marriage was incredibly strained. He sent his revisions of *Recovery* to Giroux in October in an attempt to placate his editor as best he could: "I've been over this. There are insertions & hundreds of things to be done to it. The question is—my morale is unbelievably low at present—whether it's worth going on with. Parts V–VIII will be rather different, esp. in that he gets hit for not listening to lectures, and does, so there's more [reporting?] of them. . . . A revised Delusions etc. went off to [Richard] Wilbur & Robt. Fitzgerald last Friday. Both have promised to let me know. I told them: 'Have no mercy!'"[78] He noted in a postscript, "I am proceeding w Shak's [Shakespeare's] Friend tomorrow. We'll see abt that. Teaching is onerous; I have 21 pre-professional Honors seniors (only 2 dopes), not the legal 15." The frenzied activity continued unabated, but few seemed to hear his impassioned cri de coeur.

By mid-October, Giroux had received the 172 pages of *Recovery*, which impressed him enormously, especially given Berryman's teaching responsibilities. The questions still remained: how long could Berryman keep on writing at such a feverish pace, and would the quality be as good as his previous published works? Wilbur wrote to Berryman on October 20, "I don't find all of it best Berryman, and . . . my vote, for what it is worth, is for some deletions and additions. Had you not class and continuing oomph, I would not cavil."[79] Fitzgerald returned to Berryman a copy of the typescript of *Delusions, etc.* with his critical observations, suggesting that Berryman delete certain poems.[80] Subsequently, Berryman sent Giroux the revised table of contents based on his friends' comments. At the end of the month, Berryman wrote Meredith, not in a chatty way, as he had done before, but more in the style of a biblical lamentation: "If I cd see even just you & Giroux occas'y I'd feel more human."[81] In sending Giroux a new draft of *Delusions, etc.*, more complete except for several revised sections of "Opus Dei" and a request to replace Sonnet 116 with "The Handshake, The Entrance," he signaled the disarray brought about by working on several manuscripts at the same time: "Herewith, except: (1) I can't locate the carbons of several revised sections of Opus Dei—I may come on them over the weekend—or Bob Silvers has a revised master of the whole poem at The New York Review he could throw downtown. . . . I've gone on with the novel, cheered by my talk with you and a long letter from Bellow beginning 'It's a powerful piece of writing—faulty, yes,' and ending 'You've the makings of a first-rate novel here.'"[82] While awaiting copies of Faber & Faber's edition of *Love & Fame*, he read proofs of their *Selected Poems, 1938–1968*, which would be published in May 1972; he found them fairly clean except that the conclusions of two early poems were entirely missing. He wrote to Giroux, "You cd telephone him [Bob Silvers]—I only sent them that Xtian poem on a whim anyway. You have one of the Opus Dei revisions, sent w T-P [*The Freedom of the Poet*]. Kill the parenthetical line abt [Robert] Frost early in 'Damn you, Jim D—, You Woke Me Up.'" He added other minor revisions, thus finally putting the table of contents into the order he had envisioned.

Berryman learned in early November that he had been awarded a senior fellowship from the National Endowment for the Humanities for the following year, which meant that he might have to change his lifestyle (including smoking up to four packs of cigarettes a day) and acquire a mental toughness and discipline that would, realistically, be impossible. In his application for this fellowship, he had explained the research he had done over the years on Shakespeare, sometimes with arrogant and rhetorical flourishes that failed to impress Van Doren, who told Berryman, up front and without reservation, that he would never finish the Shakespeare book.[83] Berryman informed Giroux that he would send another letter with more corrections for the Faber & Faber edition of his *Selected Poems*, but for the time being the following changes for *Delusions, etc.* would suffice:

> Here's a better table of contents. I've kept several poems Dick Wilbur strongly supported (against Fitzgerald—without of course knowing it) and I think just one he was dubious on but [indecipherable words] about. I have to trust my own judgment in the end. I'd be glad to have [yours?] too, tho'.
>
> A number have been revised since your copy, among them "Nones," which I enclose because Dick calls the top 8 lines or so of its second page "the pure note" (don't quote him) and possibly, if you want a verse quotation for the jacket-paragraph, they might do.
>
> You'll have setting-copy early next month, *suppose I live that long* [emphasis mine]. I am down to 137 lb, less than I've weighed since I was in the 4th Form, and Monday alas I'll be 57—if I get there.[84]

Giroux replied that he had received the revised poems and new table of contents and was expecting the final drafts of the "Opus Dei" poems from Bob Silvers.[85] Everything seemed to be in order for the publication, except that Giroux could not find "Gislebertus' Eve," based on a carving of Eve in the Autun cathedral in the Burgundy region of France. He also inquired about several previous magazine appearances in order to straighten out the copyrights—always an agonizing subject for a poet with little interest in keeping such records. Silvers subsequently called Giroux and read off a list of titles, including "Interstitial Office" (a title referencing a liturgical prayer hour invented by Berryman), which both Giroux and Berryman thought should be omitted.

On November 19, Giroux acknowledged receipt of "Gislebertus' Eve," one of his favorite poems in the book, which he would place at the beginning of part 3, as Berryman had indicated in the table of contents. The lines of this poem reveal an exquisite control of language: "So now we see where we are, which is all-over / we're nowhere, son, and suffering we know it, / rapt in delusion."[86] Once Giroux had dealt with three more copyright assignments, the book would be finished.

Giroux's last words to Berryman were, "Jean [Stafford] was in town yesterday for lunch, and joins me in sending you our love." Berryman taught his last class on December 7. Part of the entry in his journal notes for December 13 reveal utter desperation: "Continual thoughts of suicide—cowardly, cruel, wicked—beating them off. / Don't *believe* gun or knife; *won't*. . . . obsessed with Daddy's grave."[87] In his poem "Dry Eleven Months," a reference to the long sobriety that unfortunately did not last until the end of his life, he wrote, "Now I see sitting large / and sane and near an altogether new / & well advised tribunal," perhaps an allusion to some heavenly and considerate judge who is well advised of all the circumstances, both good and bad, and of all that is in-between, even affording a moment of peace before someone commits suicide.[88] In a copy of Bellow's *Dangling Man*, Berryman wrote on December 30, "I feel I am a sort of human grenade whose pin has been withdrawn. I know I am going to explode and I am continually anticipating the time, with a prayerful despair crying 'Boom!' but always prematurely."[89]

On the morning of January 7, 1972, fifty-seven-year-old Berryman, who had recently relapsed and started drinking again, headed toward the university, intending to cross the Washington Avenue Bridge that connected its two parts. At about 9:30, he leaped to his death from the bridge, waving to a number of students in a glass-enclosed walkway before hitting a knoll, after which his body rolled down toward the river. His death sent shockwaves through the students and faculty on campus as well as the larger poetic community. One of Berryman's students, David Wojahn, remembered this event years later in his poem "A Fifteenth Anniversary: John Berryman":

> . . . I stood on the Washington
> Avenue Bridge that day,
> an acned college kid, and in the class I took from you
> all three hundred of us,

your teaching assistants not least, feared you and your wrath,
    feared the days when,

at the desk you lectured from, you'd sleep the class's
    first half hour, waking
with a start to mumble gossip on the Medicis. Two months
    and you'd be dead,
a story we all know, waving from the guardrail to passersby,
    who must have been,

at first, quite puzzled. . . . You chose the country's
    ugliest bridge, the one

I aimlessly walked that day and every day for six
    uneventful years.

Jill Berryman telephoned Giroux with the terrible news that her son had committed suicide, mentioning in a theatrical tone that, as Giroux told me, "John has walked in under the water." Later, Giroux realized that the phrase was from the Dream Song "Henry's Understanding," which describes Henry going "down the bluff / into the terrible water" and "walking forever / under it out toward the island."[90]

In retrospect, one could well ask: what did Berryman think about suicide? Perhaps the answer can be found in the following passage, which he underscored in a copy of the 1967 *A New Catechism: Catholic Faith for Adults*: "As regards suicide, this is sometimes the result of hypertension or depressions, and we cannot pass judgment."[91] During the Mass of the Resurrection at the Church of Saint Frances Cabrini, with the Reverend Robert Hazel presiding, Giroux delivered a eulogy. Most telling were readings of Dream Songs 27 and 77, as well as the eighth of the "Eleven Addresses to the Lord." The body of John Berryman was buried in Resurrection Cemetery in Saint Paul, Minnesota. The simple gravestone, inscribed with a Celtic cross, merely gives his name, date of birth, and date of death.

In the ensuing weeks, Kate Berryman bought a duplex across the street from their old one and graciously invited her mother-in-law to live in its upstairs apartment. Jill Berryman wanted Giroux, Bellow, and Robben Wright Fleming, the president of the university, to form a committee to prove that her son's death was not the result of suicide. Needless to say, this was not done. Before long, too, it was rumored that Berryman left a note to Lowell: "Your move, Cal."[92] Lowell's elegiac poem, "For John Berryman (After reading his last *Dream Song*)," does not mention this provocation:

> I used to want to live
> to avoid your elegy.
> Yet really we had the same life,
> the generic one
> our generation offered. . . .
>
> We asked to be obsessed with writing,
> and we were. . . .
>
> You got there first.
> Just the other day,
> I discovered how we differ—humor . . .
> even in this last *Dream Song*,
> to mock your catlike flight
> from home to classes—
> to leap from the bridge.[93]

This poem recalls an unpublished Berryman poem that links death by water with the death of Berryman's father:

> My father still in my dreams uneasy I see
> Still tramping the dark beach and down at me
> Strangely looking. O my father! rest,
> For if you cannot rest
> I must rejoin you by the shameful sea.[94]

Berryman's religious faith toward the end had luminous clarity: "I fell back in love with you, Father, for two reasons: / You were good to me, & a delicious author, / rational & passionate."[95] A portion of "A Morning Prayer" reveals his simple but extraordinary effort to reunite himself with his family, friends, and especially God: "Reconcile me to my sufferings. Make tranquil my nerves. Keep Kate & me to a fuller understanding & a deeper love. Keep me active today, & grant me accuracy & insight into my work. Preserve me today from the desire to drink & if it comes enable me to lay it aside unsatisfied. Enlighten me on the problem of personal immortality. Bless everybody in the world, especially some of them, Thou knowest whom. Amen."[96]

In early May, five of Berryman's literary friends, Van Doren, Fitzgerald, Meredith, Rich, and Wright, spoke to a capacity audience in the Donnell Library in New York, reminiscing about Berryman and playing the taped voice of the poet himself.[97]

After Jill Berryman died on September 10, 1976, at age eighty-two, having suffered from Alzheimer's disease, her body was cremated and her ashes placed in her son's grave.

In looking back on Giroux's relationship with Berryman, Simpson wrote, "Bob Giroux, who continued to be [John's] editor from the publication of *Homage to Mistress Bradstreet* until his death, was the one person I could count on for a balanced picture."[98] While living and working in New York for fifteen years at the end of the last century, I came to know and admire Simpson. When she died at age eighty-four, on October 21, 2002, I co-officiated at her funeral liturgy at Saint Thomas More Church on East Ninetieth Street in New York. I also presided at her internment in Princeton, New Jersey, surrounded by her friends and relatives, including her sister Marie (now married to George C. Hall), James Childs Mabry IV, Giroux, and Reilly.

Toward the turn of the last century, Giroux and Reilly, who had lived together for many years at 10 Huron Avenue in Jersey City, moved to Seabrook Village, a ninety-eight-acre senior living community in Tinton Falls, New Jersey. Because Reilly, who grew up on Montgomery Street, across from Van Vorst Park in Jersey City, had extended family in the larger Tinton Falls area, both men found the transition fairly easy. Alert until the very end, Giroux died on September 5, 2008.[99] I presided at his funeral liturgy in Saint Elizabeth's Church in Avon-by-the-Sea before a congregation of his friends, relatives, and colleagues, including Jonathan Galassi, who became editor in chief at Farrar, Straus & Giroux in 1987 and later served as president and publisher of the firm. Giroux was buried in nearby Saint Margaret's Cemetery. After Reilly's death on October 7, 2009, I presided at his funeral in Saint Elizabeth's Church. His funeral plot is adjacent to Giroux's. Right up to the end, the two of them never failed to help others, professionally and personally, with great wit and discernment.

After Berryman's death, four volumes of his works were published, all edited by Giroux: *Delusions, etc.* (a volume of poetry, 1972), *Recovery* (a novel with one story, "The Imaginary Jew," 1973), *The Freedom of the Poet* (a collection of essays and stories, 1976), and *Henry's Fate & Other Poems: 1967–1972* (1977, with an introduction by John Haffenden). In addition, *Berryman's Shakespeare* (1999, edited by John Haffenden, with a preface by Robert Giroux) is a splendid testimony to Berryman's critical attention to the Bard, whom he and Giroux first embraced while students at Columbia.

Chapter One

1. RG was the author of *BKQ* (1982); JB was the author of *BS* (1999); MVD was the author of *Shakespeare* (1939).

2. JB also wanted to write a book on Shakespeare's friend, W. H., a primary focus of RG's book (see, for example, the letter of JB to RG, dated September 26, 1963).

3. See RG, "Henry's Understanding," for background on the friendship of JB and RG.

4. Lehman, foreword and introduction to *Shakespeare*, by MVD, x–xi.

5. See Lehman, "Robert Giroux '36," 32; Anonymous, "Interview with Robert Giroux," 6.

6. See RG, preface to JB, *BS*, ix; PM, *DS*, 77. Email from Bill Statin, Office of the Registrar, Columbia University, dated February 1, 2016, to PS verifies that RG and JB took MVD's two-semester course on Shakespeare.

7. Original essay is in Berg.

8. See David McClelland, John Poltz, Robert Shaw, and Thomas Stewart, "Interview with John Berryman," in *Berryman's Understanding*, ed. Harry Thomas, 5.

9. MVD, *Autobiography*, 213.

10. Letter is in RGPF.

11. See JH, *LJB*, 12; PM, *DS*, 6.

12. Jill Berryman, quoted in JB, *WDH*, 274.

13. See PM, *DS*, 10, 346.

14. See JH, *LJB*, 34.

15. See JH, *LJB*, 27–28.

16. JB, *WDH*, 379. See PM, *DS*, 11–13, 199; JH, *LJB*, 24–26, 32–33; the coroner's account of Smith's death, as quoted in JH, *LJB*, 28–29; ES, *PTY*, 62–65. The Saint Petersburg *Evening Independent* ran an obituary on June 28, 1926, for John Allen [*sic*] Smith, age thirty-five, which noted that a coroner's jury returned

a verdict of suicide. Smith had been living in Clearwater Beach for the previous two weeks. Mrs. Smith testified before the coroner's jury that she found an unsigned note, presumably from her husband, stating that he had been unable to sleep for three nights and had suffered from terrible headaches. Bloodstains were found on his shirt, but there were no traces of powder burns on the body. An automatic pistol, .32 caliber, was lying near his dead body. Suits for divorce had been filed by Mr. and Mrs. Smith, both charging infidelity. According to Mrs. Smith, her husband committed suicide because he had been unable to secure employment in Florida. PM states that Mr. Smith, on the verge of a divorce from his wife, "allegedly" shot himself. What really happened is perhaps beyond recovery (see PM, *DS*, 13). It should be noted that JB's poem "Of Suicide" begins with the following line: "Reflexions on suicide, & on my father, possess me" (JB, *Collected Poems*, 206).

17. See RG, "Henry's Understanding," 99–103; PM, *DS*, 13.

18. See JH, *LJB*, 192; JB, *WDH*, 368.

19. RG, preface to JB, *BS*, x.

20. See JB, *WDH*, 279–80, 283. For various versions of this incident, see ES, *PTY*, 60, 63–65, 237. RG felt comfortable telling PS his deeply felt conviction about the events surrounding the death of John's father, most likely with the intention that it would be put into print as a way of solving a murder mystery, a subject that never ceased to fascinate him, as seen in his *A Deed of Death: The Story behind the Unsolved Murder of Hollywood Director William Desmond Taylor*. In an exchange of letters with his mother in early December 1954, JB is fairly direct in asking whether his father preferred him or his brother, Robert. "Your comments," he writes to his mother in one letter, "on my father's motives in taking Bob out with him [into deep water] seem to me shrewd & just as well as justly charitable. The final thrashings of my father's life seem to me (tell me what you think of this) those of a rather cold & inexpressive man feeling both so guilty and so rejected that what had been all his life (unjustly) hidden from him boiled *irresponsibly* up and unmanageably up in such a way as to bring him before no tribunal known to us. But I can't quite *see* my father; I don't *know* him. Well, who does know his father who died when he was twelve? R.I.P." (letter probably written on December 10, 1954. JB, *WDH*, 283).

21. ES, *PTY*, 59.

22. "Tampa Stomp" was first published in *Esquire* (April 1971). See JB, *WDH*, 376–77; JB, *Recovery*, 49, 79, 81, 138, 191; PM, *DS*, 472–73.

23. JB, *The Dream Songs*, 406.

24. See CT, "A Reckoning with Ghostly Voices (1935–36)," in *Recovering Berryman*, ed. Kelly and Lathrop, 80. JB also started, but never finished, an autobiographical sketch about suicide entitled "Toward 48" (see PM, *DS*, 395).

25. Other Dream Songs that focus on JB's father include 34, 42, 76, 136, 143, 145, 235, and 384.

26. See Anonymous, "Interview with John Berryman," 4.

27. PM and JH give two different addresses for this apartment. The picture of John and Robert Berryman and Uncle Jack taken on the day of John's graduation in June 1928 reveals the steps leading up to Spanish Gardens. See PM, *DS*, 106 (D).

28. See CT's introduction to JB, *Collected Poems*, xxi.

29. JB, *Love & Fame*, 13.

30. See JH, *LJB*, 38, 48; PM, *DS*, 22.

31. JB, *WDH*, 29.

32. JB, *WDH*, 28.

33. See ES, *PTY*, 13; JB, *WDH*, 377.

34. For an overview of JB's years at Columbia, see Halliday, *John Berryman and the Thirties*, 3–42.

35. JB, *Collected Poems*, 184.

36. See JB, *WDH*, 89.

37. Halliday, *John Berryman and the Thirties*, 9.

38. RL, *Day by Day*, 121.

39. See JB, "Three and a Half Years at Columbia," in *University on the Heights*, ed. Wesley First, 51.

40. JB, *Love & Fame*, 15.

41. Dean Hawkes, quoted in JH, *JBCC*, 74. Robert Berryman, JB's brother, later wrote to MVD on December 1, 1941, that he was resigning from Columbia at the suggestion of Dean Hawkes (Berg).

42. JB, quoted in Halliday, *John Berryman and the Thirties*, 64.

43. MVD, *Autobiography*, 211.

44. See JB, *WDH*, 213. For an analysis of Blackmur's poetry, see Vanouse, "The Complete Poems of R. P. Blackmur." See also J. Bloom, *The Stock of Available Reality: R. P. Blackmur and John Berryman*.

45. JB, *WDH*, 61–62.

46. See McGregor, *Pure Act*, 33–34; JH, *LJB*, 71.

47. For a complete list of JB's publications while at Columbia, see Stefanik, *John Berryman*, 175–76.

48. RG, "Prelude," 5.

49. See Matterson, *Berryman and Lowell*, 36–40; Coleman, *John Berryman's Public Vision*, 26–27, 66–67.

50. JB, "The Ball Poem," in JB, *Two Poems*, n.p. Reprinted in JB, *The Dispossessed*, 14.

51. These poems are in RGPF. See JB, *WDH*, 33–35; CT, "A Reckoning with Ghostly Voices (1935–36)," in *Recovering Berryman*, ed. Kelly and Lathrop, 84, 109n18.

52. See RG, "Henry's Understanding," 99.

53. See letters of JB to RG, dated February 27, 1964, and "Wed," 1966.

54. RG, "Score One." This version was typed by RG and given as a gift to PS on February 7, 2000.

55. See Freed-Thall, *Spoiled Distinctions*, 49–52. "Le vent qui soufflait tirait horizontalement les herbes folles qui avaient poussé dans la paroi du mur, et les plumes de duvet de la poule, qui, les unes et les autres se laissaient filer au gré de son souffle jusqu'à l'extrémité de leur longueur, avec l'abandon de choses inertes et légères. Le toit de tuile faisait dans la mare, que le soleil rendait de nouveau réfléchissante, une marbrure rose, à laquelle je n'avais encore jamais fait attention. Et voyant sur l'eau et à la face du mur un pâle sourire répondre au sourire du ciel, je m'écriai dans mon enthousiasme en brandissant mon parapluie refermé: 'Zut, zut, zut, zut.'" (The wind tugged at the wild grass growing from the cracks in the wall and at the hen's downy feathers, which floated out horizontally to their full extent with the unresisting submissiveness of light and lifeless things. The tiled roof cast upon the pond, translucent again in the sunlight, a dappled pink reflection which I have never observed before. And, seeing upon the water, and on the surface of the wall, a pallid smile responding to the smiling sky, I cried out aloud in my enthusiasm, brandishing my furled umbrella: "Gosh, gosh, gosh, gosh!") See Proust, *In Search of Lost Time*, 1:218–19. Translation from Freed-Thall, *Spoiled Distinctions*, 50.

56. RG, "Who's Got Function," 5–6.

57. See RG, "Films."

58. See Coleman, *John Berryman's Public Vision*, 122–27.

59. RG, "On Being a Film Crank," 37.

60. Trilling, "A Recollection of Raymond Weaver," in *University on the Heights*, ed. First, 6.

61. JB, "Three and a Half Years at Columbia," in *University on the Heights*, ed. First, 55.

62. RG, "Henry's Understanding," 97.

63. See Kostelanetz, "Conversation with Berryman," 341.

64. The November 1935 issue contained a description of a car accident entitled "At the Corner" by Thomas Merton, thus making RG, still a coeditor, Merton's first editor, a position he resumed later when he edited and published Merton's highly successful autobiography *The Seven Storey Mountain*, in addition to twenty-five books by and about Merton, including his letters and journals.

65. JB, *Collected Poems*, 172.

66. Matterson, *Berryman and Lowell*, 9. See David McClelland John Poltz, Robert Shaw, and Thomas Stewart, "Interview with John Berryman," in *Berryman's Understanding*, ed. Thomas, 15.

67. In RL, *Collected Poems*, 737–38; see also *New York Review of Books* 18, no. 6 (April 6, 1972): 3–4.

68. JB, quoted in Halliday, *John Berryman and the Thirties*, 79. See JH, *LJB*, 73

69. JB, quoted in Halliday, *John Berryman and the Thirties*, 77. Some sense of Edman's philosophy can be gleaned from his 1933 essay "Man and Socialization," in which he discusses art and thought in modern society by stressing that the imaginative and creative students have the wit and insight to see the beginnings and the necessity of a new social order.

70. See M. Halsey Thomas, "The Golden Day," in *University on the Heights*, ed. First, 117; Halliday, *John Berryman and the Thirties*, 65.

71. Letter of JB to MVD, dated "Mpls. Tues. morning" [1971] (Berg).

72. JB, "Notes on Poetry," 20.

73. Henry first made his appearance in JB's poetry in 1958 and remained JB's semiautobiographical poetic persona, though many critics would nuance the figure of Henry in detail. In an interview, JB explained the origin of this name and its relationship to himself: "I'll tell you where it came from. My second wife, Ann, and I were walking down Hennepin Avenue [in Minneapolis] one momentous night. Everything seemed quite usual, but it was going to puzzle literary critics on two continents for many years later. Anyway, we were joking on our way to a bar to have a beer, and I decided that I hated the name Mabel more than any other female name. . . . We had passed from names we liked to names we disliked, and she decided that Henry was the name that she found completely unbearable. So from then on . . . she was Mabel and I was Henry in our scene." Stitt, "The Art of Poetry XVI," 193–94.

74. Letter is in PU.

75. MVD, quoted in *Columbia Daily Spectator* 59, no. 129 (May 1, 1936), 1.

76. MVD, "A Critic's Job of Work," 27.

77. MVD, "A Critic's Job of Work," 27.

78. See PM, *DS*, 70.

79. See JB, *WDH*, 43, 69, 89, 99. After writing to Yeats in the fall of 1936 and giving a talk on him on February 1937 at Clare College's Dilettante Society at Cambridge University and to the Nashe Society in Saint John's College, JB had tea with him in the Athenaeum in London in April 1937.

80. JB's second letter to AT, in which he mentions Putnam, is dated April 27, 1939. Both letters are in PU. JB's letter to Putnam is dated April 16, 1939. See Coleman and McGowan, "*After Thirty Falls*," 1. For an analysis of the relationship between Yeats and JB, see Coleman, *John Berryman's Public Vision*, 46–54.

81. JB, "Three and a Half Years at Columbia," in *University on the Heights*, ed. First, 58.

82. JB, "Three and a Half Years at Columbia," in *University on the Heights*, ed. First, 58.

83. JB, *Love & Fame*, 28–29.

84. Halliday, *John Berryman and the Thirties*, 98.

85. AT quoted in JB, *WDH*, 55, 65. See CT, "A Reckoning with Ghostly Voices (1935–36)," in *Recovering Berryman*, ed. Kelly and Lathrop, 89.

86. See JB, *WDH*, 65.

87. See PM, *DS*, 61; CT, "A Reckoning with Ghostly Voices (1935–36)," in *Recovering Berryman*, ed. Kelly and Lathrop, 91–93.

88. See PM, *DS*, 57.

89. See Halliday, *John Berryman and the Thirties*, 33.

90. JB, *Collected Poems*, 188.

Chapter Two

1. For an account of JB's student life at Cambridge, see JH, "John Berryman: The American Poet at Cambridge."

2. Letter dated October 8, 1936 (PU).

3. Letter is in PU.

4. JB amassed a large collection of books while in Cambridge, including Mathew Arnold's *Poems* and *Essays in Criticism*; The Agamemnon of Aeschylus; W. H. Auden's *Look, Stranger!*; *The Poetry and Prose of William Blake* and *The Prophetic Writings of William Blake*; Anne Bradby's *Shakespeare Criticism: 1919–1935*; A. C. Bradley's *Shakespearean Tragedy*; Van Wyck Brooks's *The Pilgrimage of Henry James*; Samuel Butler's *Notebooks* and *Hudibras: A Poem*; Thomas Campion's *Works*; E. K. Chambers's *William Shakespeare: A Study of Facts and Problems*; *The Complete Works of Geoffrey Chaucer*; Anton Chekhov's *That Worthless Fellow Platonov*; Samuel Taylor Coleridge's *Biographia Literaria* and *Lectures on Shakespeare, Etc.*; Coleridge's *Select Poetry and Prose*, *The Poetical Works of Samuel Taylor Coleridge*, and *The Table Talk and Omniana of Samuel Taylor Coleridge*; *The Poetical Works of George Crabbe*; Richard Crashaw's *Steps to the Temple*; Dante's *La Divina Commedia*; Thomas Dekker's *Plays*; *The Poems of Emily Dickinson*; Bonamy Dobrée's *Essays in Biography*; *The Poems of John Donne*; *The Dramatick Works of John Dryden*, *Essays of John Dryden*, and *Poetry of John Dryden*; T. S. Eliot's *The Use of Poetry and the Use of Criticism*; *A Companion to Shakespeare Studies*, edited by Harley Granville-Barker and G. B. Harrison; *Metaphysical Lyrics and Poems of the Seventeenth Century*, edited by Herbert Grierson; Thomas Hardy's *The Dynasts* and *Collected Poems*; *The Poetical Works of Robert Herrick*; *Holinshed's Chronicle as Used in Shakespeare's Plays*; T. E. Hulme's *Speculations: Essays on Humanism and the Philosophy of Art*; Henry James's *The American*; *The Complete Plays of Ben Jonson* and *The Poems of Ben Jonson*; *The Letters of John Keats* and *The Poetical Works of John Keats*; G. Wilson Knight's *The Imperial Theme* and *The Wheel of Fire*; *The Tales of D. H. Lawrence*; F. R. Leavis's *How to Teach Reading: A Primer for Ezra Pound* and *Revaluation: Tradition and Development in English Poetry*; Emile Legouis and Louis Cazamian's *A History of English Literature*; Menander of Athens's *Three Plays*; *The Poetical Works of George Meredith*; *The Poetical Works of John Milton* and *Milton's Prose*; *Minor Poets of the 17th Century*; Molière's *L'École des*

femmes; *The Poems of Wilfred Owen*; Palgrave's *The Golden Treasury*; Saint-John Perse's *Anabasis: A Poem*; *Three Plays of Plautus*; *Shakespeare's Hand in the Play of Sir Thomas More*; Ezra Pound's *Homage to Sextus Propertius*; Sir Walter Raleigh's *Johnson on Shakespeare and Selections from His "Historie of the World"*; John Crowe Ransom's *God without Thunder* and *Grace after Meat*; I. A. Richards's *Coleridge on Imagination*; *Shakespeare Criticism: 1919–1935*, edited by Anne Ridler; Nicholas Rowe's *Three Plays*; George Rylands's *Words and Poetry*; George Saintsbury's *Historical Manual of English Prosody*; Shakespeare's *King John*, *Love's Labour's Lost* (edited by John Dover Wilson), *Macbeth* (edited by Horace Furness), Arthur Quiller-Couch's editions of *Measure for Measure*, *The Merry Wives of Windsor*, *The Tempest*, *Twelfth Night*, and *The Winter's Tale*, *The Poems of Shakespeare* (edited by George Wyndham), *The Shakespeare Songs* (edited by Tucker Brooke), *The Taming of the Shrew*, *The Tragedy of Antony and Cleopatra* (edited by R. H. Case), *The Tragedy of King Lear* (edited by W. J. Craig), and *The Tragedy of Othello* (edited by H. C. Hart); Elmer Stoll's *Art and Artifice in Shakespeare*; John Middleton Synge's *Plays*; Allen Tate's *Selected Poems*; *The Ten Principal Upanishads, Put into English by Swami Purohit and W. B. Yeats*; *The Comedies of Terence*; J. A. K. Thomson's *Irony: An Historical Introduction*; E. M. W. Tillyard's *Milton*; *The Poetical Works of Thomas Traherne*; *Les Oeuvres de François Villon*; *The Poems of Edmund Waller*, *William Wycherley*, edited by W. C. Ward; and William Butler Yeats's *The Celtic Twilight*, *A Full Moon in March*, *Michael Robartes and the Dancer*, *Responsibilities and Other Poems*, *Stories of Red Hanrahan and the Secret Rose*, *The Tables of the Law and the Adoration of the Magi*, *A Vision*, and *Wheels and Butterflies*.

5. Lengley was a porter or "gyp."

6. Peter Monro Jack, a graduate of Cambridge, was an editor of the *New York Times Sunday Book Review Section*.

7. J. Donald Adams, also an editor of the *New York Times Sunday Book Review Section*, was not held in high esteem by some of RG's friends at Columbia College. Charles G. Poore was a reviewer for the daily *New York Times*.

8. Gilbert Godfrey and Robert Paul Smith (later known for his *Where Did You Go? Out. What Did You Do? Nothing.*) were fellow students of JB and RG at Columbia. Godfrey and Smith were then working in the scripts department at CBS; RG was working in the sales and promotion department.

9. RG told PS that he never had a chance of being the film critic at *The Nation*.

10. RG could not remember this event, which undoubtedly took place at graduation time.

11. JB took Professor Irwin Edman's courses on metaphysics and Plato at Columbia.

12. Letter is in UM. Leonard Robinson was editor of the *Columbia Review* (1934–1935); RG was associate editor that year.

13. JB, quoted in Halliday, *John Berryman and the Thirties*, 113.

14. JB, *WDH*, 103.

15. See Stitt, "The Art of Poetry XVI," 186.

16. See JB, *WDH*, 113; PM, *DS*, 72; JH, *LJB*, 89.

17. See Halliday, *John Berryman and the Thirties*, 140.

18. JB, *WDH*, 116.

19. See JB, *WDH*, 124–25.

20. JB, *WDH*, 132.

21. See JB, *WDH*, 113–14.

22. Mr. and Mrs. Berryman formally separated most likely in the summer of 1939. John Angus Berryman died on October 27, 1947, in Reisterstown.

23. For some observations about this play, see CT, "A Reckoning with Ghostly Voices (1935–36)," in *Recovering Berryman*, ed. Kelly and Lathrop, 99–107.

24. See JB, *WDH*, 135; JH, *LJB*, 109–10; letter of JB to AT, dated June 7, 1939 (PU).

25. See JB, *WDH*, 136.

26. See JH, *LJB*, 109; PM, *DS*, 104–5.

27. Letter of JB to James Dickey, quoted in Coleman, *John Berryman's Public Vision*, 56.

28. ES, *PTY*, 67.

29. According to the file for Allen Tate in Princeton's Faculty and Professional Staff Files, Tate was appointed resident fellow in creative writing for three academic years (1939–1942). His one-year contract was renewed in 1940 and 1941, but not in 1942 (ML).

30. Letter dated April 27, 1939 (PU).

31. JB, *WDH*, 142 (date of letter August 15, 1939). See JB, *WDH*, 144.

32. Letter is in Berg.

33. Quoted in Halliday, *John Berryman and the Thirties*, 189.

34. See Halliday, *John Berryman and the Thirties*, 137.

35. See PM, *DS*, 121–22; JB, *WDH*, 151–52.

36. See JH, *LJB*, 127.

37. RG, quoted in JH, *LJB*, 127.

38. See JB, *WDH*, 151–52; ES, *PTY*, 33.

39. Letter dated April 4, 1940 (PU).

40. Letter is in NYPL.

41. See JB, *Poems*, 22–23; letter postmarked June 11, 1940 (NYPL).

42. JB, quoted in PM, *DS*, 121.

43. Letter is in NYPL. See PM, *DS*, 140; information on JB's military status can be found in a letter of JB to Gordon Gerould, July 17, 1943 (ML).

44. Letter is in NYPL.

45. See JB, *WDH*, 155.

46. See PM, *DS*, 120–21; JB, *WDH*, 152–54; letter of JB to MVD, dated January 22, 1941 (NYPL).

47. JB, *Collected Poems*, 201.

48. See JB, *WDH*, 192.

49. For an account of ES's relationship with JB, see ES, *Reversals*, 167–214.

50. ES, *PTY*, 5.

51. ES, *Reversals*, 169.

52. See ES, *PTY*, 17.

53. See ES, *PTY*, for a detailed account of her life among some of America's most important writers, including JB; Delmore Schwartz; RL and his first wife, Jean Stafford; AT and his first wife, Caroline Gordon; and TSE.

54. ES, *PTY*, 32.

55. JB, quoted in Kostelanetz, "Conversation with Berryman," 343.

56. Letter dated "19 May" [1942] (RGPF).

57. Schwartz, quoted in JH, *LJB*, 132; JB, *Poems*, 18–19.

58. See JB, *WDH*, 160, 164, 170; letter of JB to RG, dated "19 May" [1942].

59. See JH, *LJB*, 158.

60. See JB, *WDH*, 170.

61. Letter is in NYPL.

62. See ES, *PTY*, 130.

63. See ES, *PTY*, 56–57.

64. See letter of JB to RG, dated "New York, 22 Oct." [1942] (Berg).

65. JB, *WDH*, 176.

66. See ES, *PTY*, 35, 38. New Directions published *Genesis* in 1943.

67. JB, *WDH*, 180. See letter of JB to MVD (NYPL).

68. Postcard is in UM.

69. See JH, *LJB*, 143 (and 158, where JH later says that Harcourt, Brace rejected a volume of JB's poems entitled *A Point of Age*); PM, *DS*, 149, 152; ES, *PTY*, 41, 45, 102; letter of JB to MVD, dated May 27, 1943 (NYPL).

70. Mizener, "Poetry from Right to Left," 156.

71. See JB, *WDH*, 192, 203, 205.

72. See JB, *WDH*, 194.

Chapter Three

1. See letter of JB to R. P. Blackmur, dated June 13, 1943 (ML).

2. Letter dated August 13, 1943 (ML).

3. See JB, *WDH*, 195–96, 199.

4. See letter of JB to MVD, dated December 9, 1943 (NYPL).

5. JB, quoted in Halliday, *John Berryman and the Thirties*, 208.

6. Letter of JB to MVD, dated December 9, 1943 (NYPL).

7. See Fraser, *A Mingled Yarn*, 129, 133.

8. See ES, *PTY*, 88. Greg was also the author of *The Shakespeare First Folio: Its Bibliographical and Textual History* and *Some Aspects and Problems of London Publishing, 1550–1650*. Among his many accomplishments, he was the Lyell Reader in Bibliography at Oxford University (1954–1955).

9. See ES, *PTY*, 215; JB, *WDH*, 208.

10. See JB, *WDH*, 211; PM, *DS*, 163.

11. RL, *Collected Prose*, 111.

12. See Air Group Nine Book Committee, *U.S.S. Essex Carrier Air Group 9*, 9, 21.

13. See letter dated May 24, 1944 (NYPL).

14. See letter of JB to MVD, dated June 13, 1945 (NYPL); JH, *LJB*, x, 157; JB, *WDH*, 223; ES, *PTY*, 154, 159, 174–75, where ES says the contract was signed in June 1946. On May 26, 1946, JB wrote to AT asking him to contact the person in charge of the American Men of Letters series and give to that person the material that JB enclosed, so that JB could receive an advance of $1,000 (PU).

15. See JB, *WDH*, 218–19; MVD, *Autobiography*, 275–76; PM, *DS*, 167–68.

16. See letter of JB to MVD, dated May 29, 1945 (Berg).

17. See ES, *PTY*, 106.

18. RG, "The Education of an Editor," 54.

19. JB, *WDH*, 222.

20. See Halliday, *John Berryman and the Thirties*, 166.

21. See JH, *LJB*, 160; JB, *WDH*, 222; letters of JB to AT, dated March 25 and May 9, 1946 (PU).

22. See Christopher O'Hare, interview with Robert Giroux (unpublished, 2000, RGPF).

23. For a picture of RG and the Lowells in Maine, see ES, *PTY*, 145. See JB, *WDH*, 223–24; Roberts, *Jean Stafford*, 241–48; Travisano, *Midcentury Quartet*, 202–11.

24. RL, *Collected Prose*, 112.

25. See ES, *PTY*, 146.

26. Jean Stafford, quoted in ES, *PTY*, 145, 152.

27. ES, *PTY*, 175.

28. Memo dated May 5, 1948 (ML).

29. Later, in 1952, JB spent considerable time and energy studying *Two Gentlemen of Verona* and the *Henry VI* plays. See JH, introduction to JB, *BS*, xxi; 179–211.

30. WM, "In Loving Memory of the Late Author of the Dream Songs," 70.

31. Letter dated July 6 [1946] (RGPF). See PM, *DS*, 173.

32. See PM, *DS*, 163.

33. *The Duchess of Malfi*, performed at the Ethel Barrymore Theatre in New York, closed on November 16, 1946.

34. A cryptic reference both to the 1946 meat shortage throughout the country and to a horse named Hampden, the third-place winner of the 1946 Kentucky Derby.

35. Letter dated October 21 [1946] (RGPF).

36. JB, "Robert Lowell and Others," in *The Freedom of the Poet*, by JB, 286.

37. See PM, *DS*, 249.

38. The original typescript of *Sonnets* was entitled *Sonnets to Chris*. For an overview of the work's complicated publishing history, see JB, *Collected Poems*, 303–6.

39. See JH, *LJB*, 169.

40. Carruth, "Declining Occasions," 120–21.

41. See JH, *LJB*, 170–71. For RG's recollections of TSE, see RG, "A Personal Memoir."

42. See JH, *LJB*, 190; PM, *DS*, 203.

43. Telegram is in UM.

44. Only a single carbon copy, dated March 20, 1947, of JB's correspondence with editor Helen Stewart of William Sloane Associates exists. She was in charge of overseeing the publication of *The Dispossessed*. See JB, *Collected Poems*, 300.

45. See PM, *DS*, 209, 213.

46. Jarrell, "Verse Chronicle," 81.

47. RL, *Letters of Robert Lowell*, 109.

48. JB, *The Dream Songs*, 137.

49. See RL, *Letters of Robert Lowell*, 3–4.

50. See RL, *Collected Prose*, 118.

51. See Coleman, "'Nightmares of Eden,'" 61.

52. JL, quoted in Coleman, "'Nightmares of Eden,'" 61. See Coleman, *John Berryman's Public Vision*, 101–2.

53. See Coleman, "'Nightmares of Eden,'" 61.

54. Golden, "John Berryman at Midcentury," 515.

55. Harry Thomas has written about this introduction: "Berryman was very slow to get to work on the selection and introduction. He was far behind schedule in writing his book on Stephen Crane. He had fallen in love with a married woman and was writing the sonnets that were published two decades later as *Berryman's Sonnets*. He was teaching at Princeton. When, late in 1948, he finally finished the work for JL, JL rejected the introduction. It was, he wrote to JB, 'too difficult and too profound for the purpose.' Pound dismissed it out of hand. JB's essay, he wrote to JL, was 'NOT GOOD. It is clumsy, unreadable, and the facts are not accurate.' In the end, JL paid JB another fifty dollars for his selection of Pound's poetry and recommended that he publish the essay in a small magazine (it came out in the *Partisan Review* in 1949). JB's name has never appeared on the *Selected Poems*, which was first published in 1949." See Thomas, "Berryman and Pound," 613; ES, *PTY*, 165.

56. See RL, *Letters of Robert Lowell*, 110.

57. See RG, "The Poet in the Asylum," 45; RG with Robert Dana, Saskia Hamilton, Charles McKinley, "Celebration of Robert Lowell," 262.

58. See letter of J. Douglas Brown to Donald Stauffer, dated June 29, 1948 (ML); letter of Donald Stauffer to J. Douglas Brown, dated June 21, 1948 (ML).

59. See ES, *PTY*, 168; JH, *LJB*, 204.

60. For a picture of TSE in front of this blackboard at Princeton, see ES, *PTY*, 172.

61. See PM, *DS*, 215.

62. See JH, *LJB*, 208.

63. See JB, *WDH*, 235; PM, *DS*, 224, 231.

64. JB, *WDH*, 242.

65. SB, "John Berryman," ix.

66. See PM, *DS*, 239. In an internal memorandum of Farrar, Straus & Company, dated November 5, 1964, RG noted that JB's critical biography of Shakespeare had not been published, that it had not been completed, and it was conjectural if it would ever be published, but he hoped it would be. The memorandum is in NYPL.

67. See JH, *JBCC*, 9; JB, *WDH*, 245. In his personal copy of this book, JB wrote, "5 July 56 – Mpls / composed 22 March '48—22 March '53!" (see Kelly, *John Berryman's Personal Library*, 32). PM maintains JB finished the poem on March 15 (see PM, *DS*, 262).

68. JB, *WDH*, 228. See Coleman, *John Berryman's Public Vision*, 99.

69. Radway, "The Fate of Epic in Twentieth-Century American Poetry," 46.

70. See JH, *JBCC*, 19.

71. JB, quoted in JB, *BS*, 280.

72. JH, *JBCC*, 5, 32.

73. ES, *PTY*, 188.

74. Coleman, "'Nightmares of Eden,'" 59.

75. JB, quoted in Stitt, "The Art of Poetry XVI," 195.

76. See Kostelanetz, "Conversation with Berryman," 345.

77. ES, *PTY*, 227.

78. See letters of JB to AT, dated February 3, 6, 1953 and April 11, 1953 (PU).

79. See PM, *DS*, 255, 257. For many of her contemporaries, Carver always remained a bit of an enigma, due in large part to her incredible work schedule and reluctance to enter into the social arena of the publishing world. Born in 1921 in Cambridge, Ohio, she received her B.A. degree in 1943 from Muskingum College in New Concord, and two years later she had obtained a job at the publishing firm of Reynal & Hitchcock in New York. Besides the praise she earned from individual authors, whose ranks also included e. e. cummings, Lionel Trilling, Katherine Anne Porter, Bernard Malamud, Leslie Fiedler, and Peter Matthiessen, Carver was given a citation by New York PEN, the writers organization, for her

"creative contributions to authors and their works." Carver, at one point, edited the works of SB, though they had a falling out after JB's death. After RG left Harcourt, Brace in March 1955, Carver edited a number of authors, including Flannery O'Connor. She moved to London in the 1960s and worked at John Murray's and Chatto & Windus before joining Oxford University Press. However, when that publisher shut down its offices in London, Carver declined to move to Oxford. Remaining in London, she worked with various publishers, including Victor Gollancz, and in the 1980s joined Trianon Press in Paris before returning to London. Carver died in 1997 in the Chelsea and Westminster Hospital in London. See SB, *Letters*, 161, 425. Her obituary can be read at https://www.independent.co.uk/news/obituaries/obituary-catharine-carver-1293892.html.

Chapter Four

1. See PM, *DS*, 272.
2. See PM, *DS*, 272, 275.
3. JB to AT, December 29, 1953 (PU).
4. See ES, *PTY*, 193.
5. Levine, "Mine Own John Berryman," in *Recovering Berryman*, ed. Kelly and Lathrop, 37.
6. See JH, *JBCC*, 42.
7. JB, *WDH*, 273.
8. JB first appears in the University of Minnesota's Board of Regents minutes of December 10, 1954, where his appointment was listed as lecturer in General Studies for the winter quarter 1954–1955, for a salary of $1,600 a term. This post continued during the 1955–1956 academic year. For the following academic year, he was listed as a lecturer in Interdisciplinary Studies under General Education. During the 1957–1958 academic year, he was listed as associate professor under English in a section titled "proportion of other departments chargeable," as well as under Interdisciplinary Studies, again under General Education. For the 1958–1959 academic year, he was listed under both English and Interdisciplinary Studies, as he was during the following academic year, but this is the first time a distinction is made that he is solely in the Humanities section. He retained this status for the next two academic years. For the 1963–1964 academic year, he was a professor in the Interdisciplinary Program (Humanities), but his name does not appear under English. He held this post until the 1968–1969 academic year. On September 16, 1969, he was promoted to Regents Professor of Humanities, with a raise of $5,000 in salary.
9. Letter dated October 25, 1954 (Berg).
10. See JB, *WDH*, 286–87, 289; JH, *LJB*, 254.

11. Letter dated March 27, 1955 (RGPF). For an extended account of RG's departure from Harcourt, Brace, see PS, "Tracing a Literary and Epistolary Relationship," 97–100; PS, *Flannery O'Connor and Robert Giroux*, 140–42.

12. Letter dated April 21, 1955 (RGPF).

13. Roger Straus, quoted in Ian Parker, "Showboat: How a Legendary Publisher Handles Writers," *New Yorker* 78, no. 7 (April 8, 2002): 60.

14. See letter of RG to RL, April 19, 1955 (NYPL).

15. Letter is in RGPF.

16. See Matthew Boswell, "The Holocaust Poetry of John Berryman, Sylvia Plath and W. D. Snodgrass," Ph.D. diss., University of Sheffield, England, 2005, 17, http://etheses.whiterose.ac.uk/4835/1/boswellm.pdf.

17. Marshall Best was an editor at Viking.

18. Most likely this refers to the loan of $120 just before Christmas 1953.

19. Letter is in RGPF.

20. JB, *WDH*, 289.

21. See JB, *WDH*, 290. Letter of Jill Berryman to RG, dated June 13, 1955 (NYPL).

22. Letter is in RGPF.

23. JB, "Shakespeare at Thirty."

24. Letter is in RGPF.

25. Telegram is in RGPF.

26. Letter of RG to JB is in RGPF.

27. JB, quoted in JH, *LJB*, 252.

28. Letter is in RGPF.

29. See letter of RG to Flannery O'Connor, dated June 10, 1955, in PS, *Flannery O'Connor and Robert Giroux*, 160–61; letter of RG to TSE, dated June 2, 14, 1955 (NYPL).

30. See letter of RG to Thomas Merton, dated June 23, 1955, in PS, *The Letters of Robert Giroux and Thomas Merton*, 196.

31. Letter is in RGPF.

32. Letter of JB to RG, dated "Thurs" [1955].

33. Letter of JB to RG is in RGPF. See JB, *WDH*, 290.

34. See letter of RG to JB, dated June 27, 1955 (RGPF). "To the degree," Coleman wrote in "'Nightmares of Eden,'" "that Berryman believed Shahn's work was essentially in harmony with his own, it is important also to consider Shahn's status at this time. When his first major retrospective was held at the Museum of Modern Art in New York in 1947, Shahn's work had been recognized for its critical exposition of 'the shortcomings of democracy in the United States,' and as recently as 1954 he had been profiled in *Life* magazine as the 'Painter of Protest.' Berryman, then, was implicitly making a particular set of claims for his own work as social commentary when he agreed to have Shahn illustrate what was the most important publication of his career in 1956. Nonetheless, Shahn's

political positioning did not deter critics from reading *Homage to Mistress Brad-street* as a poem that uncritically valorizes the American experience and the national self" (64).

35. Letter dated "Wed" [1955] (RGPF).

36. See JB, *WDH*, 291.

37. Letter of RG to JB, dated July 21, 1955 (RGPF).

38. Letter dated "3 Aug 55" (RGPF). JB provided the following notes for the stanzas of his poem:

1–4. The poem is about the woman but this exordium is spoken by the poet, his voice modulating in stanza 4, line 8 [4.8] into hers.

1.1 He was not Governor until after her death.

1.5 Sylvester (the translator of Du Bartas) and Quarles, her favourite poets; unfortunately.

5.4,5 Many details are from quotations in Helen Campbell's biography, the Winthrop papers, narratives, town histories.

8.4ff. Scriptural passages are sometimes ones she used herself, as this in her <u>Meditation liii</u>.

11.8 <u>that one</u>: the Old One.

12.5–13.2 The poet interrupts.

18.8 Her first child was not born until about 1633.

22.6 <u>chopping</u>: disputing, snapping, haggling; axing.

23.1 <u>fere</u>: his friend Death.

24.1 Her irony of 22.8 intensifies.

24.2 <u>rakes</u>: inclines, as a mast; bows.

25.3 One might say: He is enabled to speak, at last, in the fortune of an echo of her—and when she is loneliest (her former spiritual adviser having deserted Anne Hutchinson, and this her closest friend banished), as if she had summoned him; and only thus, perhaps, is she enabled to <u>hear</u> him. This second section of the poem is a dialogue, his voice however ceasing well before it ends at 39.4, and hers continuing for the whole third part, until the coda (54–57).

29.1–4 Cf. Isa. 1:5.

29.5,6 After a Klee.

33.1 Cf., on Byzantine icons, Frederick Rolfe ("Baron Corvo"): "Whoever dreams of praying (with expectation of response) for the prayer of a Tintoretto or a Titian, or a Bellini, or a Botticelli? But who can refrain from crying 'O Mother!' to these unruffleable wan dolls in indigo on gold?" (quote from <u>The Desire and Pursuit of the Whole</u> by Graham Greene in <u>The Lost Childhood</u>).

33.5,6   "Délires des grandes profondeurs," described by Cousteau and others; a euphoria, sometimes fatal, in which the hallucinated diver offers passing fish his line, helmet, anything.

35.3,4   As of cliffhangers, movie serials wherein each week's episode ends with a train bearing down on the strapped heroine or with the hero dangling over an abyss into which Indians above him peer with satisfaction before they hatchet the rope. rescue: forcible recovery (by the owner) of goods distrained [*sic*].

37.7,8   After an engraving somewhere in Fuchs's collections, Bray, above (36.4), puns.

39.5   The stanza is unsettled, like 24, by a middle line, signaling a broad transition.

42.8   brutish: her epithet for London in a kindly passage about the Great Fire.

46.1,2   Arminians, rebels against the doctrine of unconditional election. Her husband alone opposed the law condemning Quakers to death.

46.3,4   Matthew 3:12.

46.5,6   Rheumatic fever, after a celebrated French description.

48.2ff.   Space . . . outside: delirium.

51.5   Cf. Zech. 14:20.

51.6   Wandering pacemaker: a disease of the heart, here the heart itself.

52.4   Seaborn Cotton, John's eldest son; Bradstreet being then magistrate.

52.5,6   Dropsical, a complication of the last three years. Line 7 she actually said.

55.4   thrift: the plant, also called Our Lady's cushion.

55.8   wet brain: edema.

56.5,6   Cf. G. R. Levy, The Gate of Horn, p. 5.

39. Letter is in RGPF.

40. Letter dated "Thursday" [1955] (RGPF). Hal Vursell was editor of the works of Colette, Robert Graves, and Marguerite Yourcenar and a design director at Farrar, Straus & Cudahy.

41. See JB, *WDH*, 292.

42. JB, quoted in Coleman, *John Berryman's Public Vision*, 132.

43. See JH, introduction to JB, *Henry's Fate & Other Poems*, xvii.

44. See JH, *LJB*, 252. For an analysis of the rhymes and rhythm in JB's poetry, see the introduction by CT to JB, *Collected Poems*, xxxvii–xiii.

45. JH, *JBCC*, 65.

46. JB, quoted in Kostelanetz, "A Profile of John Berryman," 39.

47. See ES, *PTY*, 179; WM, "Henry Tasting All the Secret Bits of Life"; JH, *JBCC*, 6. For a more detailed evaluation of the persona of Henry, see JH, *JBCC*, 48–58.

48. Coleman, *John Berryman's Public Vision*, 142.

49. Letter dated September 7, 1955.

50. JB, *WDH*, 292–93.

51. Letter is in RGPF.

52. See telegram dated January 10, 1956.

53. Letter is in RGPF.

54. Telegram is in RGPF.

55. See JB, *WDH*, 294–95; PM, *DS*, 300.

56. Letter is in RGPF.

57. See letter of TSE to RG, dated February 28, 1956 (NYPL).

58. Letter of RG to JB, dated March 14, 1956 (RGPF).

59. Letter dated March 22, 1956 (RGPF).

60. See JB, *WDH*, 296.

61. Letter is in RGPF.

62. See letter of RG to JB, dated April 19, 1956.

63. See telegram from TSE to RG, dated April 16, 1956 (NYPL).

64. See letter of TSE to RG, March 13, 1956 (NYPL).

65. See Horgan, *Tracings*, 145.

66. Conrad Aiken, quoted in JB, *WDH*, 297. On Christmas Eve 1953, JB had attended a party at Aiken's apartment in New York. Aiken had previously read "Homage to Mistress Bradstreet," given to him by Edmund Wilson.

67. In a letter to his mother, dated June 27 [1956], JB discusses this play, entitled *It's Been Real-or-a-Tree*, which was never published (see JB, *WDH*, 297). At one point, SB thought about collaborating on this play.

68. Most likely *Henderson the Rain King*.

69. See letter of RG to JB, dated July 10, 1956.

70. Christopher Devlin, S.J., *The Life of Robert Southwell*.

71. JB and Simpson were in the process of getting a divorce.

72. Letter dated July 2, 1956.

73. See telegram of RG to JB, July 6, 1956.

74. Paul Engle was the director of the Iowa Writers' Workshop. Most likely the anthology that JB is referring to is *Reading Modern Poetry*, edited by Paul Engle and Warren Carrier, in which the final stanzas of "Homage to Mistress Bradstreet" (42–57) are reprinted.

75. Letter of RG to JB, dated July 10, 1956.

76. In the summer of 1953, John Davenport offered JB money for reading from his poems and giving a series of talks for the BBC's Third Programme on the changes that JB had seen in Paris, Rome, and London since his visits to these cities before World War II.

77. See PM, *DS*, 393. Letter of JB to RG, dated "12 July" [1956].

78. RL, quoted in the letter of RG to JB, dated July 13, 1956.

79. Letter of RG to JB, July 17, 1956.

80. See letter of RG to JB, dated July 24, 1956.

81. "The art of verse in English has been employed here by a master to grapple and hold, at a great depth, in a constant and singular intensity of spirit, one life and one past time in America. The work is classic. It serves the reader, but with austerity: hushing his inferior speech and reminding him of the precision and passion with which human reality can be known." Robert Fitzgerald, quoted in letter of RG to JB, dated July 2, 1956.

82. Telegram dated July 19, 1956.

83. SB, *Letters*, 156.

84. AT, quoted in JB, *WDH*, 298.

85. MVD, quoted in the letter of RG to JB, dated August 2, 1956.

86. Letter of RG to JB, dated December 6, 1956.

87. JB, *WDH*, 299.

Chapter Five

1. See JH, introduction to JB, *BS*, lvii. On December 11, 1956, JB had signed a memorandum of agreement with the Thomas Y. Crowell Company to publish his book *Plays of Shakespeare*; the manuscript would be delivered on or before October 1, 1957. The manuscript, more an academic text or handbook of a type that Farrar, Straus would normally not consider publishing, would contain from four to six plays by Shakespeare, plus a ten-thousand-word introduction and a three-thousand-word introduction to each play. A copy of this memorandum is in NYPL.

2. See telegram from RG to JB, dated January 15, 1957.

3. See letter of RG to JB, dated July 3, 1963.

4. Irita Van Doren, the literary editor of the *New York Herald-Tribune*, was the former wife of Carl Van Doren, Mark's older brother.

5. Letter dated February 15, 1957.

6. Letter of RG to JB, dated February 25, 1957.

7. Letter dated April 14, 1957.

8. JB's famous homecoming poem to his son, "A Sympathy, A Welcome," ends with the phrase, "poor Paul, / whose wild bad father loves you well." SB, whose *The Adventures of Augie March* received a National Book Award for Fiction, taught at the University of Minnesota from 1946 to 1948 and then again beginning in 1958.

9. Letter of RG to JB, April 22, 1957.

10. See letter of RG to JB, dated April 22, 1957; also telegram dated May 20, 1957.

11. See letter dated November 18, 1957 (PU).

12. JB, *The Dream Songs*, 9. In October 1936, JB saw the John Ford movie by this name, which is based on the life of Dr. Samuel Mudd, who set the broken leg of John Wilkes Booth in 1865.

13. See PM, *DS*, 336; JB, *WDH*, 321.

14. See JB, *WDH*, 323.

15. Berryman, Ross, and Tate, *The Arts of Reading*, 1.

16. See PM, *DS*, 339.

17. See JH, introduction to JB's *BS*, lvii.

18. A copy of this letter, dated October 22, 1958, is in Berg.

19. See JB, *WDH*, 324.

20. RL, *Collected Poems*, 192.

21. JB, "Despondency and Madness," 99.

22. RL, *Letters of Robert Lowell*, 338.

23. Wright, quoted in Blunk, *James Wright*, 121–22; AT, quoted in Blunk, *James Wright*, 174.

24. See PM, "Lowell on Berryman on Lowell," in *Recovering Berryman*, ed. Kelly and Lathrop, 63.

25. RL, *Letters of Robert Lowell*, 352–53.

26. JB, quoted in JH, *LJB*, 280.

27. See letters of RG to TSE, dated February 5, 1960; March 18, 1960; May 23, 1960; and June 24, 1960 (NYPL).

28. See PM, *DS*, 370–75; JB, *WDH*, 344.

29. See letter of RG to TSE, dated August 21, 1961; RG to TSE and Valerie Eliot, January 10, 1962; TSE to RG, February 23, 1962 (all in the NYPL).

30. See letter of RG to Thomas Merton, dated April 14, 1961, in PS, *The Letters of Robert Giroux and Thomas Merton*, 266.

31. RL, *Letters of Robert Lowell*, 406.

32. RL, quoted in JH, *LJB*, 326.

33. For a reference about not seeing one another in ten years, see RL, *Letters of Robert Lowell*, 400.

34. See JB, *WDH*, 353.

35. WM, "In Loving Memory of the Late Author of the Dream Songs," 71.

36. Greg Nelson, "Interview with W. D. Snodgrass."

37. A copy of this speech is in RGPF.

38. Letter dated September 4, 1962, quoted in PM, *DS*, 381.

39. See PM, *DS*, 392.

40. See SB, *Letters*, 425.

41. See PM, *Lost Puritan*, 323.

42. RG told PS that Roger Straus, whom PS met several times, was responsible for the decision to remainder this book.

43. E. Milton Halliday wrote *John Berryman and the Thirties*. He was a close college friend of JB and was acknowledged in JB's poem "Freshman Blues" (*Collected Poems*, 173–74).

44. Paul Thomson was a college friend who became an Episcopal priest.

45. Farrar, Straus & Cudahy bought out JB's Viking contract, and thus JB had to pay back this money from his royalties. RG wanted to publish JB's book on Shakespeare, if and when JB ever finished it.

46. Letter of RG to JB, dated March 8, 1963. Perhaps a double reference: 1) *Titus Andronicus*, act 2, sc. 3; and 2) *Hound & Horn*, a Harvard literary quarterly published between 1927 and 1934.

47. During the years that JB and RG failed to communicate with each other, RG edited the works of many other authors. With the 1996 fiftieth-anniversary catalog of FS&G in hand, RG checked off in my presence the books he had edited while at FS&G, from the winter/spring catalog of 1959 through the spring catalog of 1963. Of the 201 books he edited during this time period, two of them (*The Magic Barrel* [1959] by Bernard Malamud and *Life Studies* [1960] by Robert Lowell) won National Book Awards. Another of his authors, Salvatore Quasimodo, received the Nobel Prize in Literature in 1959. In addition, RG personally kept in contact with noted authors TSE, Isaiah Berlin, Isaac Bashevis Singer, Erskine Caldwell, Bernard Malamud, Djuna Barnes, Jack Kerouac, Edmund Wilson, Paul Horgan, Flannery O'Connor, and Elizabeth Hardwick as he edited their books during this time period. Likewise, he edited works by two former Columbia classmates, Trappist monk Thomas Merton and Ralph de Toledano, author of an autobiographical-sociological-political study with a foreword by Vice President Richard M. Nixon.

48. See letter of RG to JB, dated May 22, 1963.

49. Gerald Brenan's 1963 book was entitled *A Life of One's Own*. He also wrote *The Spanish Labyrinth* and *The Face of Spain*, perhaps causing a confusion in JB's mind as to the exact title of the book he mentioned. The Library of Congress has no record of *The Spanish Temper*.

50. See letter dated "Mon" [1963].

51. See postcard of JB to WM, dated May 26, 1963 (NYPL).

52. Letter of JB to RG, dated "Monday" [1963].

53. Letter dated July 3, 1963.

54. The reference is to JB's proposed books on King Lear and on Shakespeare.

55. Letter dated July 15, 1963.

56. The Farfield Foundation was reportedly funded by the CIA, though it is unlikely that JB knew this. JB did not receive a grant of $5,000 from this foundation; it went, instead, to SB.

57. In "The Lay of Ike," JB mentioned the names of actual people, such as J. Robert Oppenheimer, chairman of the General Advisory Committee of the Atomic Energy Commission; Lewis L. Strauss, the atomic energy commissioner, who disliked Oppenheimer intensely; and Roger Robb, counsel for the Atomic Energy Board. All were key figures in the Oppenheimer security clearance hearings in the spring of 1954.

58. Letter of JB to RG, dated August 26, 1963.

59. See JB, *WDH*, 360; JH, *LJB*, 320.

60. Letter dated September 20, 1963.

61. Letter of RG to JB, dated September 24, 1963.

62. Letter dated September 26, 1963.

63. JB's poem "Karesanui, Ryoan-ji" (Dream Song 73).

64. Mary McCarthy's novel *The Group* was a best-seller.

65. Letter dated October 10, 1963.

66. JB, *BS*, ix.

67. MVD, *Shakespeare*, 4.

68. MVD, *Shakespeare*, 11.

69. See RG, *BKQ*, 8.

70. See RG, *BKQ*, 307–15. RG, however, does not mention the following critical works that were in print when he wrote his book: G. Wilson Knight, *The Mutual Flame: On Shakespeare's "Sonnets" and "The Phoenix and the Turtle"* (London: Methuen, 1955); C. L. Barber, "An Essay on Shakespeare's Sonnets," 299–320, in *Elizabethan Poetry: Modern Essays on Criticism*, ed. Paul J. Alpers (New York: Oxford University Press, 1967), reproduced in *William Shakespeare's Sonnets*, ed. Harold Bloom (New York: Chelsea House, 1987), 5–27; Claes Schaar, *Elizabethan Sonnet Themes and the Dating of Shakespeare's Sonnets* (Copenhagen: Lund, 1962); R. J. C. Wait, *The Background to Shakespeare's Sonnets* (London: Chatto & Windus, 1972); Martin Green, *The Labyrinth of Shakespeare's Sonnets* (London: Skilton, 1974).

71. RG, *BKQ*, 52.

72. JB, quoted in RG, *BKQ*, 51.

73. See RG, *BKQ*, 100.

74. See RG, *BKQ*, 123, 155.

75. See RG, *BKQ*, 143–44.

76. RG, *BKQ*, 25.

77. See RG, *BKQ*, 221–22.

78. JB, quoted in JH, *LJB*, 85; Stitt, "The Art of Poetry XVI," 188.

79. Peter Maber, "John Berryman and Shakespearean Autobiography," in *"After Thirty Falls": New Essays on John Berryman*, ed. Coleman and McGowan, 216–17.

80. See PM, *DS*, 248.

81. See JH, *LJB*, 165; PM, *DS*, 248.

82. JB, *BS*, 275. See also xlii–lvi, 268–71.

83. See RG, preface to JB, *BS*, ix.

84. See JB, *BS*, 33–34.

85. See JB, *BS*, 49.

86. See JB, *BS*, 275–81.

87. JB, quoted in JH's introduction to *BS*, xxxv. See also 269, 275, 289.

88. JH, in JB, *BS*, xxxvii.

89. JH, in JB, *BS*, xliii. See lvi.

90. JH, in JB, *BS*, xliii.

91. See JB, *BS*, 43–44.

92. JB, *BS*, 44.

93. According to an expert on Shakespeare's sonnets, Michael Schoenfeldt, "We are not even sure what 'begetter' means here—does it refer to the patron of the poems, or to the inspirer of the poems, or to the person who helped Thorpe obtain a copy of the poems, or even to the poet himself? Various candidates for Mr. W. H. exist. He may have been Henry Wriothesley, the Earl of Southampton, whose initials may have been accidentally transposed by an otherwise careful printer, or deliberately transposed by an intentionally cagey printer. . . . Shakespeare had already dedicated his two other major non-dramatic publications, *Venus and Adonis* and *The Rape of Lucrece*, to Southampton. Nine years younger than Shakespeare, Southampton possesses an age and status that match that of the putative young man addressed in Sonnets 1–126. Sonnets 1–17 urging the young man to marry, moreover, resemble the arguments Venus uses to attempt to seduce a reluctant Adonis in *Venus and Adonis*. Mr. W. H., though, may also refer to William Herbert, the third Earl of Pembroke, codedicatee of the First Folio of Shakespeare's plays. A lifelong bachelor and a wealthy patron, Pembroke was sixteen years younger than Shakespeare. For both aristocrats, though, the term 'Mr' seems inadequate to their exalted social status, particularly in a volume so concerned with registering class markers. It is even possible that either Thorpe or Shakespeare was exploiting a deliberate ambiguity with these initials in order to ingratiate two or more patrons with one dedication" (126–27).

94. See RG, *BKQ*, 166–68.

95. See Edwin McDowell, "About Books and Scholars," *New York Times*, April 18, 1982.

96. See RG, *BKQ*, 307.

97. RG, *BKQ*, viii.

98. See letter of ES to Robert Fitzgerald, dated May 8, 1981 (PU).

99. See JB, *BS*, 392.

100. David Young of Oberlin College wrote RG on February 28, 1982, that as a professional Shakespearean expert he found his book "delightful and persuasive reading. . . . The Southampton evidence seems virtually overwhelming, and you sum it up beautifully" (NYPL). The anonymous author at *Kirkus Review*

(April 28, 1982) wrote, in part, "Fortunately, Giroux doesn't spend too much time reading the Sonnets as a roman à clef, but he nonetheless largely disregards them as art. Instead, he assembles a mass of mildly interesting but mostly peripheral data under alliterative headings. . . . It's all harmless and spasmodically informative, but more like the notes of an indefatigable student than a sustained and pointed argument." The longer review in the *New York Times* (May 31, 1982), written by Christopher Lehmann-Haupt, repeats much of RG's argument, though the final conclusion does not place him among Shakespeare's better critics: "It is by this sort of common sensical, plain-as-the-nose-on-your-face sort of reasoning that Mr. Giroux arrives at the conclusions he reaches in 'The Book Known as Q.' Because the main pleasure of reading it lies in following this reasoning, it will give little away if I paraphrase Mr. Giroux's own summary of his conclusions." There follows an appropriate summary of the book. "Of course," the reviewer continues, "this thesis of Mr. Giroux's is highly inferential. Practically everything we know about Shakespeare is inferential. The case [takes] the form of an argument that joins a chain of premises, each dependent on the next. The theory is thus no stronger than its weakest link. . . . But however strong or weak his thesis, its value lies in this: It offers us a plausible and coherent explanation of what the sonnets, personal statements that they formally are, might actually be referring to. This, in turn, gives them an added dimension of dramatic life." C. G. Thayer, writing for the *Georgia Review*, disagreed with some aspects of RG's argument, but he did agree with RG that the "onlie begetter" is the Earl of Southampton. "The book is sensible, informative on many details, and well made. . . . The problems are not new, nor should one (necessarily) expect them to be; neither are the answers, and perhaps one should not expect them to be, either" (214). In short, RG's book "is a solid, sane, sensible introduction to these endlessly fascinating poems by a professional student of the subject" (216). In his review, Frank Kermode, without giving an in-depth critique, calls RG a "well-informed layman" (32): "I suppose books of this kind are meant for a specialized kind of addict, who will not mind the omissions, the forced readings, and the lack of genuine interest in the poems themselves" (32). In "Shakespeare & Co: Reply to Frank Kermode," on June 16, 1983, RG questioned some of Kermode's statements. Later, in his letter to the editors, RG again takes Kermode to task for misreading his book: "Mr. Kermode feels my book shows a 'lack of genuine interest in the poems themselves' because I do not analyze every sonnet, but I had neither the space nor desire to do a poem by poem analysis. My opening sentence states that my book is concerned with the discrepancy between the late publication of Q, seven years before Shakespeare's death, and the circulation of the poems more than eleven years earlier, which the review never mentions." In the same issue, the last word fell to Kermode: "I am sorry to have fallen in Mr. Giroux's estimation. . . . I ought to have mentioned the theory about late publication and lack of applause. It is extremely thin and takes little or no account of the perhaps too commonplace explanation of the apparent failure of [Thomas] Thorpe's enterprise, namely that the vogue for sonnet sequences had ended a dozen or more years earlier." He concluded by trying to give a compliment: "'Well-informed layman' is complimentary, not condescending." In a letter to Harry Ford of Atheneum publishers, dated July 5, 1983, RG wrote, "I've had it with Kermode."

101. Helen Smith, "The Politics of Praise," 192–93.

102. See PM, *DS*, 399.

103. Letter dated October 17, 1963 (NYPL).

104. Letter of JB to RG, dated October 14, 1963.

105. Letter dated October 17, 1963.

106. RL, quoted in Stanley Kunitz, "Stanley Kunitz Introduces John Berryman and Robert Lowell" (PU).

107. See letter dated November 25, 1963.

108. JB, "Formal Elegy," in *Collected Poems*, 163.

109. See JB, *WDH*, 360.

110. See letter dated "Wed" [1964]; PM, *DS*, 402.

111. See letter of RG to JB, dated January 23, 1964.

112. See letter of JB to RG, dated February 15, 1964.

113. A. L. Rowse, author of *Shakespeare's Sonnets*, believed that the fair youth in Shakespeare's sonnets was the handsome and bisexual Henry Wriothesley, the third Earl of Southampton, who fell in love with Shakespeare, though their relationship was platonic. The *New York Times* ran two articles on Rowse and his theory about Shakespeare. The first appeared in September 18, 1963, by British journalist Sydney Gruson, entitled "Oxford History 'Solves' Sonnets." The article discusses Rowse's forthcoming book *William Shakespeare: A Biography*, in which he dates and analyzes Shakespeare's sonnets. This article also cites four articles written for the *London Times* by Rowse in which he explains and defends his research, refuting especially the idea that the sonnets were overtly homosexual since Shakespeare was fond of women. The second article, "Oxford Historian Meets Scholars," written by Harry Gilroy, appeared in the September 25, 1963, edition, the day after Rowse discussed his research at the Pierpont Morgan Library in New York City. It should be noted that RG also believed that the fair youth was Henry Wriothesley, though in his *BKQ*, RG approaches this relationship by noting that consideration should be given to Lord Burleigh's thwarted desire for Wriothesley to marry his daughter. When RG's book appeared, Rowse attacked it viciously in the *Spectator* (September 4, 1982). That day, RG wrote a letter to the editors of the *Spectator*, trying to explain his views on the Dark Lady of the sonnets, which he claimed had not been properly researched by Rowse. Various candidates for the Dark Lady include Amelia Lanyer, a former mistress to the Lord Chamberlain (the patron of Shakespeare's company); Mary Fitton, whom William Herbert, the Earl of Pembroke, impregnated; and Jane Davenant, mother of William Davenant, a writer who liked to claim that he was the illegitimate offspring of Shakespeare.

114. Letter dated February 18, 1964.

115. RG thought this might have been a reference to the Nazis and their use of human skin.

116. Letter dated February 27, 1964.

117. See letters of RG to TSE, dated October 18, 1963; TSE to RG, October 25, 1963; TSE to RG, November 5, 1963; and RG to John Kelly, March 6, 1964 (NYPL).

118. See JB, *WDH*, 362.

119. Letter dated April 12, 1964.

120. See letter dated April 17, 1964. Recipients included Alfred Alvarez (poetry editor for *The Observer*), W. H. Auden, Robert Bly, J. V. Cunningham (poet, teaching at Brandeis University), William Empson (poet and literary critic, teaching at the University of Sheffield), Josephine Miles (poet and literary critic, teaching at the University of California at Berkeley), Marianne Moore, Anthony Ostroff (poet, teaching at the University of California at Berkeley), J. F. Powers, Ben Shahn, and Stephen Spender.

Chapter Six

1. Letter dated "Thurs [April] 23" [1964].

2. Dudley Fitts translated parts of the Oedipus cycle with Robert Fitzgerald. From 1960 to 1968, he edited the Yale Series of Younger Poets.

3. Virginia Kirkus founded the Kirkus Service, which evaluated galley proofs of books.

4. David Posner was assistant curator of poetry at the State University of New York at Buffalo.

5. See letter of RG to JB, dated April 27, 1964.

6. Dolly Guinther was director of publicity at FS&G.

7. WM, quoted in the letter of RG to JB, dated April 29, 1964.

8. Letter dated May 12, 1964 (NYPL).

9. RL, *Collected Prose*, 104, 111. See Hamilton, *Robert Lowell: A Biography*, 368.

10. RL, *Collected Prose*, 116.

11. PM, *Lost Puritan*, 325.

12. Procopiow, *Robert Lowell*, 316.

13. JB, *The Dream Songs*, 196.

14. RL, *Letters of Robert Lowell*, 449.

15. Letter dated October 3, 1964 (Houghton Library, Harvard University, Cambridge, Massachusetts).

16. Letter of RG to JB, dated May 1, 1964.

17. RL, "Letter to the Editor," *New York Review of Books* 2, no. 9 (June 11, 1964): 23.

18. Wright, quoted in Stitt, "The Art of Poetry XIX," 37.

19. Letter dated "Sunday 10 May" [1964]. Theodore Morrison was in charge of Freshman English at Harvard when he hired JB in 1940.

20. See letter dated August 24, 1964. "[T]he book is a knockout. . . . Such bravado and such excellence calls for celebration" (*New York Times Book Review*, August 23, 1964).

21. See letter of RG to TSE, dated September 18, 1964, about RL's *For the Union Dead* (NYPL).

22. See Kate Berryman, foreword to Kelly, *John Berryman's Personal Library*, ix.

23. Letter of RG to JB, dated February 16, 1965, on FS&G letterhead.

24. Robert Fitzgerald, quoted in the letter of RG to JB, dated May 14, 1965.

25. RG was in the process of editing thirty-four books, including a handful that he felt were particularly important: *The MacArthur Controversy and American Foreign Policy* by Richard Rovere and Arthur Schlesinger Jr.; *The Myth and the Powerhouse* by Philip Rahv; *Questions of Travel* by Elizabeth Bishop; *The Old Glory* by Robert Lowell; *The Bit Between My Teeth: A Literary Chronicle of 1950–1965* by Edmund Wilson (which mentioned *77 Dream Songs*); *Seasons of Celebration* by Thomas Merton; and *To Criticize the Critic and Other Writings* by T. S. Eliot.

26. Letter of JB to RG, dated July 16, 1965.

27. Letter of RG to JB, dated July 19, 1965.

28. See letter of RG to Valerie Eliot, dated July 16, 1965 (NYPL).

29. See JB, *WDH*, 363; letter of RG to JB, dated November 17, 1965.

30. See PM, *DS*, 171.

31. RL, *Letters of Robert Lowell*, 469–70.

32. Letter is in Berg.

33. Stephen Berg was coeditor, along with Robert Mezey, of *Naked Poetry: Recent American Poetry in Open Forms*.

34. Letter of JB to RG, dated July 7, 1966.

35. Letter of RG to JB, dated July 12, 1966.

36. Letter of JB to MVD, dated "Th. Evening" [1966] (Berg).

37. JB, *The Dream Songs*, 172.

38. Letter dated "Monday" [1966]. *Sonnets to Chris*, ed. CT, in JB, *Collected Poems*, combines the sonnets from the 1940s manuscript with the later ones.

39. See JB, *WDH*, 364.

40. WM, quoted in Thornberry's appendix to JB, *Collected Poems*, 305.

41. See letter of RG to JB, dated September 28, 1966.

42. Letter of JB to RG, dated "Wed" [1966].

43. Jill Berryman, quoted in JB, *WDH*, 367.

44. Letter dated October 8, 1966.

45. See JB, *WDH*, 365.

46. See letter of RG to JB, dated October 14, 1966.

47. Letter dated "Monday, Nov?" [1966].

48. Letter of JB to RG, dated December 16, 1966.

49. The academy lists the amount of this fellowship as $25,000 at https://poets.org/academy-american-poets/winner/prizes/academy-american-poets-fellowship/academy-fellowship-53.

50. RL, quoted in JB, *WDH*, 364.

51. For a discussion of the contract for the sonnets and the galleys of the book, see JB, *Collected Poems*, 305.

52. See letter of RG to JB, dated January 13, 1967.

53. See JB, *WDH*, 366.

54. Although there is no record of a review done by WM, there was a review in the *New York Times* (June 29, 1967), by Robert Mazzocco, entitled "Harlequin in Hell."

55. Letter of RG to JB, dated February 14, 1967. In a previous letter, dated "4 Feb" [1967], JB relates to RG that his wife found two more sonnets (to be numbered 116 and 117). JB insists that *Berryman's Sonnets* have a table of contents. He ends, "Don't forget the dedicatory pages [to RG]!"

56. See Jamison, *Robert Lowell, Setting the River on Fire*, 113. Letter dated "7 Mar" [1967].

57. See letter dated March 28, 1967.

58. See Howard, "Whiskey and Ink, Whiskey and Ink."

59. Groth, *The Receptionist*, 12.

60. Letter dated June 20, 1967.

61. See letter dated June 21, 1967.

62. See letter dated July 17, 1967.

63. Letter of RG to Kate Berryman, dated July 21, 1967.

64. Letter dated October 4, 1967.

65. Letter dated October 16, 1967.

66. Letter dated October 24, 1967 (Berg).

67. Letter dated November 7, 1967. "Your face broods from my table, Suicide," "The autumn breeze was light & bright," "Go, ill-sped book and whisper to her," "Henry's Mail," "Henry in transition, transient Henry," and "I always wanted to be old" were sold to a new magazine, *Audience*, for $500. "—Mr. Blackmur, what are the holy cities?," "Henry, weak at keyboard music," and "Henry lay cold golden in the snow" were sold to *Harper's* for $150. In addition, *Mundus Artium* of Ohio University accepted two poems for $100.

68. See letter of RG to JB, dated November 21, 1967.

69. Letter dated December 5, 1967.

70. Letter dated December 31, 1967 (NYPL).

71. Letter is in Berg.

Chapter Seven

1. JB stayed at the Hotel Iroquois, West Forty-Fourth Street; see FS&G invoice, dated March 21, 1968 (NYPL).

2. Letter dated March 10, 1968.

3. See letter dated April 9, 1968.

4. Letter dated April 17, 1968.

5. See telegram from RG to JB, dated April 22, 1968 (UM).

6. RL quoted in PM, *DS*, 439.

7. RL, *Letters of Robert Lowell*, 508.

8. Martha McDowell [Duffy] wrote on performing arts for *Time* magazine. Elizabeth Kray was hired in 1963 as the Academy of American Poets' first executive director. She launched a reading series at the Guggenheim Museum, beginning in 1963. Other possible guests that RG mentioned: Kate Berryman; Roger Straus; Henry Robbins, an editor at FS&G; Michael di Capua, an editor at FS&G; Richard Holland, director of publicity at FS&G; Hal Vursell; and poet James Wright (see letter of RG to JB, dated October 2, 1968).

9. Letter dated September 27, 1968. On November 7, 1968, RG wrote JB, "Charles Monteith has just written me as follows: 'Yes, of course: we'd be very willing to pay the terms you suggest for HIS TOY, HIS DREAM, HIS REST.'" On November 9, 1968, RG sent JB a letter emending the contract of August 10, 1966, so that FS&G would have the exclusive right to license English and other foreign publishers to publish editions of this book in the English language.

10. For JB's detailed analysis of Pound's poetry, which Pound would not allow to be used as the introduction to his *Personae*, see JB, "The Poetry of Ezra Pound."

11. RL, quoted in PM, *DS*, 440.

12. Telegram from RG to JB, dated January 8, 1969.

13. JB, "Acceptance Speech for National Book Award."

14. For an account of JB's reading at Urbana, Illinois, see Laurence Lieberman, "Hold the Audience! A Brief Memoir of John Berryman."

15. See letter of RG to JB, dated April 25, 1969.

16. See letter dated June 5, 1969.

17. Letter dated "Monday" [1969].

18. See JB, *WDH*, 370–71; letter of JB to WM, dated October 11 [1969] (NYPL).

19. See JB, *WDH*, 371–72; letter of Jill Berryman to WM, dated November 16, 1969 (NYPL).

20. PM, "Broken Beauty: The Last Days of John Berryman," 21.

21. See JH, introduction to JB's *BS*, lxi. JB had drafted two hundred pages of his Shakespeare biography in 1951–1952, and he resumed working on it for twelve hours a day sometime in 1970. See letter of JB to MVD, dated "Wed. evening the 4th" [either February or March, 1970] (Berg).

22. Letter dated February 24, 1970 (Linda Lear Center for Special Collections and Archives, Charles E. Shain Library, Connecticut College, New London; copy is in Berg).

23. See JH, *LJB*, 360–62.

24. See JH, *LJB*, 384–85.

25. JB, quoted in PM, *DS*, 455.

26. See JB, *WDH*, 373.

27. JB, quoted in Stitt, "The Art of Poetry XVI," 202.

28. RL, *Collected Prose*, 117.

29. Letter dated December 27, 1970, RL, *Letters of Robert Lowell*, 563.

30. JB, *Collected Poems*, 219.

31. JB, quoted in Stitt, "The Art of Poetry XVI," 181. For a fine analysis of "confessionalism" and JB as a confessional poet, see Coleman, *John Berryman's Public Vision*, 3–21, 128–30. See also Deborah Nelson, "Confessional Poetry."

32. Letter dated May 20, 1970.

33. Letter dated "Sunday, 16? June 70."

34. JB, quoted in Rogers, *God of Rescue*, 4.

35. Letter dated June 17, 1970.

36. See PM, *DS*, 461.

37. See letter of RG to JB, dated June 25, 1970. For a discussion about the publishing history of *L&F*, see JB, *Collected Poems*, 316–17.

38. See letter of Charles Monteith to Patricia Irving at FS&G, August 17, 1970 (NYPL).

39. Letter of July 17, 1970. When JB received this letter he listed names of poets (and the dates of their births) who might be included in his projected anthology: P[aul] Goodman (1911), Eliz[abeth] B[ishop]., Randall [Jarrell], Cal [RL], [William] Meredith (1919), [Howard] Nemerov (1920), [Richard] Wilbur (1921–1956), James Dickey (1923), A[nthony] Hecht (1923), [Donald] Justice (1925), [Allen] Ginsberg (1926), R[obert] Bly (1926), [W. S.] Merwin (1927), [James] Merrill (1926), S[ylvia] Plath (1932–11 Febr. 63), as well as A[lun?] Lewis [if so, a Welsh poet], Jon Silkin [poet at the University of Leeds], and Ted Hughes. JB also noted, "I have not included any poetry after 1920, exc[ept]. RW [Richard Wilbur] and SP [Sylvia Plath] and [Andrei] Voznesenksy whose excellence seems to me to be unquestionable."

40. See JB, *WDH*, 375. For information about the publishing history of *L&F*, particularly as related to the Faber & Faber edition, see JB, *Collected Poems*, 315–17.

41. This interview, along with a number of poetry readings by JB, was videotaped. This and other recordings may be found online by searching for videos using the phrase "poetry of john berryman 1970."

42. See JH, *LJB*, 380–81.

43. Postcard is dated "Wed" [1970].

44. Jill Berryman, quoted in JB, *WDH*, 377–78.

45. JB, *WDH*, 380.

46. Hayden Carruth's devastating review of *L&F*, entitled "Love, Art, and Money," stated that JB's poems "have no real seriousness or creative force, but only a kind of edgy exhibitionism" (437). In a subsequent letter to the editor, JB was pleased that Carruth had put him in the bracing company of RL, Roethke, Schwartz, Jarrell, Bishop, and Wilbur, though according to Carruth these poets had produced "individual poems finer in poetic integrity and formal congruency" than any that JB had written (see "Letters," *The Nation* 211 [November 30, 1970]: 546). Two tickets for forty dollars were charged to JB's FS&G account on December 10, 1970; see invoice (NYPL).

47. Postcard from JB to RG, dated "Sun. morning" [December 1970?].

48. Phillips, "Balling the Muse," 73.

49. Note sent from New York (RGPF).

50. JB, quoted in RL, *Collected Prose*, 116.

51. RL, *Letters of Robert Lowell*, 563.

52. Letter dated "Wed Jan 6th" [1971]. JB provided the following list: John Crowe Ransom, Conrad Aiken, Richard Wilbur, Edmund Wilson, Franklin Reeve, Edward Hoagland, Albert Gelpi, Isabella Gardiner (Chelsea Hotel), Marshall McLuhan, William D. Snodgrass, W. S. Merwin, James Wright (Hunter College), Richard Ryan (Saint Thomas College, Saint Paul, Minneapolis), Robert Penn Warren, Allen Ginsberg, Gary Snyder, Ralph Ellison, Marianne Moore, Elizabeth Bishop, Howard Nemerov, and James Dickey.

53. Letter dated January 13, 1971.

54. Letter of RG to JB, dated January 19, 1971.

55. See JH, *LJB*, 331, 394; also PM, *DS*, 415.

56. See letter dated January 6, 1966 (PU).

57. Letter dated January 21, 1971 (PU).

58. Letter dated January 13, 1971 (PU).

59. JB, quoted in JH, *LJB*, 394. See RL, *Collected Prose*, 117.

60. Card postmarked April 12, 1971 (PU). JH notes this as the central grievance in JB's poem "Tierce," in which he laments AT's "envenomed & most insolent missive." See JH, *JBCC*, 131–32. JH mentions the tension between JB and AT. See JH, *LJB*, 163.

61. See SB, "John Berryman," xiii, in JB, *Recovery*.

62. Letter of JB to RG, dated January 25, 1971.

63. See CT, commentary on *L&F*, in JB, *Collected Poems*, 317.

64. See letter of RG to JB, dated February 10, 1971.

65. Letter of RG to JB, dated May 19, 1971.

66. See WM, "In Loving Memory of the Late Author of the Dream Songs," 73.

67. JB, *Collected Poems*, 262.

68. JB, *Collected Poems*, 263.

69. Letter dated May 11, 1971, quoted in RG, preface to JB, *The Freedom of the Poet*, viii.

70. See JB, *Collected Poems*, 322.

71. See RG, preface to JB, *The Freedom of the Poet*.

72. See letter of JB to MVD, dated "Tues. noon" [1971] (Berg); letter of JB to RG, dated June 5, 1971. JB, quoted in PM, *DS*, 487.

73. RG, preface to JB, *The Freedom of the Poet*, ix.

74. JB, quoted in RG, preface to JB, *The Freedom of the Poet*, ix.

75. RG, preface to JB, *The Freedom of the Poet*, ix.

76. JB, quoted in PM, *DS*, 492.

77. See letter of ES to RG, dated March 27, 1972, in which she shares some excerpts of letters from JB to her (NYPL).

78. Letter of JB to RG, dated October 11, 1971.

79. Richard Wilbur, quoted in JB, *Collected Poems*, 322.

80. See letter of RG to JB, dated October 15, 1971; JB, *Collected Poems*, 321. For an account of the various typescripts of *Delusions, etc.*, see JB, *Collected Poems*, 320–24.

81. Letter dated "30 Oct" [1971] (NYPL).

82. Letter of JB to RG, dated "Friday afternoon 11/12" [November 12, 1971].

83. See JH, *LJB*, 402.

84. Letter dated "Sat[turday]" [1971].

85. Letter dated November 15, 1971.

86. JB, *Collected Poems*, 246.

87. JB, quoted in JH, *LJB*, 415.

88. Poem dated December 16, 1971. See JB, *Henry's Fate & Other Poems*, 92.

89. Kelly, *John Berryman's Personal Library*, 26–27.

90. JB, *Collected Poems*, 256.

91. Kelly, *John Berryman's Personal Library*, 254.

92. See Hamilton, *Robert Lowell*, 438.

93. RL, *Collected Poems*, 737–38. In 1968, Elizabeth Bishop expressed her high regard for JB's and RL's poetry (see Travisano, *Midcentury Quartet*, 29).

94. Poem quoted in CT, "A Reckoning with Ghostly Voices (1935–36)," in *Recovering Berryman*, ed. Kelly and Lathrop, 88.

95. JB, *Collected Poems*, 221.

96. JB, *Henry's Fate & Other Poems*, xviii.

97. See Thomas Lask, "Five Poet Friends Honor Berryman," *New York Times*, May 11, 1972.

98. ES, *PTY*, 247–48.

99. I had the privilege of accompanying RG when he received the 1987 Alexander Hamilton Award at Columbia University; the 1988 Campion Award at Regis High School; the 1988 Elmer Holmes Bobst Award (along with Edward Albee, Toni Morrison, and Reynolds Price) at New York University; the 1988

Unity and Freedom Medal from the Asociación Pro Unidad Latinoamericana at the Metropolitan Club in New York; the 1989 Mayor's Award at Gracie Mansion in New York; the 2002 Award for Distinguished Service to the Arts from the American Academy of Arts and Letters; and honorary doctorates from Seton Hall University and Saint Peter's College.

Ackroyd, Peter. *T. S. Eliot*. London: Hamish Hamilton, 1986.

Air Group Nine Book Committee. *U.S.S. Essex Carrier Air Group 9: The Record of the First Two Years, from the Forming of the Air Group in March 1942 to the Return from Action against the Enemy in March 1944*. Chicago: Lakeside Press, 1945.

Anonymous. "Interview with John Berryman." *Harvard Advocate* 103, no. 1 (Spring 1969): 4–9.

———. "Interview with Robert Giroux." *Newman Journal* (Columbia College) 1, no. 2 (Spring 1987): 5–10.

Arpin, Gary. "Establishing a Tradition: John Berryman's Student Verse." *John Berryman Studies* 3, no. 4 (Fall 1977): 11–16.

———. *John Berryman: A Reference Guide*. Boston: G. K. Hall, 1976.

Atlas, James. *Delmore Schwartz: The Life of an American Poet*. New York: Farrar, Straus & Giroux, 1977.

Bawer, Bruce. *The Middle Generation: The Lives of Poets Delmore Schwartz, Randall Jarrell, John Berryman, and Robert Lowell*. Hamden, CT: Archon Books, 1986.

Bellow, Saul. *Letters*. Edited by Benjamin Taylor. New York: Viking, 2010.

Berg, Stephen and Robert Mezey, eds. *Naked Poetry: Recent American Poetry in Open Forms*. Indianapolis, IN: Bobbs-Merrill, 1969.

Berryman, John. *77 Dream Songs*. New York: Farrar, Straus & Giroux, 1964. Reprinted by Farrar, Straus & Giroux with an introduction by Henri Cole, 2014.

———. "Acceptance Speech for National Book Award." New York: National Book Foundation, 1969.

———. "The Ancestor." *Columbia Review* 17, no. 3 (April 1936): 5–7.

———. "Apostrophe." *Columbia Review* 16, no. 4 (April 1935): 23.

———. "Ars Poetica." *Columbia Review* 16, no. 4 (April 1935): 18–19.

———. *Berryman's Shakespeare*. Edited with an introduction by John Haffenden. New York: Farrar, Straus & Giroux, 1999.

———. *Berryman's Sonnets*. New York: Farrar, Straus & Giroux, 1967. Reprinted, edited by Daniel Swift, New York: Farrar, Straus & Giroux, 2014. Page references are to the 1967 edition.

———. "Blake." *Columbia Review* 16, no. 4 (April 1935): 19.

———. "The Cage." *Poetry* 75, no. 4 (January 1950): 187–88.

———. "Canto Amor." *Sewanee Review* 50, no. 1 (Winter 1947): 68–70.

———. *Collected Poems: 1937–1971*. Edited with an introduction by Charles Thornbury. New York: Farrar, Straus & Giroux, 1989.

———. "Crane's Art." In *Modern American Fiction*, edited by A. Walton Litz, 32–44. New York: Oxford University Press, 1963.

———. *Delusions, etc.* New York: Farrar, Straus & Giroux, 1972.

———. "Despondency and Madness." In *The Contemporary Poet as Artist and Critic*, edited by Anthony Ostroff, 99–106. Boston: Little, Brown, 1964.

———. *The Dispossessed*. New York: William Sloane Associates, 1948.

———. *The Dream Songs*. New York: Farrar, Straus & Giroux, 1969. Reprinted as *The Dream Songs* (complete edition of *77 Dream Songs* and *His Toy, His Dream, His Rest: 308 Dream Songs*), with an introduction by Michael Hofmann, New York: Farrar, Straus & Giroux, 2014. Page references are to the 1969 edition.

———. "Elegy: Hart Crane." *Columbia Review* 17, no. 1 (November 1935): 20–21.

———. "Essential." *Columbia Review* 16, no. 3 (March 1935): 19.

———. *The Freedom of the Poet*. New York: Farrar, Straus & Giroux, 1976.

———. *The Heart Is Strange: New Selected Poems*. Edited with an introduction by Daniel Swift. New York: Farrar, Straus & Giroux, 2014.

———. *Henry's Fate & Other Poems: 1967–1972*. New York: Farrar, Straus & Giroux, 1977.

———. *His Thought Made Pockets & The Plane Buckt*. Pawlet, VT: Claude Fredericks / Banyan Press, 1958.

———. *His Toy, His Dream, His Rest: 308 Dream Songs*. New York: Farrar, Straus & Giroux, 1968.

———. *Homage to Mistress Bradstreet*. *Partisan Review* 20, no. 5 (September–October 1953): 489–592. First book edition with drawings by Ben Shahn. New York: Farrar, Straus & Giroux, 1956. British edition: London, Faber & Faber, 1959.

———. "The Imaginary Jew." *Kenyon Review* 7, no. 4 (Autumn 1945): 529–39. Reprinted in *The Freedom of the Poet*, by John Berryman, 359–66.

———. "Ivory." *Columbia Review* 16, no. 5 (May 1935): 18.

———. "Lead Out the Weary Dancers." *Columbia Review* 16, no. 4 (April 1935): 23.

———. *Love & Fame*. New York: Farrar, Straus & Giroux, 1970.

———. "The Lovers." *Kenyon Review* 7, no. 1 (Winter 1945): 1–11. Reprinted in *The Freedom of the Poet*, by John Berryman, 344–52.

———. "Notation." *Columbia Review* 17, no. 3 (April 1936): 3.

———. "Note on E. A. Robinson." *The Nation* 141 (July 10, 1935): 38. Reprinted in *Columbia Poetry 1935*, selected by Joseph Auslander, Irwin Edman, Roderick Marshall, Elizabeth Reynard, and Mark Van Doren, 14. New York: Columbia University Press, 1935.

———. "Notes on Poetry: E. A. Robinson, and Others." *Columbia Review* 17, no. 2 (December 1935): 19–22.

———. "Olympus." *Atlantic* 226, no. 5 (November 1970): 97.

———. *Poems*. Norfolk, CT: New Directions, 1942.

———. "The Poetry of Ezra Pound." *Partisan Review* 16, no. 4 (April 1949): 377–94. Reprinted in *The Freedom of the Poet*, by John Berryman, 253–69.

———. *Recovery*. New York: Farrar, Straus & Giroux, 1973.

———. "The Ritual of W. B. Yeats." *Columbia Review* 17, nos. 4–5 (May–June 1936): 26–32. Reprinted in *The Freedom of the Poet*, by John Berryman, 245–52.

———. *Selected Poems*. Edited by Kevin Young. New York: Library of America, 2004.

———. "Shakespeare at Thirty." *Hudson Review* 6, no. 2 (Summer 1953): 175–203. Reprinted in *The Freedom of the Poet*, by John Berryman, 29–55.

———. *Short Poems*. New York: Farrar, Straus & Giroux, 1967.

———. *Stephen Crane: A Critical Biography*. New York: William Sloane Associates, 1950.

———. "A Sympathy, A Welcome." *New Yorker* 34, no. 26 (August 16, 1958): 22.

———. "Thanksgiving." *Columbia Review* 17, no. 1 (November 1935): 22.

———. "To an Artist Beginning Her Work." In *Columbia Poetry 1936*, selected by Allan Abbott, Joseph Auslander, Herbert Brucker, George Genzmer, Minor Latham, John Lyon, Henry Simon, William Y. Tindall, and Mark Van Doren, 11. New York: Columbia University Press, 1936.

———. "Trophy." *Columbia Review* 17, no. 3 (April 1936): 7.

———. "Twenty Poems." In *Five Young American Poets*. Norfolk, CT: New Directions, 1940.

———. *Two Poems*. (Season's Greetings, 1970 from Martha and Kate and John and Bob Giroux.) Contains "In Memoriam: 1914–1953" and "Another New Year's Eve (1970)." Privately printed.

———. *We Dream of Honour: John Berryman's Letters to His Mother*. Edited by Richard J. Kelly. New York: W. W. Norton, 1988.

———. "The Witness." *Columbia Review* 17, no. 3 (April 1936): 4.

———. "Words to a Young Man." *Columbia Review* 17, no. 2 (December 1935): 10.

Berryman, John, Ralph Ross, and Allen Tate, eds. *The Arts of Reading*. New York: Thomas Y. Cowell, 1960.

Blackmur, Richard P. "Commentary by Ghosts." *Kenyon Review* 5, no. 3 (Summer 1943): 467–71.

———. "The Experience of Ideas." *Columbia Review* 17, no. 3 (April 1936): 29–32.

Bloom, Harold, ed. *John Berryman*. Introduction by Harold Bloom. New York: Chelsea House, 1989.

Bloom, James D. *The Stock of Available Reality: R. P. Blackmur and John Berryman*. Lewisburg, PA: Bucknell University Press, 1984.

Blunk, Jonathan. *James Wright: A Life in Poetry*. New York: Farrar, Straus & Giroux, 2017.

Carruth, Hayden. "Declining Occasions." *Poetry* 112, no. 2 (May 1968): 119–21.

———. "Love, Art, and Money." *The Nation* 211 (November 2, 1970): 437–38.

Coleman, Philip. *John Berryman's Public Vision: Relocating 'the scene of disorder.'* Dublin, Ireland: University College Dublin Press, 2014.

———. "'Nightmares of Eden': John Berryman's *Homage to Mistress Bradstreet*." *Revista de Estudios Norteamericanos* 10 (2004): 57–70.

Coleman, Philip, and Philip McGowan, eds. *"After Thirty Falls": New Essays on John Berryman*. Preface by Richard J. Kelly. Amsterdam: Rodopi, 2007.

Conarroe, Joel. *John Berryman: An Introduction to the Poetry*. New York: Columbia University Press, 1977.

Cooper, Brendan. *Dark Airs: John Berryman and the Spiritual Politics of Cold War American Poetry*. Oxford: Peter Lang, 2009.

Corrigan, Robert A. "Ezra Pound and the Bollingen Prize Controversy." *Midcontinent American Studies Journal* 8, no. 2 (Fall 1967): 43–57.

Dorati, Antal. *The Way of the Cross: Cantata Dramatica*. Text by Paul Claudel. English translation by John Berryman. Minneapolis: Minneapolis Symphony Orchestra, 1957.

Doreski, William. *The Years of Our Friendship: Lowell and Tate*. Jackson: University Press of Mississippi, 1990.

Edman, Irwin. "Man and Socialization." *Columbia Review and Morningside* 14, no. 3 (February 1933): 3–7.

Engle, Paul, and Warren Carrier, eds. *Reading Modern Poetry*. Chicago: Scott, Foresman, 1955.

First, Wesley, ed. *University on the Heights*. Garden City, NY: Doubleday, 1969.

Fitzgerald, Robert. "Poetry and Perfection." *Sewanee Review* 51, no. 4 (Fall 1948): 685–97.

Florencourt, Frances. "Interview with Robert Giroux." In *At Home with Flannery O'Connor: An Oral History*, edited by Marshall Bruce Gentry and Craig Amason, 83–90. Milledgeville, GA: The Flannery O'Connor–Andalusia Foundation, 2012.

Fraser, Russell. *A Mingled Yarn: The Life of R. P. Blackmur*. New York: Harcourt Brace Jovanovich, 1981.

———. "R. P. Blackmur: America's Best Critic." *Virginia Quarterly Review* 57, no. 4 (Autumn 1981): 569–93.

Freed-Thall, Hannah. *Spoiled Distinctions: Aesthetics and the Ordinary in French Modernism.* New York: Oxford University Press, 2015.

Giroux, Robert. *The Book Known as Q: A Consideration of Shakespeare's Sonnets.* New York: Atheneum, May 1982.

———. "Books on Film Theory." *Columbia Review* 17, nos. 4–5 (May–June 1935): 10–17.

———. *A Deed of Death: The Story behind the Unsolved Murder of Hollywood Director William Desmond Taylor.* New York: Knopf, 1990.

———. "The Dove and the Falcon." *The Nation* 143 (August 8, 1936): 165–66.

———. "The Education of an Editor: R. R. Bowker Memorial Lecture 1981." *Publishers Weekly* 221, no. 2 (January 8, 1982): 54–60.

———. "End of the World." *Columbia Review and Morningside* 15, no. 3 (April 1934): 15–17.

———. "Films." *Columbia Review* 16, no. 1 (November 1934): 35–40.

———. "Henry's Understanding." *Yale Review* 84, no. 2 (April 1996): 96–103.

———. "Marc Connelly, Moving-man." *The Nation* 143 (July 25, 1936): 110.

———. "Novel into Movie." *The Nation* 141 (October 16, 1935): 447–48.

———. "On Being a Film Crank." *Columbia Review* 16, no. 3 (March 1935): 37–42.

———. "A Personal Memoir." *Sewanee Review* 74, no. 1 (Winter 1966): 331–38.

———. "The Poet in the Asylum." *Atlantic* 262, no. 2 (August 1988): 40–41, 44–46.

———. "Prelude." *Columbia Review and Morningside* 15, no. 2 (December 1933): 3–5.

———. "Reading Shakespeare." *New York Review of Books* 30, no. 12 (July 21, 1983): 46–47.

———. "Score One." *Columbia Review and Morningside* 15, no. 4 (special issue, May 1934): 25.

———. "Shakespeare & Co: Reply to Frank Kermode." *New York Review of Books* 30, no. 10 (June 16, 1983): 51.

———. "Taxidermy on the Screen." *The Nation* 141 (October 2, 1935): 391.

———. "Unsettled Accounts." *The Nation* 142 (June 24, 1936): 821.

———. "Who's Got Function?" *Columbia Review and Morningside* 15, no. 5 (May 1934): 3–6.

Giroux, Robert, Robert Dana, Saskia Hamilton, and Charles McKinley. "Celebration of Robert Lowell: Lowell off the Page." *Kenyon Review* New Series 22, no. 1 (Winter 2000): 255–74.

Golden, Amanda. "John Berryman at Midcentury: Annotating Ezra Pound and Teaching Modernism." *Modernism/modernity* 21, no. 2 (April 2014): 507–15.

Groth, Janet. *The Receptionist: An Education at* The New Yorker. Chapel Hill, NC: Algonquin Books, 2012.

Haffenden, John. *John Berryman: A Critical Commentary*. New York: New York University Press, 1980.

———. "John Berryman: The American Poet at Cambridge." *Cambridge Quarterly* 8, no. 2 (1978): 129–150.

———. *The Life of John Berryman*. Boston: Routledge & Kegan Paul, 1982.

Haffenden, John, and Richard J. Kelly. "John Berryman: Contributions to Periodicals & Annuals." *John Berryman Studies* 3, no. 3 (Summer 1979): 49–51.

Halliday, E. M. *John Berryman and the Thirties: A Memoir*. Amherst: University of Massachusetts Press, 1987.

Hamilton, Ian. *Robert Lowell: A Biography*. New York: Random House, 1982.

Heyen, William. "John Berryman: A Memoir and an Interview." *Ohio Review* 15, no. 2 (Winter 1974): 46–65.

Horgan, Paul. *Tracings: A Book of Partial Portraits*. New York: Farrar, Straus & Giroux, 1993.

Howard, Jane. "Whiskey and Ink, Whiskey and Ink." *Life* 63, no. 3 (July 21, 1967): 67–68, 70, 72–74, 75–76.

Hulbert, Ann. *The Interior Castle: The Art and Life of Jean Stafford*. New York: Knopf, 1992.

Hyde, Lewis. *Alcohol and Poetry: John Berryman and the Booze Talking*. Dallas, TX: Dallas Institute, 1986.

Jamison, Kay Redfield. *Robert Lowell, Setting the River on Fire: A Study of Genius, Mania, and Character*. New York: Knopf, 2017.

Jarrell, Randall. *Randall Jarrell: 1914–1965*. Edited by Robert Lowell, Peter Taylor, and Robert Penn Warren. New York: Farrar, Straus & Giroux, 1967.

———. "Verse Chronicle." *The Nation* 167 (July 17, 1948): 80–81.

Kashka, Boris. *Hothouse: The Art of Survival and the Survival of Art at America's Most Celebrated Publishing House, Farrar, Straus and Giroux*. New York: Simon & Schuster, 2013.

Kelly, Richard J. *John Berryman: A Checklist*. Foreword by William Meredith. Metuchen, NJ: The Scarecrow Press, 1972.

———. *John Berryman's Personal Library: A Catalogue*. Foreword by Kate Donahue Berryman. Washington, DC: Peter Lang, 1999.

Kelly, Richard J., and Alan K. Lathrop, eds. *Recovering Berryman: Essays on a Poet*. Ann Arbor: University of Michigan Press, 1993.

Kermode, Frank. "Reply to Mr. Giroux." *New York Review of Books* 30, no. 12 (July 21, 1983): 47.

———. Review of *The Book Known as Q* by Robert Giroux. *New York Review of Books* 30, no. 7 (April 28, 1983): 32.

Kirsch, Adam. *The Wounded Surgeon: Confession and Transformation in Six American Poets*. New York: W. W. Norton, 2005.

Kostelanetz, Richard. "Conversation with Berryman." *Massachusetts Review* 11, no. 2 (Spring 1970): 340–47.

———. "A Profile of John Berryman." *American Poetry Review* 9, no. 6 (November–December 1980): 39–43.

Lehman, David. "Robert Giroux '36." *Columbia College Today* 14, no. 3 (Fall 1987): 30–33.

Lieberman, Laurence. "Hold the Audience! A Brief Memoir of John Berryman." *John Berryman Studies* 1, no. 3 (July 1975): 8–11.

Lowell, Robert. *Collected Poems.* Edited by Frank Bidart and David Gewanter with DeSales Harrison. New York: Farrar, Straus & Giroux, 2003.

———. *Collected Prose.* Edited by Robert Giroux. New York: Farrar, Straus & Giroux, 1987.

———. *Day by Day.* New York: Farrar, Straus & Giroux, 1977.

———. *Letters of Robert Lowell.* Edited by Saskia Hamilton. New York: Farrar, Straus & Giroux, 2005.

———. *Life Studies* and *For the Union Dead.* New York: Farrar, Straus & Cudahy, 2007.

———. *Notebook: 1967–68: Poems.* New York: Farrar, Straus, & Giroux, 1969.

Mancini, Joseph. *The Berryman Gestalt: Therapeutic Strategies in the Poetry of John Berryman.* New York: Garland, 1987.

Mariani, Paul. "Broken Beauty: The Last Days of John Berryman." *Commonweal* 140, no. 1 (January 1, 2013): 21–23.

———. *Dream Song: The Life of John Berryman.* New York: William Morrow, 1990.

———. *Lost Puritan: A Life of Robert Lowell.* New York: W. W. Norton, 1994.

Matterson, Stephen. *Berryman and Lowell: The Art of Losing.* Totowa, NJ: Barnes & Noble, 1988.

McGregor, Michael N. *Pure Act: The Uncommon Life of Robert Lax.* New York: Fordham University Press, 2015.

Melville, Herman. *Billy Budd.* Volume XIII of the Standard Edition of Melville's *Complete Works.* London: Constable, 1924.

Meredith, William. "Henry Tasting All the Secret Bits of Life: Berryman's Dream Songs." *Wisconsin Studies in Contemporary Literature* 6, no. 1 (Winter–Spring, 1965): 27–33.

———. "In Loving Memory of the Late Author of the Dream Songs." *Virginia Quarterly Review* 49, no. 1 (Winter 1973): 70–78.

Merton, Thomas, O.C.S.O. "At the Corner." *Columbia Review* 17, no. 1 (November 1935): 8.

———. *The Seven Storey Mountain.* New York: Harcourt, Brace & Company, 1948.

Mizener, Arthur. "Poetry from Right to Left." *Kenyon Review* 5, no. 1 (1943): 154–60.

Nelson, Deborah. "Confessional Poetry." In *The Cambridge Companion to American Poetry since 1945*, edited by Jennifer Ashton, 31–46. Cambridge: Cambridge University Press, 2013.

Nelson, Greg. "Interview with W. D. Snodgrass." *Phoebe* (Fall 1984). http://phoebejournal.com/interview-with-w-d-snodgrass.

Phillips, Robert. "Balling the Muse." *North American Review* 256, no. 4 (Winter 1971): 72–73.

Pohl, Frederick. "On the Identity of 'Mr. W. H.'" *The Shakespeare Newsletter* 8, no. 6 (December 1958): 43.

Procopiow, Norma. *Robert Lowell: The Poet and His Critics*. Chicago: American Library Association, 1984.

Proust, Marcel. *In Search of Lost Time*. Translated by C. K. Scott Moncrieff and Terence Kilmartin. Revised by D. J. Enright. 6 vols. New York: Random House, 1992.

Radway, John North. "The Fate of Epic in Twentieth-Century American Poetry." Ph.D. diss., Harvard University, 2015. https://dash.harvard.edu/handle/1/26718713.

Roberts, David. *Jean Stafford: A Biography*. Boston: Little, Brown, 1988.

Rogers, Tom. *God of Rescue: John Berryman and Christianity*. Oxford: Peter Lang, 2011.

Samway, Patrick, S.J. *Flannery O'Connor and Robert Giroux: A Publishing Partnership*. Notre Dame, IN: University of Notre Dame Press, 2018.

———. "John Berryman's High Regard for Gerard Manley Hopkins." Lecture at the 2017 Hopkins Literary Festival, Newbridge, Ireland. http://www.gerardmanleyhopkins.org/lectures_2017/berryman_and_hopkins.html.

———, ed. *The Letters of Robert Giroux and Thomas Merton*. Notre Dame, IN: University of Notre Dame Press, 2015.

———. "Tracing a Literary and Epistolary Relationship: Eudora Welty and Her Editor, Robert Giroux." *Eudora Welty Review* 8 (2016): 69–108.

Schoenfeldt, Michael. "The Sonnets." In *The Cambridge Companion to Shakespeare's Sonnets*, edited by Patrick Cheney, 125–34. Cambridge: Cambridge University Press, 2007.

Schwartz, Delmore. *Genesis: Book One*. New York: New Directions, 1943.

———. *In Dreams Begin Responsibilities*. New York: New Directions, 1938.

Silverman, Al. *The Time of Their Lives: The Golden Age of Great American Publishers, Their Editors and Authors*. New York: St. Martin's Press, 2008.

Simpson, Eileen. *The Maze*. New York: Simon & Schuster, 1975.

———. *Orphans: Real and Imaginary*. New York: Weidenfeld & Nicolson, 1987.

———. *Poets in Their Youth: A Memoir*. New York: Random House, 1982.

———. *Reversals: A Personal Account of Victory over Dyslexia*. Boston: Houghton Mifflin, 1979.

Smith, Helen. "The Politics of Praise." *The Cambridge Quarterly* 32, no. 2 (2003): 187–93.

Smith, Robert Paul. *Where Did You Go? Out. What Did You Do? Nothing.* New York: Pocket Books, 1958.

Stafford, Jean. "Influx of Poets." *New Yorker* 54, no. 38 (November 6, 1978): 43–52, 55–56, 58, 60.

Stefanik, Ernest. *John Berryman: A Descriptive Bibliography.* Pittsburgh, PA: University of Pittsburgh Press, 1974.

Stitt, Peter. "The Art of Poetry XVI: John Berryman 1914–1972." *Paris Review* 14, no. 53 (Winter 1972): 177–207. Reprinted in *Berryman's Understanding,* edited by Harry Thomas, 18–44.

———. "The Art of Poetry XIX: James Wright." *Paris Review* 16, no. 62 (Summer 1975): 35–61.

Thayer, C. G. Review of *The Book Known as Q* by Robert Giroux. *Georgia Review* 37, no. 1 (Spring 1983): 214–16.

Thomas, Harry. "Berryman and Pound." *Michigan Quarterly Review* 45, no. 4 (Fall 2006): 613–16.

———, ed. *Berryman's Understanding: Reflections on the Poetry of John Berryman.* Boston: Northeastern University Press, 1988.

Travisano, Thomas. *Midcentury Quartet: Bishop, Lowell, Jarrell, Berryman, and the Making of a Postmodern Aesthetic.* Charlottesville: University of Virginia Press, 1999.

Van Doren, Mark. *The Autobiography of Mark Van Doren.* New York: Harcourt, Brace, 1958.

———. *Collected Poems: 1922–38.* New York: Henry Holt, 1939.

———. "A Critic's Job of Work." *Columbia Review* 17, no. 3 (April 1936): 27–28.

———. *Shakespeare.* New York: Henry Holt, 1939. Reprinted with a foreword and introduction by David Lehman. New York: New York Review of Books Classics, 2005.

Vanouse, Allison. "The Complete Poems of R. P. Blackmur." Ph.D. diss., Boston University, 2014.

Vinh, Alphonse, ed. *Cleanth Brooks and Allen Tate: Collected Letters: 1933–76.* Columbia: University of Missouri Press, 1998.

Waldron, Ann. *Close Connections: Caroline Gordon and the Southern Renaissance.* New York: Putnam, 1987.

Wilson, Edmund. *The Bit Between My Teeth: A Literary Chronicle of 1950–1965.* New York: Farrar, Straus & Giroux, 1965.

Winters, Yvor. "Three Poets." *Hudson Review* 1, no. 3 (Autumn 1948): 402–6.

Wojahn, David. "A Fifteenth Anniversary: John Berryman." *Poetry* 151, no. 1–2 (October–November 1987): 194–95.

awards and prizes
Pulitzer Prize, 100, 110–12, 156,
157–58, 161, 187, 188
Ramparts's first prize, 124, 126, 130
Shelley Memorial Award (Poetry
Society of America), 71

Baker, Carlos, 56
Baker, Howard, 46
Baldwin, James, 154
Bard College, 59, 78
Bargebuhr, Frederick, 187–88
Barnard, Mary, 43
Barnes, Djuna, 61, 71, 226n47
Barrault, Jean-Louis, 47
Barzun, Jacques, 2, 30, 60
Baxter, Warner, 131
Baylor School, 141
BBC, 105, 124, 166, 168, 223n76
Beckett, Samuel, 189
Beilenson, Peter, 94, 96, 97, 98
Bellow, Saul, 100, 121, 134, 186, 202,
203–4
Berryman acknowledgement of,
120, 177
on Berryman poems, 101, 107, 113,
184, 185
dedication of Berryman book to,
133, 145, 185
description of Berryman by, 73, 192
at University of Minnesota, 224n8,
114
Bennett, Arnold, 191
Bennett, Jean, 13, 32, 39, 42, 48, 50, 52
Bentley, Gerald Eades, 140
Berg, Stephen, 160–61
Bergner, Elisabeth, 65–66
Berlin, Isaiah, 226n47
Berlind, Bruce, 66
Berryman, Charles Peter (nephew), 49
Berryman, Jill (Martha) (mother), 4,
9, 28, 40, 123, 127, 144, 197

on Allyn's death, 6, 188–89
Allyn's rape of, 5
death of, 205
Giroux and, 6–7, 203
intrusive presence of, 13–14
and JB books, 163, 179
JB death and, 203–4
JB letters to, 12, 15–16, 39, 43, 49,
60, 62, 73, 74, 80, 84, 90, 96, 108,
119, 208n20
John Angus and, 5–6, 42, 214n22
remarriage to Jack Lemon, 52
Berryman, John
alcoholism of, 13, 39, 67, 79, 114, 116,
117, 118, 119, 148, 168, 174, 179–80,
181, 182, 190, 191
apartments and residences, 13, 42,
43–44, 46, 47, 48, 54, 55, 77, 79,
112, 116, 121, 155
appearance, 73
autobiographical themes in, 25–26,
42, 95
Bellow and, 73, 101, 107, 113, 120,
133, 145, 177, 184, 185, 192
Blackmur and, 15–16, 28–29, 56, 68,
70–71
burial, 203
as Cambridge student, 30, 35–36,
38–39
childhood, 4–6
as Columbia student, 2–4, 13–32
as Columbia teacher, 42
eccentric behavior, 63, 180
Eliot and, 40, 68, 73, 97, 98, 100, 115,
178
European trips, 77, 114
father's death and, 6–8, 19, 31–32,
183, 204
father's relationship with, 25–26
fellowships and scholarships, 12,
15, 30–31, 39, 59, 62, 73, 108, 136,
156

Mayer, Peter, 146
McCallum, John, 81
McCarthy, Mary, 133
McDiarmid, E. W., 115
McDowell, Martha, 176, 234n8
Melville, Herman, 22
Mencken, H. L.
  American Language, The, 29
Meredith, William, 121, 143, 154, 159,
    181, 198, 205
  Berryman friendship with, 64, 120
  on Berryman sonnets, 162, 163
  Berryman visits with, 120, 122, 123,
    128, 168, 196
  on Dream Songs, 95, 151, 167, 171,
    172, 173, 181
  works
  —*Love Letter from an Impossible
    Land*, 64
Merrill, James, 144, 150, 151
Merton, Thomas
  at Columbia, 4, 16, 23
  Giroux as editor of, 82, 119, 158,
    210n64, 226n47, 232n25
Merwin, W. S., 66, 128
Michigan State University, 178
Miles, Josephine, 231n120
Miller, Perry
  New England Mind, 74
Milton, John, 36
  "Lycidas," 47
Minneapolis, MN
  Abbot Hospital in, 112, 114, 148, 151,
    155, 157, 158, 159, 170, 172, 180
  Berryman apartments in, 79, 112,
    116, 155
  See also University of Minnesota
Mizener, Arthur, 53–54
Moe, Henry Allen, 139
Monk, Samuel, 115
Monroe, Harriet, 24
Monteith, Charles, 146, 179

Dream Songs and, 124, 165, 175,
    234n9
  Love & Fame and, 165, 187, 190,
    192–93
  Mistress Bradstreet and, 98, 107
Moore, Douglas, 2
Moore, Marianne, 41, 111, 231n120
Moravia, Alberto, 81, 145
Morley, Frank V., 44, 45, 53, 70
Morris, Alice, 145
Morrison, Theodore, 45, 51, 53, 154
Moses, W. R., 43
Moss, Howard, 183, 185
Mulligan, Eileen Patricia. *See*
    Simpson, Eileen
Munford, Howard, 113
Muni, Paul, 114, 124, 131
Murray, Nicholas, 36
Mussolini, Benito, 33

Nash, Ogden, 124
National Board of Review of Motion
    Pictures, 20
National Book Award in Poetry, 110,
    111, 112, 120, 177–78, 188
National Endowment for the Arts,
    172
National Endowment for the Hu-
    manities, 197, 201
National Institute of Arts and Letters,
    71, 154, 155
National Poetry Festival, 121, 124
Nation, The, 26, 29, 46, 63, 102, 169
  Berryman as poetry editor for, 42
  reviews of Berryman works in, 24,
    57, 189
Nazi Germany, 32–33, 41
Neff, Emery, 30, 193, 194
Nemerov, Howard, 155
New Catechism, A, 203
New Directions, 41, 44, 50, 69–70
New Poems, 1940, 47

Thorp, Willard, 56, 62
Thorpe, Thomas, 136, 137, 228n93
Thurber, James, 60
Tillyard, E. M. W., 36
Time, 55, 90, 157, 169
Times Literary Supplement, 92, 105,
107, 128, 199
    on *Mistress Bradstreet*, 110, 130
Toledano, Ralph de, 226n47
Tolstoy, Leo
    Anna Karenina, 74
    Master and Man, 197
Trilling, Lionel, 2
Trinity College, 170
Tully, Charles, 52

United States Information Agency,
113
University of California at Berkley,
117
University of Chicago, 192
University of Cincinnati, 73, 74
University of Michigan, 44
University of Minnesota
    Bellow at, 224n8, 114
    Berryman status at, 57, 79–80, 84,
        99, 114, 121, 158, 179, 219n8
    lectures by Berryman at, 79, 97–98,
        99–100, 115, 116, 177, 219n8
    sabbatical from, 127, 144
    Tate at, 79, 100, 117
University of Notre Dame, 178
University of Rochester, 158
University of Utah, 116
University of Vermont, 73
University of Washington, 72, 178
Untermeyer, Louis, 187
Updike, John, 154

Van Doren, Carl, 29
Van Doren, Dorothy, 14, 29, 40–41
Van Doren, Irita, 111

Van Doren, Mark, 14, 59, 172, 186, 193,
201, 205
    aid to Berryman by, 30, 31, 40, 45,
        48, 55
    Berryman and Giroux as students
        of, 2–5, 15, 30, 31
    Berryman interest in views of, 181,
        198
    Berryman visits with, 40–41, 120,
        122
    on Blackmur, 27–28, 96
    celebration honoring, 60
    on Dream Songs, 128, 171, 172
    as film critic, 29
    on Frost, 123–24
    as Giroux mentor, 31, 36, 136
    Giroux relations with, 31, 37
    influence on Berryman, 3, 31
    on *Mistress Bradstreet*, 107–8, 111
    poetry philosophy of, 28
    on Shakespeare, 2, 3, 25, 135–36, 137
    works
        —*Collected Poems: 1922–38*, 3
        —"Critic's Job of Work, A," 27–28
        —*Shakespeare*, 2–3, 135–36
        —*Winter Diary, A*, 3
Varsity Review, 3–4
Vassar College, 181
Vidor, King, 20
Viking, 73–74, 78, 82, 83–84, 85, 86,
    88–90, 226n45
Virginia Quarterly, 175
Voice of America, 146, 147
Vursell, Hal, 94, 222n40, 234n8

Walcott, Derek, 61
    Selected Poems, 145
Warren, Robert Penn, 39, 41, 61, 79,
    121, 159
    as Southern Fugitive, 32, 62
Watson, Wilfred
    Friday's Child, 99, 101

PATRICK SAMWAY, S.J., professor emeritus of English at St. Joseph's University in Philadelphia, is the author or editor/co-editor of fifteen books, including *The Letters of Robert Giroux and Thomas Merton* (2015) and *Flannery O'Connor and Robert Giroux: A Publishing Partnership* (2018), both published by the University of Notre Dame Press.

CPSIA information can be obtained
at www.ICGtesting.com
Printed in the USA
LVHW091508281020
670065LV00004B/82

9 780268 108410